BITTER ALMOND

Best wishes
Doug
July '25

Bitter Almond copyright © 2025 Doug Terry

Doug Terry asserts the right to be identified as the author of this work in accordance with the Copyright Designs and Patents Act 1988. All rights reserved.

No part of this publication can be reproduced or transmitted in any form or by any means, electronic, mechanical or otherwise, without the express written permission of Doug Terry.

British Library Cataloguing in Publication Data.

A CIP catalogue record for this book is available from the British Library.

Foreword

His name was Robert, or it may have been Robin, I forget now. Anyway, it was Robert (I'll stick with Robert) who first suggested I write an account of my early years, and my time in care.

The two of us, Robert and I, met, briefly as it turned out, at a leisure centre in West Wales in, well, it must have been 1994 or 1995. By then I was thirty years and three hundred miles (the distance was no coincidence) from Eastry, and Robert, who had spotted me playing table tennis, suggested a match, best of three.

It had all started out innocently enough. A youth worker in my early forties, I'd taken a group of teenagers to St Clears for an indoor sports session; badminton, five-a-side football, that sort of thing. It was a regular Wednesday evening excursion this, two staff and a dozen or so youngsters; Coke or Red Bull from the vending machine for the keen and, for the bored or disaffected, shoulder shrugging and sneaking outside for a fag and a fondle; the usual, and not unnoticed, sort of behaviour.

White ball on green table. We'd hardly begun a knock up when Robert began to question me about my background.

'So where were you in care?' he asked, as the ball went back and forth.

'Eastry,' I replied, without thinking. 'Eastry, in Kent. How did you know?'

'I've been watching you,' he said. 'The way you play; the aggression, the will to win. Nobody plays like that, unless they've been in care - or prison,' he added, with a laugh. 'And I'm guessing care. Am I right, or am I right?'

It may, or may not, have been a lucky guess, but Robert had found me out. Not only had I spent two years in care, and, indeed, nearly all my childhood in the spotlight of social services, I'd never spoken about it to anyone - and I mean not anyone, not even my wife.

The stigma, the shame and guilt I'd felt as a child I carried forward to my adult years. It took a stranger to get me to admit that I'd been one of the thousands – there must have been tens of thousands – of "looked after kids", to get me to come clean, so to speak.

'You should write it all down,' Robert said, using the distraction of our game to press home his advantage, and to encourage me to talk. By the end of the match, I was both physically and mentally exhausted. He beat me two-one, though, long term, perhaps, I was the real winner. Maybe we should call it a draw.

Eastry. Robert had sown the seeds, but how was I to put it all together, to rebuild my past? Well, I had my own memories, and those of my brothers - four of them - to call upon. And six months after that chance meeting in St Clears, I took a trip down to East Kent, coming back with maps, community newsletters, parish magazines, and photographs of the home, now a quiet, eerie, residential spot, reinvented as Eastry Park. But none of what I was able to gather provided me with the information I needed for a dependable, and readable, narrative.

Then came the Data Protection Act (1998). This piece of legislation, I quickly realised, had the potential to unlock all sorts of secrets, to provide me with a way into the past, to harvest what I felt was pertinent. Now I was able to get Kent County Council to release my personal files, something which, despite the law, and the passing of the decades, they, initially at least, were reluctant to do. Those photocopied papers, including care home and school reports, were priceless.

From the National Records office in Kew, I obtained copies of HM Inspectors' reports pertaining to Eastry and, for comparative purposes, from a raft of other homes in Kent and the south-east.

Meanwhile, the archives of the University of Hull yielded the papers of Anne Kerr, Labour MP for Chatham, and Rochester (1964-66), a woman who, along with others, had led a long campaign on behalf of the residents of King Hill hostel, where I'd spent time in 1963.

Further research gave me a fresh insight into the former workhouse at Newington Lodge, including press and television interest, and the part it played in the influential drama *Cathy Come Home* (1966). The film, viewed by more than twelve million people, did much to bring the plight of the homeless into the public arena. It was also a catalyst for the setting up of the homelessness charity Shelter.

Coincident with the passing of the Data Protection Act, and a real game changer, came the growth of the internet and social media. Need a name or a date? Just log in and begin typing. It was via the internet that I discovered Douglas Welby and his book *The Kentish Village of Eastry* (2007), which provided useful background on the Eastry

Union Workhouse, and the origins of the children's home. Another breakthrough came via the Care Leavers Association, their website enabling me to contact one or two former Eastry residents. 'Old gits now,' wrote one of them. Speak for yourself, Mr. MacDonald.

George Orwell (*Why I Write*) proposes a series of motives for writing prose, which include 'a desire to seem clever, to be talked about, to be remembered after death, to get your own back on grown-ups who snubbed you in childhood, etc. etc.' While I wouldn't disagree with the first three of these suggestions - I am, I'm sure, as egotistical as the next person - I can say, hand on heart, that I have no wish to "get my own back" on those adults who did so much to shape my young life; not least because most, if not all, the staff and officials from my time at Eastry have long since passed away. What I *am* concerned with are the historical and political perspectives – using the word "political" in a non-party sense. Having spent more than twenty years working in adult care and teaching I can report, from personal experience, that the abuse of power, the pettiness, the "don't do as I do, do as I say" attitude still prevails, just as it did at Eastry in the sixties.

Indeed, it seems to me that wherever, and whenever, vulnerable people – children, the aged, those with learning difficulties or mental health issues - are placed in the care of others, you should not be surprised to find – as I have found – abuse or, at the very least, the potential for abuse. This includes financial manipulation or plain neglect, as well as physical or sexual harm. Sadly, the devious, the bullies and the authoritarians continue to flourish. We - parents, carers, the authorities - can't afford to be complacent.

And here I must say that working with disadvantaged and vulnerable people has taught me that decent, compassionate folk - often too busy working hard, trying to make a difference, and a living (many front-line staff are paid at less than the National Living Wage) to get involved with the politics of it all - are, nevertheless, in the majority. Three or four examples turn up in the following pages. I hope you recognise them and take them to your heart, as I did all those years ago.

Doug Terry

Pembrokeshire 2025

*For my brothers
Edward, Andrew, Malcolm, and Ian*

And for Jo

No child under twelve years of age shall be punished by confinement, in a dark room or during the night.

Article 136 of Poor Law General Order
24th July 1847

CHAPTER ONE

A dot. An object in the far flat distance. But is it coming on, travelling towards us, or moving away, about to sink below the horizon? Squinting, I raise my hand to my brow. The dot blinks, expands, and then shrinks back, before lighting up again, pulsing like a flying saucer in the declining sunlight.

'Did you see that flash? Must be a mirror – or a mudguard. It's *him,*' I cry. 'It's Dad. It's his bike!'

A minute or so brings certainty. It *is* Dad coming home from his job at the brewery in Faversham. He's late, but then he's always late on a Friday; often it's seven o'clock before he gets home. Friday, you see, is pay day, and Dad, in common with the other men, must wait for his wages. Afterwards, the workers are given a free beer. For Dad, there is a five-mile cycle ride home.

'Bring up the radio.' Edward's reaction to the news of Dad's imminent arrival is to continue our game. Putting aside his imaginary binoculars, he adjusts his imaginary goggles, running a hand over the imaginary scar on the right side of his face.

He appears to have all the time in the world. Certainly, there is time to inform HQ, to shake the desert sand from tunics and equipment, and to set a trap.

Eventually the officer moves, and we, Andy, and I, follow, retreating into the field, squatting down in the flattened nest of corn that is our hideout.

'You there, Private Douglas. Creep forward. Go on, move up and report back.'

'I can't,' I say, clutching my thigh. 'It's my leg. I've been hit.'

'Nein, Nein, Nein,' snaps our exasperated Capitan (it seems we're the Germans this time round). 'This isn't El Alamein; we finished that battle before tea, and you lost. So, go back out there. You're the lookout. It's your turn.'

Following orders, I go down on my belly and inch forward, propelling myself along on elbows and knees, scratching my arms and legs on the flinty field surface.

'Where are the Britishers?' says our leader, in a half-whisper.

'Hold on.'

I'm listening for a squeaky pedal, an oil-parched chain, the tell-tale sound of a puncture repair kit dancing to the rock and roll of a rear-mounted saddle bag. It's a sure give away, that.

And, suddenly, there he is – a motor-cycle outrider! Experience – allied to a vivid imagination – tells me that a convoy of armoured cars and tanks, survivors of the minefield and quicksand, can't be far behind.

'Wait for it...Wait for it,' says the officer.

Action at last!

'Rous. Rous. Schnell. Schnell!' comes the comic-book command. The three of us boys rush out onto the road, machine guns blazing.

'Gotcha! Bang, bang, you're dead!'

'Oh no, I'm not,' says the enemy. A shake, a swerve, and a fistful of Milky Way stick grenades land at our feet. 'One each,' says Dad, and with a further wobble he is on his way home to Mum.

'Get you next time,' I shout to a flickering rear lamp. But the moment has passed.

'Don't be late. I want you home before dark,' Dad calls over his shoulder. 'Do you hear me, Edward? Before dark.'

Edward signals his compliance with a curt 'Jerval, mein Colonel.'

'And you can stop that silly language,' says a fast-disappearing Dad, in response.

Edward sticks out his tongue and gives a Nazi salute. He likes playing at Germans; they have Rommel, and the smartest uniforms.

*

Home was Doddington, an isolated settlement on top of the North Downs, six hundred feet above sea level. To the east ran, and runs, a series of ancient lanes and tracks, the old Pilgrim's Way leading to Canterbury, near to where Dad was born.

Dad's given name was Albert, so Mum called him Ted. Mum herself hailed from Marden, away in the valleys of the Medway and the Weald, twenty miles to the south and west. She was proud of her origins, and boasted that she shared her maiden name, Fuggle, with that of a Kentish hop.

'Every pub and off-licence in the country stocks bottles of beer with my name on them,' she'd say. But, like Dad, Mum never touched alcohol and hated her first name. 'Doris! What was your gran thinking of? It makes me sound like a blowsy barmaid, or a tart from one of those old war films.' Dad called her "Lovey".

We lived, surrounded by orchards and cornfields, in a small council-owned cottage on the outskirts of the village. 'If anyone asks, tell them you're from up the hill, a mile on from the Chequers Inn,' was how Dad told us to give directions. Not that I remember being stopped. There was little traffic – the postman or a bread van, or Mr. Doughty the butcher dropping off meat for Mum; lamb's liver or mince, when the housekeeping allowed.

Every now and then a green Maidstone and District bus - a single decker - sailed past on its way down to the village, from whence it continued to the main road, the A20, and from there on to Lenham, Charing or Ashford in one direction, or to Maidstone, our county town, in the other. But the service was sporadic, a motor bus too big a target for ambush and, since we boys went everywhere on foot, easily ignored when playing outdoors.

Yet everything, it seemed, was connected; something I was reminded of the day we came close to losing our sister.

'Is that your pram in the middle of the road, missus?' asked a breathless bus driver, appearing in the back garden. 'Be a love and come and shift it.'

'Oh, my God, Claire!' In one movement, Mum, who'd been in the garden attacking the sitting-room rugs, dropped her carpet beater, dumped her clothes-prop, and went off down the garden path like a thing possessed.

'It's okay, darlin,' called the bus driver. 'I had a peek. She's fast asleep.'

Following Mum down the sloping path to the road, the driver helped haul Claire's pram back up the garden steps.

'There,' he said, 'no harm done.'

But Mum didn't see it that way.

'Why can't you boys behave?' she said. 'I've got Malcolm and Ian indoors, there's the rugs to finish, the washing and ironing...Can't I leave your sister out for five minutes? Is that too much to ask?'

Someone was in for it when Dad got home. Edward, we decided.

War games. That was what we were playing in 1962, the year I've chosen to begin my story. That and Cowboys and Indians (Claire's pram made an excellent chuck wagon). Oh, and I seem to recall that we were expecting an alien invasion, probably from Mars, at any moment. But the monsters wouldn't get *us*. We were ready and waiting, and heavily armed, with cap guns, pea shooters and water pistols.

1962. There were six children by then. Edward (Teddy) was born in October 1953, six months after Mum and Dad's hastily arranged wedding. I was the second eldest, born in 1955, when there was still rationing, and Churchill was Prime Minister. Andy (Ned) came along in 1956, quickly followed by Malcolm (1958), Ian (1959), and Claire (1961).

Bringing up six children would be a challenge at any time, but for Mum it was a real struggle, not least because everything must be done without the benefit of electricity. It may have been 1962 but modern conveniences like gas and electricity still hadn't reached rural properties like ours, though pipes and cables had gotten as far as the village proper in the late fifties. Water via the mains arrived in 1960, but we were still waiting for a bathroom and an inside toilet.

Without electricity, we depended on a range. Lighting this big black monster, and "keeping it in" was a job for Dad, though we boys got into the habit of bringing home twigs and bits of wood to burn.

One of my earliest childhood memories is waking to the sound of Dad preparing the kitchen fire – riddling and raking and cleaning out the accumulated ash before lighting it with newspaper and kindling, to which Dad added cinders – lumps of coal, often still warm, that had survived incineration the night before. But it would still be late morning before the range was hot enough to boil a kettle or cook a meal. The best way to keep the fire in was by banking it up at night with coal and shutting the damper, so that it would still be alight the following day.

The living room fire, the family's only other source of heat, Mum had to light, except in winter when Dad kept it alive by damping down before bed. Then, in theory at least, it only needed someone to rake and stoke. A struggling fire would have a fistful of sugar thrown at it, and if this failed, Mum would cover the front with a sheet of newspaper which she pushed up against the tiled surround, holding it there until the fire began to roar. 'Come on, come *on,*' she'd say, impatiently willing the coals to burst into flames.

Once, and only once, Edward chose to lend a hand. 'Don't tell,' he whispered, quietly pulling back the wire mesh guard. But there was an art to rekindling a fire – you had to know when to stop – and Edward held the newspaper too near and for too long. All at once a brown scorch mark appeared in the middle, then quickly spread outwards until, suddenly, the paper burst into flames – just like the map at the beginning of *Bonanza,* I recalled afterwards.

'Mum,' we shouted. 'Come quickly. The house is on fire.'

Mum rushed in to find the room full of smoke and her three eldest sons engaged in a war dance, stamping charred paper and soot into the fireside rug, and making matters worse. 'You boys will be the death of me,' she said, thrusting Claire into my arms. 'Just wait until your father gets home!'

But it was a long day, with plenty of scope for distraction, and by the time Dad walked in, the living room was clean, Mum having gone about with a brush and pan, turning the rug over to hide the scorch marks.

Meanwhile, her three Indian braves, not so brave after all, sat squeezed up on the old horse-hair settee in front of a crackling fire, all smiles, and angelic faces, looking like butter wouldn't melt. Andy was reading, I was pretending to read, and Edward was bouncing Claire up and down on his knee in time to music from the old battery-powered Bakelite radio which lived in the corner. And to complete the scene, a couple of strategically placed candles, backed up by the light from a paraffin lamp, illuminated a collection of vases, jam jars and milk bottles filled almost to tipping point with honeysuckles, dog-rose and dusty-faced daisies, the fruits of an afternoon's reparation work.

'You won't get around me like *that*,' Mum said as I launched yet another armful of daises in her direction. But we did.

*

Wash day, following tradition, should have been Monday, with the ironing done on Tuesday (pronounced *choose day*), sewing, and mending on Wednesday, and so forth. But for Mum everyday was wash day and ironing day, and cleaning day. And with none of the labour-saving devices we take for granted today, it must have been a hard slog.

Looking back, I don't think Mum would have managed for as long as she did without help from her mother-in-law.

Gran Terry, baptized Alice Amelia, was known by the more familiar name Millie. Physically she was a tall, 'handsome' woman and, at the time of which I am writing, in her mid-fifties. She lived in a row of terraced cottages at West End, on the opposite side of the village, but came up most days to help Mum with the housework.

Although there was little love lost between them, Mum, as I have said, would have struggled without Gran. Closing my eyes, I can still see her, bent over the kitchen sink, rubbing away at collars and cuffs with a big bar of green soap, a burning cigarette hanging from her mouth, the ash threatening to fall into the wash.

And while Gran dealt with the washing, a large saucepan of dirty nappies, left to soak overnight, would be boiling away on the range. Once this lot was ready and rinsed everything would be taken outside to go through an old mangle, before being put on the line. Wet days were a disaster. Then the washing was draped over the fireguard in the living room, steaming nappies, romper suits, all of it, five or six items at a time. Meanwhile, larger items like sheets and pillowcases were strung across the kitchen or, weather allowing, aired outside on a wooden clothes horse or, when this was full, draped across the garden fence or convenient hedge.

Gran was a determined woman with a "can do" attitude, one that came with a whole dictionary of chivvying expressions. 'Come on, Douglas,' she'd say, pointing to a heap of dirty crockery. 'Get stuck in. Life's too short for peeling mushrooms.' Then she'd throw me a cloth. All of us older boys had to help with the chores, or look after the younger ones, while Gran sorted the washing, and Mum did the ironing or made tea. Any sign of rebellion meant a reminder that children should be seen and not heard.

Mostly, of course, we just wanted to finish and go out to play, but you had to pick your moment.

'I've done the dishes, Gran. Can I go now?'

'What about the rubbish? Have you taken out the ash, like I asked?'

Start whining or, worse still, interrupt Gran when she was talking, and she'd tell you to hush up. 'Little boys' tea doesn't run yet' she'd say. Or, along the same lines, but for a bit of variety, 'You'll have to be patient.

Rome wasn't built in a day.' Then, just when you'd given up hope, Gran would relent. 'Go on then, off you go. But don't wander off.'

Playing in the front garden, we made daisy chains, teased each other with dandelion clocks (one puff, one chance; fail and you were doomed to wet the bed), went through the buttercup test, struggled, but eventually mastered, the arts of hat and paper plane making, and learned to communicate over huge distances – about twenty feet - using old bits of string and a couple of tin cans.

A particular challenge - something I'm sure I'd fail now - involved making a moving vehicle, made of a cotton reel, half a clothes peg, and an elastic band. When summer came, Dad carved us a pair of crude, but serviceable, cricket bats.

The back garden was given over to food production. Paths, made of concrete slabs, separated strips of cabbage, carrots and potatoes, and there were runner beans too, one year grown in rows, the next in wigwams. There was also an old garden shed. This was Dad's private den, which he kept locked. It held dangerous things; sharp garden tools, as well as chemicals needed for dealing with pests - though the best thing for slugs, Gran advised, was beer, poured into saucers.

At the very rear of the garden, beyond a rough area surrounded by weeds and brambles, the ground, topped by rickety fencing, led up to a cherry orchard. Here, atop the bank, and on permanent, proud display, lay the things I'd dug out of the soil: broken clay pipes, bits of animal bone, and my best finds, two clay flagons with maker's marks pushed into wet clay, the largest, and latest, dated 1887.

After days of pestering, Dad had set aside a small patch of vegetable garden for me, encouraging the propagation of carrots, lettuce, and radishes, sown from seed. I was pleased, of course, but the main attraction, for me, were the man-made things I'd found and pulled out while turning the soil. My laid-up bottles were more than seventy years old and had once held cider. Just think, I told myself, seventy years! Decades back a couple of farm hands had drunk from these same containers. Afterwards, with no eye to the future, they'd tossed the empties away, leaving them abandoned, waiting, almost intentionally it seemed, for me to lift and celebrate, and begin to think about how I too might be remembered.

Inspired, I set about preparing a time capsule of my own, a more deliberate message to the future. A few days later, in a private and solemn ceremony (looking over my shoulder to see that I wasn't being watched), I buried a tin containing a farthing (a coin that had gone out of circulation a year or so before), some pages from a comic, and a scrap of paper, folded into a matchbox, giving my name and date of birth. For all I know, it's still there today.

The garden, front or back, couldn't hold us boys for long; outside an entire world waited, inviting exploration. A high plateau under a big, wide sky was our stage; our props – Claire's pram aside – anything we could beg, borrow, or steal from the house, the hedgerows or nearby woods, farms, and fields.

Not that we had to go far to find adventure. Across the road, at the T-Junction, stood Cuthbert's Farm. Old Cuthbert and his family had lived there for years, generations probably, and, over time, had accumulated a veritable miser's hoard of oil drums, broken gates and fencing, buckets and barrels, wheels, and wheelbarrows. And, dominating the corner, half hidden by thistles and ragwort, stood an old, abandoned tractor, an ideal base for hide-and-seek and a dozen other games. The first one over there was the king of the castle.

That tractor became a tank, a racing car, a motor torpedo boat - the possibilities were endless. And when our collective imaginations faltered, there were farm cats and chickens to torment, moving targets for homemade catapults and pea shooters, made from the dry stems of hogweed.

At the end of May, an internal clock, with which we boys were fully in tune, sent farmer Cuthbert out a-wassailing, visiting his orchards, there to oversee that annual, religious country ritual: the garlanding of the year's blossoming fruit trees.

Each tree was visited in turn, a favoured few being draped with twisted lengths of rope, decorated with bright-red cylinders. These ropes, we discovered, were bird-scarers, the orchard equivalent of a scarecrow, set alight and smouldering, high up among the branches.

The staggered cylinders, shotgun cartridges, were set to go off at intervals, one every fifteen minutes or so. Why not take a bag full, Edward suggested, and use them for our own purposes? Live explosives would add a whole new dimension to our war games; from now on fights and battles would be played out for real. So, we planned and plotted, watched, and waited - and got caught red-handed dragging one of the ropes from a tree. Perhaps it was just as well.

Later in the year, the fire brigade sent an officer to inspect the bonfire we had built, in August, ready for Guy Fawkes night. Someone from the village had reported the pile as a potential danger. Mum was livid and demanded to have the name of the person responsible. 'Bloody fox hunters and whist drivers,' she said.

But Officer King didn't know or wasn't prepared to say. Yet he was a kindly enough man, accepting the offer of a cup of tea and letting Ian climb all over him, playing with his cap and counting the shiny buttons on his tunic.

'And how old are you, little man?'

'Three.'

'And when will you be four?'

'On my birthday.'

Officer King went out to the garden, to examine our bonfire. 'Do you boys know what happens when rubber burns?' he asked, pulling an old bicycle tyre out from the middle of the stack. 'No' I said, in innocent denial. But I did. Only a week before, we three older boys had built a woodland fire which included, as its centrepiece, a worn, abandoned car tyre, lighting it with a box of matches stolen from home, just to see what would happen.

It began slowly, with a smoulder of newspaper sheets and larch shavings, then nothing, just smoke and a momentary, dying glow from a handful of twigs. So, we tried again. And again. Finally, with a last handful of paper and matches came fire.

Yellow at first, then a lazy blue, followed by an oily, iridescent green, we watched as the flames grew and grew, snake tongues forking out from within. Reconnoitring, they rose up to consider us, a waiting, expectant audience of three, before disappearing, darting, weaving, and writhing back towards the hidden centre of things. Then came a pause, a last chance to prod and poke, or even to walk away, before a sudden burst of sound and light announced the beginning of the show proper.

Wood crackled, sparks flew skyward, green branches and wet leaves spat and hissed. For long minutes, flames shot outwards and upwards in all directions. Soon, with the temperature reaching melting point, came a final, magical transformation, as the rubber tyre, our star performer, began to ooze and liquify. A stinking mess, a mass of molten lava, the tyre boiled, erupting, and flowing like the delta of a volcano cone.

Now it was too late. There was no going back, no making things right, no doing anything other than to stand and watch, awestruck and choking, careless of burning faces and running eyes, mesmerised by the fierce heat, lost in an explosion of seething, violent colours. And panicked by the arrival of Charlie Finn, the local gamekeeper.

'I found these little savages in my wood!' Charlie didn't bother to knock, just bundled the three of us through the front door of our cottage and into the living room. Before Mum could react, he had Edward by the ear. 'And this one,' Charlie said, *'this one* - he could hardly get the words out – had the cheek, the *cheek* I tell you, to call me *paleface*! Said they were only playing Cowboys and Indians, he did. And he *smirked.* Answered back and smirked! If you ask me the three of them deserve the belt. And if I had my way, that's exactly what they'd get. I'd give them a bloody good hiding - one they'd never forget.'

Charlie reeled off a list of other woodland transgressions. It was, I must confess, a long one, ranging from trampling saplings and dismantling piles of cleared and stacked logs to springing traps and interfering with a holocaust of cadavers; magpies, crows, weasels and stoats, creatures slaughtered and pinned up on the branches of trees, both as a deterrent and as trophies, showing just who was boss.

Regular intruders, Edward, our leader, had rejoiced in taking down any crucified creature he found, insisting on giving the stoats and weasels a Christian burial, complete with improvised memorial. The birds fared less well, their wings and feathers removed in a scientific effort to discover how they got airborne and managed to fly.

Such outrages, Charlie said, went back to the spring, when our trespassing had taken us even deeper into the woods, to the areas where his pheasants were sitting. He'd found dozens of eggs crushed.

Mum promised that Dad would have words when he got in from work, then "forgot" all about it.

*

At home for the evening, away from temptation and trouble, we boys made our own entertainment; reading, or teaching each other to read, putting together jigsaws or playing dominoes and cards.

Every now and then, if one of us pestered long enough, a box of photographs would appear. 'Be careful,' came the warning, as a much-cherished pile of pictures was passed round. We would wait impatiently to hear, for the umpteenth time, the stories behind them, each snapshot, no matter how dog-eared, receiving respect, if not reverence.

'That's your dad,' Mum would remind me, and I'd gaze again at a young boy holding a rifle, and wearing a helmet, standing to attention. Dad's borrowed kit belonged to one of the soldiers billeted with Gran when the family lived over at Birchington.

It was 1940, Dunkirk, and thousands of troops needed somewhere to sleep. And how did that work? Well, the military just knocked on the door, Mum explained. Any spare rooms, missus? Then, looking a bit sheepish, and very, very tired, a soldier was handed over to Gran Terry. Dad was eight years old, my age, and had enjoyed every moment of it.

Ten years later Dad had his own uniform. He'd left school to join the RAF and went to train at Halton in Buckinghamshire (it was the furthest he ever went from home). Dad was an apprentice armourer, with the rank of corporal, tasked with loading bombs onto a new generation of jet fighters and bombers.

Dad seldom mentioned his past. Mostly, it was Mum who talked about his service history and the friends he made. From Dad I learned I owed my name to one of them. 'His nickname was Jock, but to me he was always Douglas, or Doug.'

Alas, Dad's Airforce career was destined to be a short one. A year or so after signing up, Dad was diagnosed with kidney problems. After various tests and examinations, surgeons removed his right kidney, and he was discharged from the service.

On Mum's side of the family, there were pictures of Uncle John and Auntie Betty, Mum's elder siblings. John, the first born, was something of an enigma. Based in Cyprus, he was a civil servant, seconded to the War Office. As for rank, title, or job description, well, that was anybody's guess; it was all very hush-hush. Uncle John had signed the Official Secrets Act, and, according to Mum, never spoke about his work.

Auntie Betty's life was, by comparison, an open book. Ten years older than her sister, there were half a dozen pictures of her, often with friends, at the seaside, and studio portraits, more formal and posed. She was short and slim, and had dark wavy hair and blue eyes, an older version of Mum.

With the outbreak of war, Auntie Betty joined the Land Army, as shown by another series of photographs featuring Betty and her co-workers, five or six athletic-looking girls draped over a five-barred gate, hair pinned up, dressed in dungarees of regulation corduroy.

Again, the picture seemed posed, and it is easy, now, to imagine the photographer's instructions: 'Go on, girls, shake your spades, axes, and rakes in Adolf's direction. Show him what you're made of!'

Then Auntie Betty moved to America. A war bride, hers was a classic wartime romance. It all happened at a dance arranged to welcome the US Army; two starstruck young people, an engagement and, in 1946, marriage in the United States.

Now Auntie Betty lived on a farm near Chattanooga, in Tennessee, where Uncle Harold hired out earth moving equipment, and traded knives and guns. Once, by a sort of serendipity, the song "Chattanooga Choo Choo" came on the wireless as we were admiring some well-thumbed photographs. Dad was tuning in, looking for *Friday Night is Music Night*, and there it was: "Pardon me boy, is that the Chattanooga Choo Choo?" After that we all learned the lyrics and it became a family anthem.

Mum's war included a spell as an evacuee. Aged just four, she found herself packed off to South Wales. 'Thousands went,' she explained. 'We must have been quite a sight, with our little suitcases, name tags and gas masks hanging round our necks. Somewhere near Merthyr Tydfil is where I ended up. I went from the train to a community hall, joining a line of other children, each of us in need of a home.

'I was one of the youngest and was taken in by a family called Williams. They were nice enough – Mr. Williams was a bank manager I seem to remember – but I couldn't get used to the place. There was the language of course, and the Welsh accents. And I had to go to chapel on Sundays. But the worst thing about it was the countryside, and the weather.

'Wales is a wild and windy place, not a country for fruit or hops. We lived among little valleys of sloping terraced houses, overlooked by slag heaps from the coal pits. And grey; everything was grey. The pit ponies were grey, the miners were grey, and the roofs were covered with grey slates. The only colourful things were the bracken in the autumn and the yellow gorse that covered the hillsides in the spring.

'I was young, of course, much too young to understand, but I couldn't see why anybody would choose to live in such a place. Even the trees looked unhealthy; they were small and scrubby and bent over in the wind. They almost looked as though they were trying to run away!'

I was spellbound – like children everywhere I found it hard, even faced with the photographic evidence, to believe that any adult had, once upon a time, also been a child. In any case, what I was really waiting for was the story about the bombing. This one never failed to hold my attention, even after the umpteenth telling.

'What about the plane, Mum?'

'What about it?'

'Well, what could you see? Could you see the pilots' faces?'

'No,' Mum would say. 'I've told you. The bombers were much too high. But you could hear them overhead and we children were taught at school to know the difference. Our planes, the fighters, were faster and lighter, while the Germans came over slowly, with a sound like a heavy droning.

'But this morning, the one you're asking about, there was another noise, a loud bang – more of a thud, really. A bomb, a single bomb, they said later. Probably, it was one the crew forgot to drop on Swansea or Cardiff.

'Anyway, I was looking up the street, searching for "Jones the Milk," as they called him. And Thomas, Jones' horse, well, it was twenty years ago, but I can still see him, the poor creature. He was standing on the hill, on the other side of the cobbles, his head buried in a nose bag, as good as gold. Then, wallop! He was gone. I heard a sort of whistle, then up in the air it went - horse, cart, churns, the whole lot. Thomas was never seen again, and nor was Jones the Milk.

'Then, well, Mrs. Williams was at the door, pulling on my sleeve, telling me to come away. She wanted me to get under the kitchen table, in case more bombs dropped. But I couldn't move. And after Mrs. Williams saw the damage, she couldn't move either. We stood there, the two of us, awestruck, rooted to the spot. Shock, I suppose.

'Soon, as we watched, one of the two big wheels from Jones' dogcart came spinning down the road; just like a child's hoop it was, rattle, rattle, down the middle of the street. And close behind came a stream of milk, washing through the gutter; white, streaked with red blood.

'Then the front of the bombed house fell away – collapsing like a pack of cards. It made me jump, it did. There was smoke and dust everywhere, a big plume mushrooming upwards; I'll never forget it, if I live to be a hundred.

'Afterwards, you could see right into the building, into the rooms. I remember the iron bedsteads, and the wallpaper, peeling off the walls. And in the sitting room, a settee and two armchairs, with not a mark on them.

'But the thing I remember most was the piano. I wanted to reach in and touch the keys; I had an overwhelming urge to move all the furniture around, like playing in a giant doll's house.

'Then, after a second or two, Mrs. Williams came to her senses and pulled me away. She was obviously surprised by the piano. "I never knew the Pritchards were musical," she said. "There's posh, isn't it!"

'When your Gran found out about the bombing, she brought me home. I think she'd taken the Luftwaffe's attacks on South Wales personally, deciding that I might as well be back in Kent. And, of course, she'd missed me.'

Other photographs from the family collection included a picture of Mum and Dad on their wedding day. It was April 1953, and their marriage was followed by a two-day honeymoon – a trip to Maidstone Zoo and the Easter-time point-to-point races at Charing.

Older still, and well-faded, was a photo of Grandad John Fuggle, who'd died of pneumonia when Mum, born in 1936, was 11 years old.

Most memorable was the picture and story relating to Ellen Paige, Mum's grandmother. Middle-aged in her photograph, Ellen, born Ellen Button, had once, Mum said, been a real beauty, so much so that a local artist asked to paint her portrait. At the time Ellen was a pupil at a Maidstone charity school and the artist in question had begged permission to capture Ellen's likeness; in return he offered to donate a sum to school funds. 'Her picture is hanging in Maidstone Museum,' Mum said. 'When you're older you should go and have a look for yourselves.'

Books, games, and family history aside, the family's main source of entertainment was the wireless set. It was a real beast of a machine this, and frustratingly slow to warm up; once turned on it was a good minute or two before a set of valves began to glow through the brass mesh. Then a list of strange sounding destinations, Hilversham, Allouis, Athlone, Luxembourg, engraved along the top of the cabinet, lit up, tempting a young listener to tune in, and dream of foreign travel.

I remember turning the dial back and forth, taking my time, keeping the whistles, crackles, and hisses to a minimum, trying to find Radio Luxembourg. Then Dad would intervene, telling me to put the radio back on to the BBC Light Programme; he wanted to catch the early evening news and the weather forecast. Afterwards Dad insisted on listening as a posh sounding man broadcast a "general synopsis" for sea conditions in some more distant, foreign places; Dogger, Fastnet, Biscay, and Trafalgar; alluring destinations, though regularly pounded by storms and gales, it seemed.

Closer to home, we had our own share of harsh weather; autumn rains that slashed at the cottage windows howling and moaning, rattling at the doors, shaking the roof, creeping in through a smoking, seldom swept chimney, as if desperately looking for somewhere to hide.

Then, in late December 1962, came warnings of a cold snap, with the possibility of ice, hail, and snow. In for the evening, we listened and shivered, then moved closer together, paying little heed; the fire roared, the front door curtain and doorstop held; the family was settled, safe and snug, cheered by a warming drink and that ever-comforting voice of the man from the BBC. Maybe we'd get a white Christmas?

*

The snow began falling late on Christmas day, at bedtime. Thin, sleety stuff at first, the snowflakes were soon coming down thick and fast. Filled with excitement, Andy and Edward joined me at the bedroom window, the three of us making plans for the morning, to go out and play with our toys – Winchester rifles, a wigwam, balsa wood planes, presents delivered by Santa the night before.

But Boxing Day brought blizzards, keeping the family shut up indoors. For me, all thoughts of playing out, of Cowboys and Indians, snowballs, and snowmen, disappeared before I'd reached the outside toilet. By mid-morning, the garden outbuildings were only accessible using a shovel to keep the short walkway open.

Dad, fearing the worst, had risen early, fetching a box of kindling from the shed, piling up wood and the remains of our coal supplies outside the backdoor, just in case.

And Dad was right to be worried. Within three or four hours, the snow lay more than a foot deep; by the end of the day the temperature had dropped to minus twenty, and the drifting snow had closed the road. Only our excitement melted away; Christmas was no fun anymore.

Soon the days began to run into each other, and the focus was one of simple survival. A week in and the household coal stock, seriously depleted, was being rationed. Soon we were down to the last bucket. Dad fetched in an old paraffin heater, but the fuel only lasted an hour or two and, besides, it was dangerous; a paraffin stove is not designed to be used in a confined space, without ventilation. We children pushed and shoved, playing a silent game of musical chairs, fighting to be nearer to this extra heat source, not knowing that it was the paraffin that caused our drowsiness, headaches and, eventually, nausea.

Ultimately, the best way to keep warm was to go to bed, Edward, Andy, and I sharing a mattress, with old army coats thrown on to give more warmth. We took turns to be the one in the middle, which was the snuggest place to be.

Waking in the mornings, like three bears disturbed during a winter hibernation, the end of the bad weather seemed a long, long way off. The bedroom window, fascinating at first, was frosted with strange patterns and whirls, while outside, beyond the cottage confines, the world was one of hushed silence, with swords of ice hanging from the windows and porch.

During the day, the family's time was spent trying to keep the fire going. Anything which would burn was thrown into the flames. An arctic expedition out to the garden shed yielded two apple boxes, fork and spade handles and a dibber; an old pair of Dad's working boots went onto the fire, one at a time. The Christmas tree, long since stripped of its chocolate decorations, was next; the pine branches flaring and crackling, dropping needles in protest, releasing a final, farewell Yuletide aroma.

Next, the kitchen bin was raided; chicken bones, discarded crackers, wrapping paper and school-made paper chains making a desperate, and meagre addition to fuel supplies. Finally, Dad splintered Claire's highchair, and that too found itself consigned to the flames. At one point cannibal eyes were directed at the wooden cavalry fort Malcolm had been given for Christmas. But that was where Dad drew the line. We needed to find other sources of fuel, and quickly, before the fire went out.

With the snow continuing to fall, trapping the family indoors, the larder shelves were quickly stripped and left bare. Extra bread and milk had been bought ready for Christmas, and a search of the kitchen produced tins and jars, corned beef, pilchards, macaroni cheese and such like. Dad boiled the kettle on the open fire for cups of tea, or a hot drink of Bovril, but lighting the kitchen range and cooking a warm meal was out; it would mean using up precious fuel, and besides, none of us could raise the energy. A miserable New Year was welcomed in with half-empty boxes of Melbury Fruits, dates and orange and lemon slices, leftover Christmas fayre Dad got in every year, and which the rest of us usually turned our noses up at.

Help arrived when a labourer from Cuthbert's Farm came dragging a sled loaded with logs. He didn't need to open the garden gate; it was no longer there, his sleigh glided over feet of snow, which seemed to cover the entire world.

The next day a snow plough came through, and for a week or so it was possible to get down to the village, but only by arranging a lift on a tractor. It was now that the snow fences went up; then the snow returned and these barriers, intended to prevent drifting, proved to be quite useless.

Work was out of the question. Dad couldn't get to Faversham; the North Kent coast was cut off by the snow and was completely inaccessible. At Whitstable, the man on the radio told us, the sea had frozen over. Nationwide, trains, buses – the whole transport system – had ground to a halt. People were already calling it "the big freeze". It went on for nearly three months.

*

For Dad, no work meant no wages. He had to claim National Assistance, trudging miles through the snow and ice to the Labour Exchange in Sittingbourne, battling through winds that whistled in from the east. Luckily, he soon managed to organize a ride, joining other men facing the same challenge.

And so, it went on. Sometimes, between spells of sleet and snow, two or three milk bottles would appear on the doorstep, attracting a mob of blue tits, tapping at the silver tops. They had to be quick. In no time at all the milk froze, expanding, mushrooming up, leaving the bottles topped with strange-shaped, Cappadocian fairy castles.

One afternoon, the coalman arrived and dropped off a sack of rationed coal and there were sporadic deliveries of mail. Then the skies turned leaden, more snow fell, and the milkman, the coalman, and other trades ceased to trade. Muffled silence closed us in again, the only signs of life being the arrow footprints of birds, and yellow streaks of animal urine staining the snow which, morning fresh, once again blanketed the garden.

A new school term came, but attendance was sporadic, to say the least. The school boiler broke down; the infants' toilets froze over; staff couldn't get in from outlying districts; morning milk and lunchtime meals didn't materialise; the weatherman warned against all but essential travel. Was school essential? No, Mum decided.

Then, at the beginning of March, with snow still on the ground, Gran died. It was cancer; a slow death, long in coming.

We'd all knew Gran was ill. She didn't come up at Christmas, though her presents for us, wrapped in advance, were found under the tree. At first Dad, in denial, made excuses, blaming the weather. But one night he sat the family down and told us that Gran had been admitted to a sanatorium, a sort of hospital, he explained.

Dad visited when he could, coming back looking pale, tired, and crestfallen. He seemed hunched, smaller somehow. Gran was getting better, he'd say, and sent her love. Soon we learned not to ask.

*

Gran's cottage had been a refuge, somewhere we boys knew we would always be welcome. A regular Saturday afternoon destination, calling on Gran was both a treat, and a break for Mum and Dad, as well as giving them a little space. Attractions included the village shop, and a play area, with swings and slides and a roundabout, and room to kick a ball.

But the main draw was the television. Gran, like so many others of her generation, had bought a TV for the queen's coronation, and it was still in good working order ten years later, in 1962. On Saturday afternoons we boys would sit and watch Grandstand - horse racing, speedway and wrestling, and the rest. Mostly, though, we played in the village park, coming back in time for tea. But silence was the rule when the football results came on, since Gran "did the pools" and was due to win a fortune any day now, if not sooner.

Fortunately for us, though I'm not sure it was appreciated at the time, Gran owned a bathroom, with a bath, toilet, and sink, installed and plumbed in. At home we made do with an old tin tub, taken down from the back wall then checked, at Mum's insistence, for bugs and spiders before Dad brought it in and set it down in front of the fire. Filling the bath with water, and keeping it warm, was demanding work and took time. Often, we just stepped in and stood still while Dad gave us a "strip wash". Cold weather often meant "a lick and a promise".

But for Gran, sending her three oldest boys home scrubbed and clean was a matter of personal pride. Complain as we might, she had standards, and she expected them to be kept.

Looking back, one of my strongest memories of Gran is the leaving of her. It was late October, and we were headed home. Edward decided that it was his turn to carry the battery-charged Chinese lantern torch Dad had put together to light us through the gathering gloom. It was here, homeward bound, that we halted, Gran insisting on one last round of hugs, kisses, and cuddles.

Half-way up Chequer's Hill, out of range of further "soppy" assaults, we turned, chorusing our thanks and goodbyes, waving as Gran's tall, slightly stooping figure was swallowed up by the dusk. 'Go on, get yourselves home,' came the echoing reply.

And then she was gone.

*

It was left to Mum to account for Gran's death. 'Gran's in heaven,' I was told. Then, after I pressed for more information, Mum promised that I would see Gran again one day. As an explanation I found this far from satisfactory. It left me worried and confused, with a whole raft of further questions. After all, for a future reunion to come about I too had to die, and since I had no plans to do so until I was very, very old - if not older - I couldn't see how Gran would recognise me when, like a naughty schoolboy sent to wait outside the headmaster's office, I was eventually, and inevitably, obliged to turn up. Only, I wouldn't be eight anymore, would I? No, I'd be ancient. Gran, on the other hand, wouldn't have aged at all. Or would she? And what about heaven itself? How much room was there? What if it was full up when I arrived? Suppose it was full up when *Mum* got there?

And I wasn't finished. 'Mum,' I asked, with some anxiety, 'has Gran really gone to heaven?'

'Of course, she has.'

'Well, how come she still visits me, then?'

'Don't be silly, it's just your imagination.'

But I persisted. 'Gran does come, honest. Nearly every night.' Unable to get me to change my story, Mum made me agree to keep Gran's "visits" to myself. On no account was I to say anything, especially to Dad.

As far as I remember, I kept my promise, but I am willing to swear, even now, that Gran did come. She sat at the end of the bed, sideways on, just as she did when she came upstairs to say goodnight or read a bedtime story. I could smell her perfume and feel the weight of her body pressing on the mattress. I'd lie still, propped up on the bolster, while Gran, in turn, sat looking at me, smiling an enigmatic smile. No words passed between us; I was incapable of speech, nor could I move or reach out to touch her. But I wasn't into the bedroom to meet my sister. 'She'd get one too,' she added, 'if this was the Soviet Union.'

The Russians, it seemed, valued mothers of large families very highly. Women like Mum were treated as heroes of the state; feted, much photographed, and rewarded with a home for life.

Now, following Gran's death, Dr. Wall called again. He was after Mum, and she knew it. Seeing him at the door, she turned and rushed towards the stairs but the doctor, arms flapping like he was shooing a goose back into a farmyard, quickly had her cornered. Now he needed Dad's help. 'Come on man, keep her still while I find a vein...'

And Dad cooperated. 'Do what he says, lovey. It's for the best, I promise. It's only Valium.'

A syringe appeared, and a bitter liquid shot into the air. Mum became hysterical, struggling like a frightened animal. 'Ted, Ted, get him away. Make him stop.' But the doctor persevered. 'There now, that wasn't so bad, was it?'

Dr. Wall returned the next day, and again before the end of the week. Soon Mum gave up struggling, becoming docile and withdrawn. She was being prepared for what was to come.

Towards the end, any number of other people turned up. The rent man, Mr. Crabb, was the most persistent, and had been calling at the house once or twice a week since early March. At first, Mum, seeing him coming, tried to make a game of it; 'Hush up,' she'd say, and we'd all duck down behind the furniture. It was great fun, and a relief when Mr. Crabb turned around and walked back down the garden path. But the arrears were mounting.

Mr. Doughty the butcher called, and the milkman as well; both had long since stopped delivering and were growing tired of Mum's vague promises of payment. Under pressure, Mum agreed to hand her creditors something on account on Family Allowance day, so they took to coming to the house on Tuesday mornings, before she had a chance to spend it.

One evening, just before bedtime, Mr. Smith, the village shopkeeper, knocked at the door, asking for Dad. 'I've come to offer my condolences,' he said.

'You'll have to take us as you find us,' Mum replied, as our caller stepped into the front room. Then, leaving Mr. Smith with Dad,

Mum turned the radio down, whipped away four or five steaming nappies from the fireguard and, sending us boys upstairs, made herself scarce, disappearing into the kitchen.

It soon became clear that this was more than a social call. 'Now look here,' Mr. Smith began, producing an all too familiar red exercise book. 'I don't want to make things worse than they already are, but, well, there are rumours in the village. My customers are saying you're moving away. I hope you're not planning to do a "moonlight". There's the money…I can't afford the loss…I'm not a charity…'

There was more. As well as providing for herself, Gran, like Dad, had obtained supplies for the family "on tick". Now she was gone and although Mr. Smith sympathised, well, business was business; he couldn't live on fresh air. He expected Dad to settle both accounts, so much a week on top of the usual bill.

I remember sneaking out of bed and sitting near the bottom of the stairs listening to the conversation as it unfolded.

A child, unable to see the bigger picture, I felt partly responsible. Had I helped give the game away? Earlier in the day, Mum had sent me down to the shop to buy tea. Six packets, and it had to be Brooke Bond.

Packets of Brooke Bond tea carried Dividend Stamps - orange in colour, about two thirds the size of a standard postage stamp, and Mum needed six more to complete a savings card, which could then be exchanged for cash. So off to the village I went, and then back again, trading in the completed card for twenty Embassy. My reward? A sherbet dip – and the certain, and embarrassing, knowledge that I had provided Mr. Smith with evidence of our family's poverty.

Mr. Smith, you see, refused credit for cigarettes; he considered them a luxury, and like all "non-essentials" only accepted cash. Unfortunately, the list of banned goods didn't stop with cigarettes and, indeed, seemed to increase week by week. Peanut butter, potato crisps, chocolate spread... Mr. Smith took care, always, to work his way down the list. A shake of the head, a raised eyebrow, and a much-used red pencil appeared from behind his ear, with which he crossed through the offending items. Bacon, cheese, and such were acceptable purchases, because they needed weighing, and because Mr. Smith thought we children didn't know the difference between ten ounces and twelve. He was wrong.

Thinking about it now, it must have been quite a mental struggle, Mr. Smith balancing the loss of trade against the possibility, or otherwise, of getting paid. Mum used to rage about it. 'Isn't our money as good as the next person's?' she'd say. For his part, Mr. Smith had probably concluded that the "next person" was almost certainly a better bet. Mum, I remember, use to refer to him, with real spite, as "an old Jew Boy".

*

Mr. Tremain, from the NSPCC, came during the last week of May. He took us, Edward, Andy, and I, out to the back garden for a chat. 'We need to make some changes,' he began. 'This house is too small...your mum can't cope...'

The three of us sat on the bank and listened, dumbstruck, while Mr. Tremain explained what was going to happen next. Everything, it seemed, had already been settled.

'There's a council run hostel at West Malling, a few miles away, on the other side of Maidstone,' we were told. 'You'll be moving in there with Mum.'

And Dad? Well, fathers weren't allowed, but separation would give Dad an opportunity to look for a new home, a bigger house, with room for everyone. Any questions?

'Is it our fault?' I asked. 'Is it because of Mr. Finn's pheasants? Is that why we've got to leave?'

For a moment I considered asking for a host of other crimes to be taken into consideration; among them trampling corn, kicking over feeding troughs, and interfering with milk churns, but thought better of it.

Mr. Tremain, smiling, put his arm round my shoulder. 'Now look,' he said, and went on to repeat his words about Mum and the house. The rent arrears went unmentioned.

Is there ever a suitable moment for a family to be evicted? Of course not. But turning us out now, in the spring, when the world, our world, the garden and the fields and orchards, was coming back into new life seemed, even at the time, to be particularly harsh. Our young lives ran with the seasons; we lived by the country calendar, a rural almanac with continuity written at the top of every page. And why should it end? Already the swallows were returning, the same pairs, Gran had told me, that nested with us every year, flown thousands of miles over the curve of the earth, across jungle and desert, leaving South Africa, determined to reach their northern summer home, beneath the eaves of our cottage.

There were other annual miracles. Across the road, the cornfields, after long weeks carpeted with snow, had come back to life, their brown winter stubble sprouting green, stretching away into the distance. Already the maythorn in the hedges had begun to fade, soon to give way to honeysuckle, dog roses, hips, and berries. In the woods, early anemones, celandine, and primrose bowed to purple foxgloves, while all along the chalky roadside verges, bright red poppies conspired to take advantage of convenient cracks and crevices. Come July, I knew, these poppies would be everywhere, invading the fields, a splash of life-giving blood among the golden corn which swayed and rustled, with ears fit to burst, in the high summer breeze.

Signalling the end of summer came the harvesters; big machines going up and down, back, and forth, stripping the fields. Taking advantage of the dry weather, the work went on until dusk, the men stopping only for a swig of beer or cider, their day's labour ending with Massey Ferguson lights blazing, picking out the last of the rabbits as they broke cover. Then came the noise of the shotguns, followed by silence.

Leave? We couldn't leave. Forget idyllic ramblings and nostalgia, Edward, who'd been deep in thought, put forward his own, more prosaic argument. What about school? It was May half-term but next week we'd have to go back. We *had* to go to school. Every child went to school. It was the law.

Mr. Tremain listened, but it was no good. Legal matters, he explained, were for other people, grown-ups, to worry about. And besides, there was a school in West Malling, near to our new, temporary, home. He was sure we'd soon settle in and make new friends. It was up to us boys to help things go smoothly, to look after the younger ones, and not to upset Mum. He'd sort the rest.

Then Dad came and joined us. 'Don't worry about me, I'll be alright,' he said, in response to Edward's questioning. 'You boys just make sure you look after your mother and your sister.'

Mr. Tremain went over the practical arrangements, while Dad sat quietly by, head bowed, occasionally nodding his agreement. The day of our departure, we learned, was just forty-eight hours away. Mr. Peters, a removal man from Sittingbourne, had been booked and was coming tomorrow to drop off a pile of tea chests. And since Mum had refused council transport, he'd also agreed to deliver the family to King Hill, to the hostel. 'You boys will have to choose one or two toys to take with you...'

I didn't want to listen, didn't want to hear. Thrown into a state of panic and confusion, I could hardly imagine life without Dad, or, for that matter, Mum being able to cope on her own. Yet fathers weren't allowed to live with their families at the camp. Why was that? 'Your Dad's got digs, in Maidstone,' I was told. 'But you'll still see him at weekends.'

'What's digs?' Andy asked. 'And what's the NSPCC?' I added. Mr. Tremain said the letters NSPCC stood for National Society for the Prevention of Cruelty to Children. 'So why are you letting the council throw us out?' asked Edward. 'Isn't *that* cruel?'

Not only had Mr. Tremain failed to stop our eviction, but he'd joined in, taken a lead, arriving with a car full of cardboard boxes, ready for Dad to start packing. And yet, despite everything, he seemed to be on our side. It was all very puzzling.

Two days later, Mr. Peters turned up, as agreed. Determined not to help, I sat on the garden bank pulling at clumps of white thrift, watching the removal van filling up, the end drawing ever closer. Nagged to "shift myself" and with anxiety levels rising, I chose instead to escape, taking refuge in the back garden, where I sat propped up against the shed, comforted by familiar sights and sounds. A song thrush, half-hidden under the leaves of a rhubarb plant, hammered a snail against a stone; a pair of white butterflies nosed at last season's cabbage stalks; a bee came buzzing around my head, then went on its way. Life went on as before.

Then Dad came to fetch me. Mr. Peter's van was ready, the engine running; it was time to go.

*

A locked-in journey of twenty miles or so took the family to King Hill, where the van came to a halt. There were voices, a door banged, the vehicle shook as its rear shutters went up. I rubbed my eyes, struggling to adjust to the light. At first all I could see were rows of trees, fruit trees, on either side of the road. I gazed out, looking back at the way we'd come, and saw line after line of cherry and plum and apple. Late falls of blossom scented the air, a breeze sending pink and white petals dancing across the road, kissing my arms and face, and sticking to the side of the van like blown confetti.

Surely, we were back at home, hadn't we? It all seemed so familiar. We'd sat in the dark, our backs bent, limbs pulled this way and that, fighting to hold off tables, chairs, beds, and bedsteads, all of which threatened to come crashing down on top of our heads at every junction and with every twist and turn of the road, and now we were home, back where we'd come from. Mr. Peters, charged with frightening Mum and Dad, teaching them a lesson, had taken the family on a sort of macabre Blossom Tour: pay your rent, or next time...

But no. There was to be no next time, no last chance or stay of execution. 'All change,' said a cheery Mr. Peters, as he helped Mum down from the van. 'Whoops a daisy...there you are, missus, ...littluns next.' Then, with an expansive sweep of his arms, he introduced a group of bushes, shrubs, and trees. 'Welcome to the Stalag,' he said. Turning to Dad, he reminded him of their arrangement. 'I can't hold on to this stuff forever. You've got my number. Five bob a week.'

'Watch your backs.' Mr. Peters had spotted an escaping mattress, Mum and Dad's double, his raised foot kicking the guilty item back the way it had come. Then, before it could fall forward a second time, he quickly pulled down the shutters, climbed up into his cab and turned the key. 'Chin up, it might never happen,' he called out of the window as, with a lurch, the van moved off.

Mr. Peters was clearly in a hurry. I glanced at the side of the van: *Peters and Sons*, it read. I expect he needs to get home to his family, I concluded.

CHAPTER TWO

And that was that. The authorities had ordered the family removed, and the removal van had removed us. We were left abandoned at the side of the road, two battered suitcases, two or three toys and other thin possessions at our feet, looking on as the familiar contents of our home disappeared into the dusty distance.

What came next? An eerie silence, punctuated by bird song and an incessant chirrup of grasshoppers and crickets, descended. Rooted to the spot, not one of us, it seemed, was able to react. We were, I think, too stunned. To have spoken, to have moved, to have shifted as much as an inch would have been to acknowledge the finality of what had just happened.

Only when Mr. Peters and his van had gone beyond the last bend in the road was the spell lifted. It was Edward who broke the silence. He'd spotted something behind the trees; a hut and a striped pole, 'Like the one outside the barber's shop in Sittingbourne.'

Edward was right, though not about the pole. Mr. Peters had deposited us twenty yards before the main hostel entrance, where there was a hut, a guard house as it turned out, and a barrier - the stripy pole - which came down across an entrance way. There was a high chain-link fence too. The greater part of the fence was hidden by trees and bushes, but the top, crowned with spiky strands of barbed wire, was visible, even from the road. 'Come on then,' said Dad. 'Let's get it over with.' We ducked under the red and white barrier and entered King Hill hostel.

"Ello, 'ello! Where do you think you're off to, then?'

A few paces in and a disembodied voice boomed out, challenging us to stop and show ourselves. 'See this?' A tall, thin man in a dark blue uniform and peaked cap - which he pointed to now - and who looked like he was a bus inspector or belonged to the St John's Ambulance, stepped out of his hut, carrying a clipboard and a mug of tea. 'This cap means halt. Respect, see. Respect the uniform. Here, hold on to this a mo,' he said as, changing his tone, he passed the mug to Dad.

A quick glance at his clipboard, a head count followed by a nod in the affirmative and we'd arrived. 'Let's see. Terry? Mother and six kids. Okay, up you go. You're looking for the big red-brick building. It'll be to your right, opposite the billets on the other side of the square. You can't miss it. Ask for the matron, Mrs. Lipscombe, or Mrs. Abbot, the assistant warden. If you can't find them, it's the welfare officer, Nan Lynch you want. *She'll* soon sort you out.' With that he took back his mug of tea and, touching his cap, returned to the hut. A second or two later the pole went up.

Next came the walk, the long walk of shame, as back through the barrier the family went, following the roadway round a sweeping bend. Here the vista broadened, the screen of trees and bushes left behind, the birdsong and crickets lost to another world.

Now the whole camp lay exposed before us; a wide expanse with not a tree or flower in sight, just a group of huts, and the red-brick building, just as the gate man (his name was Tom, I learned later) had described.

That red-brick building, all tall chimneys, and gables, peeling paint and spreading ivy, dominated everything. From here two rows of high windows looked out like eyes over the huts below, watching over a scene, it seems to me now, worthy of a Bruegel painting; busy, and crowded with extras.

A middle-aged man in a leather jerkin stood at the rear of a Bedford lorry, heaving a sack of coal on to his shoulder. Nearby, some boys scrambled about in the nettles and dock and dandelion clocks that erupted from the cracks in the crumbling road surface, squabbling over lumps of stray coal that had fallen by the wayside. A group of girls, my own age or a little older, played at hopscotch, using an improvised patch marked out with a lump of chalk on the tarmac. Another little set of children ran about in the afternoon sun, playing tag, ducking between lines of washing that fluttered like flags of surrender between rows of wooden huts.

There were numbers of these huts. I lost count at twenty. One or two, including a toilet block, bathhouse, and laundry, stood a little apart, while the others, the ones with the lines of washing, clustered together in groups of four, each surrounding an inner quadrangle and a patch of rough grass.

More than half of the shelters, from what I could see, had windows cracked or boarded over, their rotten planking, the lower parts covered in a rising patina of green mould, evidence of neglect and the steady march of time. 'Are we going to live in one of *those*?' I asked, thinking aloud.

It was difficult, that walk. Nothing was said, but we all knew that, at the finish, when we reached the main building, Dad would have to leave, to turn and go back the way we'd come, retracing his steps, heading out of the camp, back to the digs Mr. Tremain had told us about, in Maidstone. It was to be the end of family life.

Meanwhile, I was aware that the family was being watched. Outside the first of the huts, groups of women and children clustered round a standpipe, queuing for water, filling anything that came to hand. One runny-nosed toddler, wearing nothing but a grimy vest, played in a mud pool that had formed beneath the solitary tap.

As we drew near, I offered up a silent prayer: 'Please, *please* let us get past without being noticed.'

It was a forlorn hope. Almost at once, the pots and pans fell silent as, one by one, the women at the standpipe stopped to gawp at us, a family of newcomers.

One of the younger girls, eyeing up Dad, called out to Mum, 'He's a bit of all right that one. I'll have him if you've finished with him, love.'

A second woman, a brunette sporting an untidy beehive, added, 'What do you say, Brylcreem boy?'

After that, the whole scene descended into chaos. There was laughter, wolf whistles, pushing and shoving. One woman, bigger and louder than the others, pulled up her sleeves, picked up a saucepan of water and poured it over the head of a bare-footed blonde. 'That'll cool you down, missus.'

We hurried on. Close by, at the first accommodation block, a tall lean woman, arms crossed, stood against a door jamb, surveying the scene. A turn of her head revealed a pair of large dangly earrings; when she drew back her lips a gold tooth appeared, glinting in the sun. Nearby, a younger, scissor-wielding girl, seemingly oblivious to the commotion at the water pipe, sat in a scrap of shade hacking away at her hair, which fell into a metal bucket. She gave a half smile, perhaps in sympathy for our shared plight; more likely out of embarrassment.

'We're all lousy here,' the gold-toothed woman called, reading my mind. 'You'll be wanting Mrs. Lipscombe, I suppose? Try the main building.'

Mrs. Lipscombe was waiting in the square. Anticipating the family's arrival, she'd taken a chair outside and sat dozing in the early June sunshine, manilla file clutched to her bosom.

First impressions? Well, there was the uniform (all the staff, I was to learn, wore a uniform), a white blouse, dark jacket, and dark pleated skirt. Then there was the woman herself; thin, with a sour face framed by dark hair, which she wore pulled tightly back, and which was speckled with streaks of grey. Her eyes, when she opened them, were also grey. A smudge under her nose suggested the beginnings of a moustache.

'I'll have your Family Allowance book,' the matron said, pointing a heavily veined hand in Mum's direction. There was no welcome, just a silent head count. Matron ignored Dad altogether. 'Don't worry, you'll get your book back. It's just for identification.'

Mum, anxious to please, fished about in her handbag, while Mrs. Lipscombe, relaxed to the point of indolence, continued her enjoyment of the afternoon sun, fanning herself with our file. 'I'll need the rent of course. Five shillings a night for mothers, and half again for each child. A week in advance,' she added, lest Mum should think she could put off parting with her cash.

Mum found her purse, but in her hurry to follow the matron's demand for payment, fumbled, with the result that the contents ended up on the ground. There was an instant reaction. Mum, going down on her knees, recovered half a dozen coins and, while Dad chased a rolling half-crown, I went after a shilling, which had disappeared beneath Mrs. Lipscombe's chair. Matron, looking down, caught my eye but I couldn't, or rather wouldn't, acknowledge her; instead, I stared at the floor, then across at her flat sensible shoes.

It was now, following Matron's long legs upwards, that I made a shocking discovery. She had hairy calves! From her ankles to her knees, dark strands of hair pushed against the inside of a pair of nylon stockings. 'Let us out,' they seemed to cry. 'It's hot in here. We can't breathe.' I turned away in disgust.

Mrs. Lipscombe, I decided, was fifty-four, a number arrived at, when I got to my feet, by the simple expedient of reversing the figures on her silver lapel badge, which read forty-five. I didn't like her.

I didn't like Nan Lynch much, either. She was the second official we met, coming out of the office building behind the matron to see what was going on. 'Ellen Patch,' she called, 'you missed your ten o'clock appointment. Where were you? Dorothy Martin, I need to see you. Report to me tomorrow at nine. Understood? Don't let me come looking for you.'

Nan Lynch, it was clear, had eyes in the back of her head; she was quite capable of helping Matron with our induction while at the same time engaging with the movement of other women in and around the square behind us. Nan, as Tom the gate man had told us, was the welfare officer, the person the hostel inmates must suck up to if they wanted to be rehoused.

It was Nan who found the family a place in Hut Thirteen. 'Pat, come here; I've got a job for you,' she called across the square. 'I'll put you in a hut with Pat,' she said, turning to Mum. 'Pat knows the score.'

A tall, sun-tanned character, answering Nan's call, came loping across the square in response. It was the woman with the gold tooth and earrings we'd seen before.

Nan soon had us sorted out, her first job being to dismiss Dad, inviting him, with firmness, to say a quick goodbye before leaving the premises. 'Your husband can come on Saturday afternoon,' she told Mum. 'Two hours, from two to four, but not earlier.' Anyone found on the premises out of official visiting hours, Nan threatened, was likely to face a permanent ban.

I find it difficult, even after all this time, to think about, yet alone describe, that separation. It was the first, but by no means the last. Dad began to walk away; Mum, distraught, begged him to come back. 'Don't leave me, Ted,' she said. Dad turned and took Mum in his arms, telling her everything would be all right; Malling was only temporary, he would soon find us a proper home. After more sobs and struggles, Dad managed to extricate himself. Then the whole scene repeated, with Mum sounding increasingly desperate. Eventually, with Claire becoming hysterical, and after trying to intervene, Nan agreed to let Dad come to the door of our new home. But no further.

'That's enough of that.' Sitting at the table, I looked up to see a large female standing at the open-door, taking the light away. It was Mrs. Abbot, the warden, who came into Hut Thirteen followed by a second uniformed officer carrying a large cardboard box. With Mum distracted, Dad was told to disappear.

'Put it on the table,' Mrs. Abbot ordered, referring to the box, before dismissing her junior colleague in the same perfunctory manner. 'We do our best to make every new family feel at home,' she said. 'And that includes giving you this, your welcome pack. A hand if you will, Pat.'

Between them, Mrs. Abbot and Pat unloaded a loaf of bread, a wrap of Echo margarine, a box of tea, a small packet of sugar and a variety of tin cans – condensed milk, corned beef and two tins of baked beans. 'There you are. If you need anything else, Pat, I'm sure, will sort you out.'

Pat nodded her agreement but stuck out her tongue as Mrs. Abbot turned away. 'They'll charge you for that lot,' Pat whispered to Mum, in an aside. Pat, I decided, was a friend.

'Oh, before I go, a few rules,' said Mrs. Abbot, spinning round. 'You can have a full, written list in the morning, but in the meantime, I want to remind you that there are to be *no males*. No men, husbands or otherwise. Understood? Remember, you are here at the taxpayers' expense. Mr. Terry can visit on Saturday afternoons, but not during the week. Monday to Friday we expect him to be working, and when he's not at work he should be looking for alternative accommodation. Yes? You've only got twelve weeks, remember.'

Mrs. Abbot's monologue was interrupted by a loud "humph" from Pat, who sat at the end of the table, one arm wrapped round Mum's shoulders in a gesture of support and solidarity.

'Look,' said Mrs. Abbot, softening somewhat, 'even I'm obliged to obey the rules. We all need to follow the rules. Take alcohol, for example. I mean, I'd love to sit here drinking a glass or two of stout with you girls, of course I would. But what if there was an emergency? And how are you going to look after your children if you're inebriated? Then there's the music. The walls in these huts are thin, paper thin, so noise must be kept to a minimum. That means no wireless, gramophones, or musical instruments. It's all about respect, you see. Pat, I'm sure, will go through it all with you. At the end of the day, the rules, all the rules, are here to help us all get along as a community...'

With Mrs. Abbot rattling on about rights and responsibilities - it seemed, and seems, to me that the King Hill rules were mainly, if not exclusively, about responsibilities - I managed to get behind her and out through the door.

I was tempted to go through the main exit, to follow Dad. But then I remembered my promise; namely that, along with Edward and Andy, I would look after Mum and the younger ones, Malcolm, Ian, and Claire. Besides, I knew that by now Dad would be long gone. So instead, I went exploring the rest of our new home. I didn't get far.

The passage down the corridor, I discovered, led to a door, beyond which was Pat's side of the hut. At one time the top half had held a pane of glass; now it was boarded over with a sheet of ply and kept locked. Before this dividing door, on the left, there were two other rooms, both of which, I concluded, must be ours. There wasn't much to see. In the corner of the biggest room stood an old utility-style wardrobe; it looked like an upturned coffin. Out from underneath, laid over bare boarding, crept a scrap of carpet, which expired a foot or so before a rust-framed double bed. Cracks travelled down the main window. In the centre of the room, a length of flypaper hung from a bare light bulb. There was no other furniture.

The second room, smaller, had no furnishings at all, not even a light bulb. The only things our predecessors had left behind were two thin mattresses and a pair of stripy, greasy-looking pillows. Newspaper sheets had been spread across the floor, and there was a stub of candles, a saucer full of old wicks, burnt matches and wax which must, I assumed, have also belonged to the hut's earlier occupants.

I went back, confused, into the main room. 'I think there's been a mistake,' I began, interrupting Mrs. Abbot, who was in full flow, 'we've only got one bed.'

Mrs. Abbot cut me short. 'I do *not* make mistakes, young man,' she said. Then she instructed me to follow her across the square to one of the other huts, which served as a storeroom. Edward and Andy came too. There we were handed blankets and sheets and, making a second journey, used the box that had held our food donation to carry back a collection of mismatched cutlery and crockery. There was also an old wooden highchair for Claire. 'Tell your mother she'll have to sign for this and pay for any damage,' said Mrs. Abbot. 'And don't go blaming *me* for the conditions. It's the inmates who break up the beds; they burn anything they can. Frankly, I was surprised to find that Hut Thirteen still had a table and chairs.'

After a meal of corned beef sandwiches, washed down with a choice of orange squash or sweet tea, four of us boys, shattered and still disorientated after what had been a long and strange day, retired to the smaller bedroom, kipping down as best we could atop the available two mattresses. Mum took Claire and Ian with her into the bigger room, and the double bed.

Our first night away from home. It was frightening, but we had no choice but to make the best of it. Pat had handed Edward a piece of candle and the four of us, open to distraction, used the guttering light to make rabbit and dog shadow shapes on the walls. But the room was hot and stuffy - none of the windows opened - and with the candle burning down, we soon began to flag.

And the mattresses! Hard and alive with creepy crawlies, trying to sleep was nigh on impossible, our young flesh providing a midnight feast for a myriad of bugs and insects.

For an hour or so we dozed and talked, sometimes changing places. I for one couldn't sleep; indeed, having had no time to wind down from the events of the day, my body fought against it. Instead, I lay quietly talking and questioning, the response times becoming more stretched - Are you awake? Why don't you answer me? - until, at last, all that remained was the indifferent sound of regular breathing.

Lying there, together yet alone, the enormity of what had happened hit me, and hit me hard. With Dad gone I wanted my Gran. Silently, I willed her to appear. 'Come on, Gran, you can do it, I know you can.' I was desperate to conjure Gran's spirit, longed to receive a promise that all would come right in the end, needed to feel engulfed by the feelings of wellbeing I'd experienced when, following her death, she'd visited me in Doddington.

But Gran didn't come, not on that first night, or any other night. It was hard, but eventually I had to accept that she was lost to the past, to memory and time. Gran belonged to Doddington, and, despite my best efforts, couldn't follow me to King Hill. I tried and tried, but she never made herself known to me again.

*

The next morning, after a breakfast of bread and jam, Pat's two sons were told to show us over to the toilet block. I should say at once that, aside from the first day or two, we had little to do with Roger, or his brother Jack. There were, I think, good reasons for this. Firstly, they were older - eleven and twelve I should estimate (three younger siblings lived with an aunt in London, I learned later); secondly, they had their own little gang, the family having arrived at King Hill two or three weeks prior to our own incarceration; and thirdly, and most importantly, they possessed a go-cart, the ownership of which conferred upon them tremendous status and meant that all their time and attention was taken up waging war on another group of older boys and girls who owned wheels –

by which I mean old, discarded prams with wooden boxes and string-driven steering attached.

But on that first morning we all trooped over to the toilets together, before returning to the huts and, arming ourselves with an array of receptacles, joining the queue of women and children at the water tap. It was to become a regular morning routine.

The toilet block was disgusting. There were no urinals; instead, women and children, male and female, must use the cubicles provided. There were two rows of these, and I remember going from door to door, tentatively looking for one that was vacant, where the locks weren't broken and where there was still a seat to sit on. Several of the cubicles, I discovered, had holes punched in their plasterboard partitions, while others, pipe work blocked with God knows what, had floors swimming in urine, and walls smeared with excrement. The sinks too were filthy, half a dozen basins being made to serve more than a hundred inmates. The roller towels supplied were grey and greasy and there was no toilet paper.

Roger and Jack laughed at my reaction. 'Shit, shit and shit,' Jack shouted as he kicked open the individual toilet doors. Then, almost at once, two women came in with their children. 'Watch your 'effin language,' one of them said. Jack stuck two fingers up, and the five of us made a quick exit.

Next to the toilets stood a bath block, five tubs for a hundred people. Roger and Jack, determined, I think, to expose us new boys to the worst King Hill had to offer, insisted we went in to have a look.

Each bathtub, I remember, had what Mum called a "tide mark" - a filthy black line, made up of human dirt and body fat, encircling the upper rim, while dripping taps had stained the bath enamel copper green. Off-white wall tiles, squared off with mould-blackened grout, echoed to Jack's youthful scorn and laughter. 'What did I tell you? Shit, shit and more shit.' Nan Lynch would have condemned us for our ingratitude.

I rarely went back to that place. No, if I went anywhere near water, it would be in the afternoon, when our gang made a game of sticking our heads under the communal water tap to get a drink and, on hot days, cool ourselves down. The toilets we couldn't avoid altogether, but for myself I only ever went first thing to do "a number two". A daytime call of nature meant dodging behind a hut or wall. Most nights we went to bed without a wash, sometimes wearing the clothes we'd had on during the day.

Back at Hut Thirteen, the mornings took on a routine of their own, with groups of women gathering to gossip and show solidarity. They brought their children with them, of course; mostly toddlers but also babies in prams.

It was risky, but sometimes one of the women would produce a transistor radio. Then the older children took turns keeping watch, looking out for the warden or her staff, who would certainly confiscate the offending item if it were discovered.

Shy at first, I soon became part of this regular morning arrangement, helping to drag chairs and rugs outside. Some of the women sat under the protective shade of the inner quadrangle, while others, more welcoming of the summer sun, preferred the open air, lounging on the grass.

Afterwards, free to play, I joined groups of other children, kicking a ball about, dodging in and out of a cat's cradle of washing lines which, during fine weather, were full of sheets, pillowcases, and nappies.

Yet none of us older kids evaded the day-to-day chores altogether. Once, I remember going off to hunt down a sewing needle, a substitute stylus for a smuggled-in gramophone. I remember too Pat trusting me with a knife and, after receiving instruction, spending an afternoon scraping out a collection of furred up kettles, layered with the chalky minerals of the hard water of West Kent. I caught snatches of adult conversation while taking on the task of pram rocking, trying to get a baby to sleep, and a girl named Rosemary showed me how to change a nappy without stabbing her baby sister with a safety pin. 'You can kiss me if you like,' she said afterwards. My response was a silly grin - and a fleet-footed getaway.

Of the women themselves, one of the most memorable was June, a small bubbly blonde afflicted with freckles and a French nose.

June's problems, leaving aside the freckles and nose, she traced back a year or more, when her husband George had been killed in an accident at work. George had been employed in a paper mill and, it seemed, found himself in the wrong place at the wrong time. 'Stupid bugger got himself flattened by a huge roll of paper. It was like being crushed by a giant toilet roll it was.'

June used to talk at length about compensation and how, when her money came through, she'd treat Mum and the other girls to a day out down on the coast. 'How about Folkestone; or Hythe if you like, or maybe Hastings?' she'd say. 'Stick of rock, cockles and whelks; Babycham or Cherry B, and a fish and chip supper to round things off.' It was all a pipe dream, of course.

Millie was another girl who sought company in the quadrangle. Six months pregnant, she hated the heat of summer. 'Trust me to get bloody knocked up at Christmas!' Yet, leaving aside her gripes, her maternal instincts were clearly strong, since much of her talk was about the baby things she'd managed to put together. 'I've got a shawl. I've got a feeling it'll be a boy, but I got it in neutral white. My sister gave me blankets and nightgowns and I've got nappies, a dozen altogether, six of them towelling, and the rest muslin.'

Millie did her best to appear positive, but she had other children, three sons, to worry about. On one occasion, I remember she turned to Mum and, in a half-whisper, confided, 'Well, I don't know about you but I'm afraid to show my kids too much affection. After all, they might be taken from me in three weeks. See, I've even started counting the days. Twenty-two we've got. And, after that, well, who knows, I might never see my boys again.'

Mum's response was to cling more tightly to Claire and to throw me a look of near despair. It was one of those daily, if not hourly, reminders that time was running away from us.

Elsie, known as a "bit of a character" hailed from Bromley, and was teased for it. 'Bromley? That's London that is,' Pat would say. 'You shouldn't be here; you don't bleedin' belong. Does she belong, girls?' Pat would laugh, appealing to the comic sensibilities of the assembled company. And the other women, with a nod and a wink, would continue the ragging. 'Yeah, it's a London borough is Bromley. You've got the Underground and red buses, so it's London, not Kent.'

Then Liz, born in Sidcup, would join in, taking Elsie's side and reminding everyone of their shared plight. 'We got red buses too, but you try and get help from any other borough. Especially the London ones. I'm off the housing list now. As soon as I moved to King Hill, they struck me off. Three bloody years I was waiting and now I'm back to square one.'

The complaints went on. Behind the banter and the gallows humour, there was real, genuine bitterness, anger about the way the

Malling families found themselves forced to live.

'Look what happened when those boys threw stones at my Michael,' June said. 'Little buggers. I don't care whether they meant it or not. The fact is Micky ended up with a split head. And the medical help? Nowhere. There's no nurse to turn to in an evening emergency. And no phone box for nearly two miles, down in the village. 'And' she continued with growing vehemence, 'if they think I'm going to send my boys to school, with no bus and no pavement to walk on, they've got another think coming.'

I never did work out who "they" were, but Mum obviously shared June's concerns, since we boys didn't go to school either.

Ivy told another, by now familiar, tale. 'The only way I could get help for my Johnny when he had the fever was to have my oldest boy go and stand in the road and flag down a car. Delirious Johnny was, temperature over a hundred, lying there calling out, wanting his dad. But they wouldn't let my old man in, not without the police being present. My kid might have been at death's door for all they cared.'

Pat, as always, was the most expressive. 'It's a diabolical liberty, that's what it is. A bleedin' diabolical liberty. Know what I mean?" It was, she said, a diabolical liberty that the office, which housed the only telephone, was closed after six at night; it was a diabolical liberty, too, that there were no power points in the huts, with no proper cooking facilities, save for the old solid fuel ranges, which were a fire hazard; that most of the outside lights didn't work, and that the electricity meters had been fixed so that the girls paid more than double the electricity company's official rate. Above all, it was a diabolical liberty that husbands were kept out. Know what I mean? The question - Pat invariably ended her observations with the phrase "Know what I mean?" – was followed by a pause, a split second of silence, which ended when someone, anyone, agreed that Pat's grievances were justified; the way the King Hill families were treated was indeed "a diabolical liberty". After that it was someone else's turn to pitch in.

*

It would, no doubt, make for a more exciting story if I were to tell you how the King Hill families, inspired by inmates like Pat, fought back. How they formed a Residents' Committee; how some husbands, like father of six Roy Hill, were jailed for moving in with their wives, refusing to acknowledge court orders and staying put until the police came to arrest them; how these same families, with the support of local action groups and MPs, including Labour representative Ann Kerr, and Eric Lubbock, a much respected Liberal party spokesman who labelled King Hill "a concentration camp", decided on collective action; how the Friends of King Hill, a group made up of residents, socialists and other left-wingers, campaigned for change, determined to fight for family unity.

But all of this, along with the barricades, the protests, and the marches, belong to 1965. By then all the children and mothers from our time had long since left. Yet the emergence of a group calling itself "Friends of King Hill" was far from being a spontaneous response to hostel rules and conditions. No, the talk of rebellion went back to the summer of sixty-three, much of it taking place in and around Hut Thirteen, with Pat in the role of leader. 'We shall overcome,' she used to sing. All that was lacking were political links and outside support.

The newspaper photographs from 1965 are instructive. They show the Friends of King Hill marching on the London home of Kenneth Robinson, Minister of Health, and, on another occasion, to Brixton Prison, where three fathers "guilty" of moving in with their wives and families were confined. There were placards too. One little girl's sign reads, "My daddy is in prison for being a good daddy", another, "Kent councillors stop smashing up families at King Hill". But when the protesters, desperate to be heard, tried to lay their grievances before a housing committee meeting, they were violently ejected, particularly harsh treatment being handed out to anyone wearing a CND badge or, horror of horrors, sporting a beard.

The most poignant newspaper picture, perhaps, shows a group of children; scruffy, defiant urchins, lined up behind a barricade of dustbins, defending the roadway into the hostel, armed with a variety of weapons, mostly rotten fruit and vegetables. Despite their best efforts, it was to be a long time before any real changes were made, and another seven years before the camp was finally closed. Nevertheless, there are times when I can't help wishing myself eight years old again, back there helping to defend the barricades, being arrested for chucking a cabbage at a policeman, or a dustbin lid at a Tory councillor.

We boys had our own share of excitement, of course. Like all children we were inquisitive; people, places, ideas, smells, sights, and sounds; we were hard-wired, primed to investigate it all. "Nosiness" the adults called it, but it was part of our DNA.

So, when, a week after our arrival, the talk turned to the man, or men, who'd been detected sneaking about the camp the previous night, my ears pricked up. A prowler had disturbed huts of women; lights had been shone through windows; word had spread, and many of the inmates had taken precautions, pushing bedsteads, prams - anything heavy - up against their bedroom doors.

Who were these intruders? The chief suspects, the women agreed, were American servicemen from a nearby US base, trying to take advantage, preying on the young and vulnerable, wives who'd been forcibly separated from their husbands. The Yanks had tried it on before.

Could it be true? Were there American servicemen camped just along the road? It hardly seemed possible. I'd always equated Americans with the heroes of the stories, films, and comic strips I, like children everywhere, had been brought up on: Midway, the Japanese Islands, the Normandy beaches. Mothers at risk? All thoughts of intruders went out of my head as I contemplated a new adventure. I didn't need to persuade Edward and Andy: one look and we had an unspoken agreement: let's go and explore.

A day or two later, wearing homemade paper hats, and making a point of saluting Tom, on duty at the hostel barrier as we went past, the three of us marched off into the afternoon sunshine.

'Left, left, he had a good job, but he left. Left …Left…' It was the same rhythmic chant we boys invariably used to keep in step when playing at soldiers. We continued all the way to the base, only halting half a mile or so along the road, when the airfield came into view. 'There's a plane… Last one there's a nutter!' And then, breaking ranks, we ran off towards the main gate where, outside, stood a mounted Spitfire.

A Spitfire! This was the stuff of dreams. A real-life Spitfire, complete with its markings, angled on a plinth like a giant Airfix model, pointing towards the skies. It was a public reminder that this site, like the hostel, had been an RAF base before the US military took over after the war.

Here too there was a high fence, a guard house, and a barrier, just as at the hostel. But there the similarities ended. The US guards were impeccably dressed, wearing crisp blue and white Navy uniforms which included polished belts and buttons. They sported crew cuts and, thrill of thrills, carried guns. Real guns.

Beyond the guard house sat planes and jeeps and tanker lorries, all of them parked up on the shimmering tarmac; the only movement, as far as I could see, being a revolving radar, along with a set of mesmerising, flashing lights emanating from a watchtower. The maintenance hangers, too, seemed deserted.

Closer to the fence, the planes, Dakotas, Convairs and Neptunes, familiar to us from comics and picture cards, found themselves dwarfed by a Hercules transport plane, twice the size and boasting four huge propellers. I remember sitting on the bank opposite the guard house, chewing on a stalk of grass, watching the sunlight glinting on the glass nose of the nearest Neptune, waiting, in vain, for the Hercules crew to appear and prepare for take-off.

How could something the size of a Hercules get off the ground? I never did find out, since the American planes only flew at night; they could be heard above the hostel's huts, heading south, their mission, I know now, being to supply NATO bases and ships in the Mediterranean. The base itself closed two years later, in 1965.

As for the facility's personnel, some instinct told us boys to keep our distance, while they were, of course, content to ignore us, three scruffy children in paper hats, in turn. That is until the day one of the men, like an alien from outer space, decided to make contact. What to do? What to say? How to react?

'He's coming this way,' said Edward. The serviceman crossed the road, heading towards the position we held, on the bank.

Edward wanted to run. 'Come on, scarper.'

'No, don't,' I said, pulling at Edward's shorts as he stood up. 'Don't move. Stand still. He's got a gun. We might be arrested - or shot.'

'What for?' Andy asked.

'For spying of course,' Edward said.

Seeing that we were, indeed, about to make a run for it, the soldier lengthened his stride; he was upon us as we reached the road.

'It's okay, guys' he smiled, noting our discomfiture. 'You're not in any trouble. I'm a friend. My name's Joe, Alabama Joe.

'So, where y'all from?'

'From the hostel,' I said. 'We're homeless.'

'Gee, I'm sorry to hear that. But say, that gives me an idea. How about going on a secret mission?'

Without waiting for a reply, Joe produced an envelope. 'Who's in charge here?'

Andy and I glanced at Edward. 'I am, I suppose,' he said, avoiding eye contact.

'No, no. If you're in charge you must speak with *authority*. Okay?' Joe said. 'So, let's go again. Who's in charge here?'

'I am, *sir*,' Edward said, pushing back his newspaper hat and saluting. Then Joe saluted and the three of us saluted him back.

'Your mission is simple,' Joe said. 'Just give this envelope to Amy, in Hut Eight. Nobody else, just Amy. Amy Ruck. Ask for her by name.'

Joe handed over an airmail envelope, with thin airmail paper inside. After trying to hide it under his hat, then in his sock, Edward tucked the letter into a back pocket.

Relieved that we weren't in trouble, anxious to please and carry out Joe's orders, the three of us ran all the way back to the hostel, stopping only when Andy pulled up complaining of a stitch, giving us the opportunity to take a rest, calm down, and march into camp looking as innocent as possible.

None of us boys knew an Amy Ruck – we were new, and Hut Eight wasn't in our block - and we were wary of asking in case we aroused suspicion. What if Joe's letter was handed to the wrong woman? We needed a plan.

'Well,' Edward said, 'we'll just have to go and knock and ask. If she's not there we'll leave a message next door, saying that the warden sent us and wants to see Mrs. Ruck in the office. Then we'll keep an eye out and speak to her when she turns up.'

As it happened, we didn't have long to wait, catching up with Amy as she came out of her hut, struggling with a pram and two toddlers.

Edward stepped forward. 'A letter for you,' he said, removing his paper hat before taking the crumpled missive from his pocket. For a second, I thought he was going to bow.

An embarrassed glance round and Amy, her face hidden under a headscarf, took the proffered envelope, shoved it down her front and, putting a warning finger to her lips, walked quickly away.

'Charming,' said a deflated Edward.

What did we expect? Well, I for one thought this might be the start of something big, an adventure that would lead to, well, who knew what. Certainly, a chance to meet with Joe again. I was convinced, wrongly as it turned out, that Amy would send one of us back to the base with a reply. Perhaps, I thought later, she'll call on me, the keenest, to be her go-between.

I really wanted to talk some more with Joe and found myself rehearsing all sorts of questions and answers. Where was Alabama? Did Joe have a map he could show me? I needed to know how close Alabama was to Tennessee. Had Joe ever been there, to Tennessee? Maybe he'd taken a train to Chattanooga, the nearest halt to Pikeville, where Auntie Betty lived with Uncle Harold and my cousins (I fell asleep trying to remember their names).

With no letter of response, the three of us marched back to the base anyway, the very next day, and for many days afterwards, lazing on the bank opposite the gate, its fenced-off woodland and the afternoon sun at our backs, listening to the sound of a late cuckoo, smelling wild garlic, chewing on lengths of long grass, waiting for a man who never came.

It was all very trying. I had dozens of questions I wanted answered – questions about the base and the planes, and about Amy, of course. Beyond that, this, I thought, was my chance, an almost unbelievable chance, to quiz a real live American about America; about John Wayne, the Statue of Liberty, General Custer, and Sitting Bull. Mostly, though, I wanted to ask Joe about Joe. What was it like being black?

*

I don't remember how it started, but some afternoons I'd wander off alone down to the hostel gatehouse and, when he was on duty, chat with Tom. It was one way of avoiding the regular evening hunt for firewood. Perhaps, too, I was looking for a father figure, while for his part, Tom, who spent his days alone, probably welcomed the company. He certainly didn't seem to mind me asking questions or quizzing him about the past, and his war service.

Tom's war had been spent in the deserts of North Africa, fighting for Monty against the Germans.

'Both sides had respect for each other,' he said. 'And little wonder. We were all in it together, see. Back and forth across the desert we went, fighting for Tobruk, for El Alamein, giving ground, taking ground, each side determined on victory.'

And of course, Tom explained, the two armies were fighting a mutual enemy, struggling with the same conditions - the heat, the insects, the sand. It was all about surviving the heat of the day and, later, getting your "scoff" before facing a freezing night, often spent under a tank.

'And Jerry faced the same challenges,' a thoughtful Tom said. 'We shared too much to hate them. If we had to use our rifles, we'd aim to hit their legs, below the knees. Respect, you see.'

Interrupted by an arriving car, Tom would spring into action, grabbing his cap, straightening his tie and, regardless of the warm weather, donning his jacket. Then, he would step outside for a moment to raise the barrier, salute and, when he thought it necessary, ask the driver of the vehicle to explain their business.

I remember looking round while Tom went outside (occupants of the hut weren't visible from the road, otherwise there would, I'm sure, have been trouble). I found a radio, and, behind the radio, neatly lined up, a row of cowboy books. There was also a daily newspaper, a lunch box, and a drawing pad and pencil.

'So, you've caught me out, lad,' Tom said, finding me with the drawing pad in my hand. 'Now you know what I do all day.' He laughed. 'Well, I need to take it easy. It's the shrapnel, you see. Little pieces of metal, a memento from Tobruk. That's why I took this job in the first place. The bits of metal, they're in my body, floating about. One false move and, well, it'll be goodnight, Vienna.'

Seeing my concern, and confusion – I didn't see what Vienna had to do with anything – Tom changed the subject, gently taking his pencil and pad from my hand. 'Do you like drawing?' I nodded my assent; I did, though Edward was the artist in the family. What followed was a lesson on how to sketch a street of houses, following the lines to achieve a sense of perspective.

'Pass me a sandwich, will you?' asked Tom.

'Now watch,' he said. Breaking off a piece of bread, Tom rolled it into a ball. Moistened, it made a perfect eraser. 'Now skedaddle,' he said, 'before the warden finds you here. And you might as well take this sandwich with you,' he added, as an afterthought. 'I don't want it now your sticky prints are all over it.' Tom threw the offending item in my direction, and I plucked it out of the air. 'Good catch' he said as the sandwich stuck in my hand. It was cheese and pickle, the first food I'd seen since the previous day.

*

If Dad couldn't come to us, it seemed only right that we should go to him. We'd easily discovered the place where he was working (he had no reason to hide it from us) and marching up to the US Airbase only to be ignored was no longer enough to satisfy our curiosity and need for adventure. In the background, too, was the notion that we might get something out of it: namely, a place to live. Dad was helping to build blocks of new flats and houses. We needed a home. So why not go and ask someone in charge if a place might be put aside for us, the Terry family? Simple.

The trip needed planning. Maidstone was seven or eight miles distant from the hostel, too far to walk without arousing suspicion. We older boys were supposed to be in school - the term didn't end until half-way into July – though no one had made us, or any of the other King Hill children attend, at least on a regular basis.

What we needed was money, and fundraising ideas. And that's how we became involved in the Express Milk float heist.

*

The plan came from Roger and Jack. 'It's easy,' said Jack, outlining his scheme. For him it was a game, like Cowboys and Indians. 'All we need to do is get the go-cart up to speed then head the float and its driver off at the pass.'

'Yeah,' Roger said. 'You lot follow on foot but stay close or milky will see you in his side mirrors. Once he's stopped, grab a few bottles of pop, and make a run for it.'

For a day or two the plan worked like a dream. Waiting for our chance, we watched until the milkman strode off with his milk crate, then grabbed half a dozen bottles and legged it, hiding behind the nearest hut until our victim returned to his float, and moved on.

Afterwards, drunk on the contents - Dandelion and Burdock and Vimto were my personal favourites - we took it in turns to take the empties to the village grocery store and get the deposit money back. It was win-win.

But other children, it seemed, had being playing the same game and it wasn't long before our gang was spotted and chased off. After that milk, pop, bread, and other supplies, essential or otherwise, had to be collected from the square, under the ever-watchful eyes of staff. When Pat led a delegation to the office in protest, Mrs. Lipscombe and the milkman met her. A real-life flesh and blood character named Eric, with a family of his own to support, Eric had little time for cutthroats, cowboys, and desperados. 'You need eyes in the back of your bloody head in this place,' he said.

Thwarted by Eric, we boys stepped up our game, launching a raid on one of the local pubs. It all came about by accident really. One weekday afternoon, wandering about the village, Edward picked up the sound of rattling bottles. The three of us followed the noise to a high-sided wall, topped with shards of broken glass, and peering through a crack in a side door, which, it turned out, was unlocked, discovered the pub landlord crating up his empties. It was a lightbulb moment. 'Wow, get a load of that! All those bottles...hundreds I bet, better than the milk float. Think of the money we could get back on *those*.'

So, we waited and, five minutes later, once the coast was clear, snuck into the yard and lifting a dozen or so empty bottles from their crates, carried them round to the pub's off-licence counter, asking for the deposit money back. It was a brazen piece of deception, and the whole episode left me feeling physically sick. We got close to two shillings, but none of us was brave enough to try it a second time.

After this we adopted less risky strategies. Mostly this meant banging the sides of cigarette and chewing gum vending machines, hoping to dislodge a few coins. It was a long shot, but sometimes the money had failed to drop, luck was on our side, and we collected. We used the same method with the village's three red telephone boxes, two of us standing watch outside while Edward, under protest, went in. Maybe an earlier user had failed to press button B, leaving behind the two penny coins which came back after a failed call? Edward made sixpence like this one afternoon; we celebrated with a visit to the newsagents and spent it on Sherbet Dips, quite forgetting that the money was supposed to be saved for visiting Dad.

Then, for a while at least, our financial problems seemed to have been solved.

'How would you boys like to earn a bit on the side, no questions asked?'

Pat had a money-making plan of her own. 'It's all legit and above board,' she said, reading Mum's mind.

Mum was aghast, her immediate response, head buried in hands, being to withhold consent, asking Pat why she didn't use her own boys. 'They were helping,' Pat said, 'but the little sods have gone on strike.'

It wasn't as respectable as, say, fruit or vegetable picking; indeed, it wasn't respectable at all. Yet Mum, sometimes barely able to dress in the mornings or get through the day without Pat's help or encouragement, quickly capitulated, allowing Pat to have her way. There was money in it, and we needed to eat.

And so, the next day saw us, the usual trio, wandering round Malling village, limping along, right foot on the pavement, left foot in the gutter, looking for fag ends.

'When you spot a big, fat juicy one, bend down and pretend to be tying a shoelace or sandal buckle,' was the advice. So, we followed Pat's instructions, putting a fist over our best finds, waiting for an opportunity to get the burgeoning stubs into a Golden Virginia tin before being chased away.

Pat provided basic training and, as for the rest, the three of us soon picked it up. We learned early on that there was no point in leaving the hostel unless the weather was favourable. Wet or damp cigarettes would disintegrate in the hand, like soggy blackberries or strawberries, gathered in with reluctance, and only suitable for jam. Conversely, if the days were dry, something moist, like a wet cabbage leaf must be added to the tin, otherwise the tobacco simply wouldn't roll. 'Try swiping something from the vegetable stand at the grocer's,' was Pat's suggestion. So, we did.

The joy at finding a discarded, half-smoked butt, or, better still, a packet with one or two cigarettes still contained within the foil wrapper, was thrilling. Indeed, the prospect of such rich pickings meant that the three of us soon forgot our reluctance, and the shame of being condemned by potential observers. In fact, the whole thing became a competition, so much so that we even began squabbling over territory, each boy quickly learning that pub doorways, phone boxes, shop entrances, anywhere where a smoker might linger, were likely to yield the best returns.

We took pride, too, in our ability to strip the tobacco away from its filter, harvesting a tube of tightly packed tobacco for the day's collection, without including burnt ends or pieces of cigarette paper.

But it was demanding work, an expedition of three or four hours being more than enough. Agreeing to stop for the day, we'd find somewhere private to sit and blend our crop, pulling, rubbing, stretching, and teasing the tobacco between tired fingers to give a good mix, looking for a strong, dark colour, and, after a poor day, fluffing up the tobacco to make our haul seem bigger than it really was.

But there was no fooling Pat. When it came to tobacco, Pat was an aficionado and had the nicotine-stained fingers to prove it. She could fill a cigarette paper with tobacco, roll it, lick it, seal it and light it, and all with the flick of one hand, the other invariably being occupied with a mug of strong tea.

I can well remember sitting at the hut table waiting while Pat emptied our proffered tins on to a sheet of newspaper. I remember being desperate for her approval too, holding my breath while she examined the goods, pulling and kneading, stretching, and sniffing, commenting on the value, or otherwise, of the blend.

Satisfied, Pat would divide the tobacco, depositing our harvest into a line of other containers, their owner's names scratched on the lids. 'How does four pence each sound?' she'd say, opening negotiations. I once asked for eight. 'That's a diabolical liberty that is,' she said. But at heart Pat was a real softy. 'Oh, all right then me ducks,' she'd say. 'I know how you boys like to haggle.' Then, before we could open our mouths, she handed us sixpence each. 'There, that's a bob and a half, and you can double your money by taking on the deliveries.'

After presenting Mum with her share of the profits, in the form of both money and a handful of rollies, Pat sent us on our way, her instructions being to visit the other huts, knocking on doors, distributing the goods. 'Just tell them your Auntie Pat sent you; they know the score.'

Pat had it all organised. The three of us boys were handed small buff envelopes for cash payments. Anyone asking for credit, or new inmates expressing an interest in getting in on the scheme, must go to her in person.

'And don't get caught by the bloody screws,' was Pat's parting shot.

As always, we made a game of it, waiting to make our rounds until later in the evening, flitting between the lines of huts, like POWs dodging German searchlights and guard dogs. It was exciting.

*

Six shillings, Edward calculated, would get us to Maidstone, with money left over for food and sweets. The village bus stop was easy enough to find – it was a prime location for fag ends – and there was a timetable and shelter. What none of us knew was where to get off, so on arrival in Maidstone we simply joined the first exodus of passengers, climbing down from the bus after it crossed the Medway, at the bottom of the High Street.

With an hour or more until lunch, exploring the Medway seemed just the thing. Who knew what we might discover?

Trooping along the towpath, the outlook, at first, was disappointing. Close to the town, the waterside was shut-in and crowded, the view populated by residential properties and modern offices. Further along came groups of old brick-built factories; the facades of former commercial buildings, tall chimneys, the arches of the Fremlins brewery site, dating from Victorian times.

Then, after an unexpected, but welcome, bend, the vista expanded; the Medway widened, with room now for a row of barges and houseboats: *Moonraker*, *Morning Sunrise*, *Evening Star*; a galaxy of astronomically named vessels strung out along the river.

Things were quieter now, business and industry giving way to the natural world. A convoy of mallards, disturbed, sailed off, making its way to the other side of the water; a kingfisher, ready for lunch, sat watching and waiting on a gnarled branch.

Soon the towpath, already narrow, began to close in: progress involved fighting a cloud of midges, while at the same time brushing through a thicket of overhanging trees.

As we moved forward, tentacled roots spread above the thin soil and bumpy surface, probing their way towards the water. All at once Edward followed, tripping on the woody growth. 'Pike!' he called, then, pitching forward, fell into the river.

Andy and I laughed. We laughed at Edward's cries for help. We laughed when, seeking a landing, he grabbed hold of a bunch of stinging nettles. We laughed at his screams and his thrashing about, at his kicking and gurgling, which served only to take him out into the river. We laughed out of panic; we laughed because we were frightened and helpless; we laughed because not one of us could swim.

Suddenly, as if from on high, a young soldier appeared, striding along the towpath. 'Stand back,' he said, seeing at once what was going on. Wading into the water, which came up to his waist, he grabbed Edward by the scruff of the neck and hauled him on to the bank, leaving his catch lying there gasping for air (much as Edward's pike might have done, had it existed). Then the khaki-clad squaddie went back and fished out Edward's sandals. The rescue took less than a minute from beginning to end.

Afterwards came the inquisition. 'Sit down,' our rescuer said, and Andy and I joined Edward, squatting under a growth of elderberry bushes, as far back from the water's edge as the path allowed.

There were more questions than answers. Where were Mum and Dad? 'Shopping,' I said. Hadn't we seen the warning signs? 'The river is dangerous; there are sudden currents and eddies, the bank shelves suddenly in places...'

'Well, we'll leave it there, kids,' said the soldier, seeing that we were upset, and more than a little shaken by what had happened. 'I hope the three of you have learned a lesson. Be more careful in future.' As he walked away, he called back over his shoulder, 'Oh, and if I were you, I'd ask Dad for swimming lessons.'

That soldier became an instant hero. Here was a character – tall, firm of jaw, fearless - straight out of *The Hotspur* or *The Eagle*, it seemed. And what a story he would have to tell his mates and comrades! With his ruined tunic, muddy boots, and shrunken, soaking beret, he'd be sure to get a medal when he got back to barracks, I told myself. Now I'm not so sure.

'I can't go anywhere like this,' Edward said, spreading his arms in a gesture intended to invite sympathy.

'Yuck, you stink,' said Andy, as the two of us began to wipe our older brother down. Handfuls of grass were tried, after which we picked some nearby dock leaves (the antidote being always, it seems, found growing close to the culprit) to ease the nettle rash on his limbs.

'I can do that,' Edward said, snatching the leaves.

Leaving Edward to it, Andy and I stood back, teasing and taunting. We were merciless.

'You look like a drowned rat,' I said.

'Yeah, from now on we'll call you Ratty,' Andy said.

'Ratty, Ratty, Ratty', we sang, making sure to keep our distance.

All this, of course, was a nervous reaction to what had just happened, and what might have happened, if the soldier (we never did learn his name, just that he served with the Royal Engineers), taking a shortcut back to barracks, hadn't come along when he did.

'Listen,' said Edward, adopting a confidential tone, 'keep quiet about this, right? It's a secret, something between the three of us. Agreed? Never talk about it.'

'Yes, Ratty,' we said. But we kept our collective promise.

*

Architecturally, Maidstone was, and is, a Georgian town, its main streets boasting rows of plate glass-fronted shops, coloured awnings, a Kentish Bank and, in our day, a fleet of trolley buses advertising products such as Oxo, Aspro, and Paxo (along with a range of other goods their manufacturers had been persuaded might profitably end with the letter "O"), the whole place being ripe with the pervasive aroma of malt and hops. In short, it was a traditional market town, quite a stylish place as it happens, and certainly not one in which the shopkeepers were likely to find Edward's Harry Worth impression amusing.

Chased away from the window fronting Smiths, we wandered over to a plinth-raised cannon - a weapon, boasted its plaque, captured at Sebastopol, and erected here, at the top of the High Street, to celebrate a British victory in the Crimean War. We couldn't know it, but this was a Frith moment; a stepping back in time, the view from the monument down towards the Medway a panorama hardly changed in more than a century.

Moving on, our wanderings took us to Earl Street, where we discovered the town museum. 'Let's go in and find Ellen Button,' Edward said. 'You know, the Blue Coat school girl. Remember what Mum told us about her picture being on one of the walls?'

Andy and I weren't keen and said so. The museum was housed in a big, imposing, half-timbered Elizabethan building; it was a long way from the street to the heavy wooden entrance doors, with two wings and, I imagined, prying eyes looking out at us from every side. What if unaccompanied children weren't allowed? There was no way to get in unnoticed.

'I bet it's free,' said Edward. 'And besides,' he said, 'we've got a right. Our great-grandmother is in there. If anyone asks, we'll say we've come to give the museum information about Ellen Button, how she became Ellen Paige, how we're related.'

I stayed hesitant, recalling my reflection in the window of Smiths. 'Look at us,' I said. It was not a pretty sight. Despite his earlier efforts, Edward's legs remained smeared with river mud; Andy had a broken buckle on his right sandal - he walked with a kind of sliding limp - while I was wearing a pair of worn-out wellies, in July. Eventually, though, it was agreed. 'But only if I don't go first,' I said. We settled things in the traditional way: *Eeny, meeny, miny, mo...*

The museum was fascinating. Tiptoeing our way around, we began exploring the ground floor. The first room, just off the entrance, we found full of stuffed birds, while a second had skewered moths and butterflies. Hundreds of them. On the next level, space was given over to cabinets of Japanese porcelain, a collection, valuable no doubt, guarded by a life-sized Samurai warrior, complete with helmet, armour, and sword. I had to fight an impulse to knock him over.

Uneven floorboards of dark wood led to a dimly lit Egyptian room which, designed to suggest the darkness of a tomb, was both scary and irresistible. In the centre of the chamber, on a raised platform, lay an open, beautifully carved and colourful sarcophagus, containing a bandaged Mummy; while all around were examples of the items (copies no doubt) of the sort of things the deceased would need in the afterlife - everything from drinking vessels to golden chairs and board games. There were canopic jars too, along with embalming equipment, including implements used to pull a dead Pharaoh's brains out via his nostrils. Yuck!

Our noises of delighted disgust were interrupted by an elderly grey-haired woman who'd drifted, unnoticed, into the room from behind us. A lanyard declared her name – Mrs. Fry, employed as a museum curator.

Mrs. Fry peered at us for a moment or two, glanced at the "do not touch" signs, opened her mouth to speak, then closed it again. A trio of scruffy children left unattended in a room housing the museum's most valuable exhibits was not, I think, what she had expected. It was certainly not something she was about to encourage.

Taken off guard, Mrs. Fry's tone was firm. 'Can I help you?' she asked.

'Yes,' I said, remembering our mission. 'My mum's gran is in here.'

'In here?' said Mrs. Fry.

'Not in this room,' I said, 'but somewhere in the museum.'

'Yes,' Edward said.

Invited to continue, Edward told the story of Ellen Button. The pictures on the stairs, one of them, he was sure, was the Blue Coat School girl.

'Show me,' was the blunt response.

Edward led the way. 'That one,' he said, pointing to a prominent oil painting. And there, in her bonnet, ribbons and blue cape, just as Mum had described, was Ellen Button.

'Mum says she was chosen by an artist who came to the school in Loose because she was pretty, and because she was named Button and had a button nose,' Edward said.

'Well, she is certainly pretty,' Mrs. Fry said, with a smile of amusement at this last detail. 'Come to the office and I'll make some notes.' Then she took us down a flight of steps to a small room where, producing a pen and paper, she set down the other information we were able to provide.

'Mum says there are two pictures,' Edward said. 'Our gran saw one hanging in the council offices during the war.'

'Oh, that's interesting, I'll certainly follow that up,' the curator said, before shepherding the three of us out of the building.

After passing a series of unexplored repositories, dusty rooms labelled *Numismatics*, *Ceramics*, and *Textiles*, we found ourselves outside, leaving through the museum's back entrance, which opened into a large formal garden.

Today, a council-sponsored website describes Brenchley Gardens as "an ideal location to spend a lunch break away from the office". So, it was all those years ago, in 1963, the park's benches being occupied by hassled workers consuming their sandwiches, along with the contents of their newspapers, amid formal, ornate squares filled with thousands of flowers - petunias, pansies, and wallflowers among them - a bandstand and a war memorial.

Armed with Edward's penknife, a loaf of bread, sliced ham, and a lump of cheese, all of it obtained from a nearby corner shop, we followed their example, choosing a spot near the water fountain to sit and eat.

I was happy and proud to have provided a name for the Blue Coat School girl, adding to local historical records, playing my part in increasing the sum of human knowledge, despite the fact that Mrs. Fry, having jotted down a brief note of what we boys had to say, had made a point of personally escorting the three of us to the exit. 'You need a wash and some new shoes,' she'd told Edward.

Now, half an hour later, Edward, stung by this observation, did his best to wash his legs clear of the last vestiges of the Medway, splashing himself with water from the garden fountain.

*

Boxley Road, where Dad was working, wasn't hard to find. After asking once or twice ('Go on, it's your turn, I asked last time.'), a passer-by pointed to the outside of the prison, directing us to follow the wall. And so away we went, running our hands along the rough, uneven stones of the jail, discussing the chances of escape. All you needed, we agreed, was a high-sided lorry or a laundry van, or a giant trampoline. It was a month after the Great Train Robbery.

I had my own idea of what Dad did all day. It was just a moment in time, yet if I closed my eyes, Dad was there, kitted out with a hard hat and donkey jacket, negotiating a jungle of scaffolding, or jumping down from a concrete encrusted dumper truck. Either that, or he was pushing a wheelbarrow full of cement over heavy duckboards, his calloused, barnacled hands, evidence of hard graft. Between tasks, during rest breaks, I visualised him sitting in a wooden hut, reading his newspaper, drinking tea from a thermos.

Imagination aside, what Dad was doing, I knew, was working hard to earn the money his family needed to rent a new home. Surely, he'd get one of the houses. After all, he was helping to build them, wasn't he? I was first across the road, determined to find out.

The building site was overwhelming. Everything - new, unfamiliar sights, smells, and sounds - hit us in a simultaneous assault. From above came the clang of metal against metal. I looked up, then found myself pulled out of the way by Edward, dodging a man who came past carrying a window frame.

Next, the three of us circled a big red cement mixer which coughed and spluttered with a repetitive turn, turn, turn. Further on we took it in turns to jump a puddle of liquid, its oily surface betraying spilled fuel. It was one of dozens of holes pock-marking a surface of caked clay and crushed brick. 'Go around the ladder,' I said, 'or it's seven year's bad luck.'

We didn't get any further.

'Are these boys yours, Ted?' a hod-carrying man called from a doorway. 'Well, get them off the bloody site. Pronto.'

A moment or two later, Dad appeared from within. He was not impressed. 'Here I am, slogging my bloody guts out, and you go and pull a stunt like this. Does your mother know where you are? Well?'

Confronted, Edward admitted that Mum knew nothing of our adventure.

How did we get here? Where did the bus fare come from? Told to speak up, I put our money down to refunds on empty pop bottles.

What to do? Dad was in a difficult position. He wasn't prepared to let us return to King Hill unaccompanied and, put on the spot, had little choice but to ask if he might knock-off early.

'Walk,' came the order, and Dad took us to a large wooden hut, full of muddy boots, tools, and safety equipment. It smelled of damp clothes, pipe tobacco and sweat, the territory of workmen.

Inside, Dad spoke to a man he called his "ganger" who passed him on to the site manager; the site manager, in turn, went and whispered to another man, the only one wearing a jacket and tie, and who occupied a privileged position, sitting at a table, examining drawings. 'Looking for a job, boys?' he said. 'Well, come back when you're a bit older.' Then he gave Dad the nod to take us home.

Leaving the hut, I recalled our plan; namely, to find someone who might give us a place to live. But my thoughts were interrupted by the site manager, who told Dad that leaving early would mean his pay would be docked by three hours. After that I didn't bother.

Dad took us back to King Hill, but he, like all other adult men, was, as I have said, banned from entering the hostel during the week. Nor was he allowed to loiter at the gate. Instead, he had to stand outside, talking with the other fathers who came during the afternoons and evenings, until, fetched by Edward, Mum came down.

Reunited, Mum and Dad joined other couples, looking for a gap in the bushes and weeds that grew up against the fence, desperate to find a space which allowed them to touch their fingers or kiss through the mesh, to whisper sweet nothings, or discuss the future. Gifts, presents, or supplies, anything too big to go through the fence were lobbed over the top, or left at the gatehouse with the promise, not always kept, that it would be passed on to its intended recipient via the office.

Friday night was the busiest. On Fridays, payday, Dad would bring us our treats. Waiting, we joined a group of other children, picking teams, passing the time playing cricket with a balding tennis ball and a lump of wood, or a football constructed from a newspaper wrapped up in a sock; we always managed to improvise something. When Dad arrived, he would throw us our Milky Way bars, just as he had at Doddington. 'Catch, boys,' was the cry and over the barbed wire came the missiles.

Later, years later, I tried to talk about moments like this with Dad, inviting him to live them again, to share his thoughts, from his personal perspective, with me. But he stayed tight-lipped. He saw no point in raking over the past; indeed, our Doddington eviction, King Hill and what followed had become a taboo subject for him. So, in many ways the fence remained between us.

*

Saturday was visiting day. During the afternoon, a steady stream of fathers came up from the gate to spend precious time with their families.

From the square, visitors went to the nearby Community Hut – a converted accommodation block kitted out with groups of tables and chairs and a small café area. Husbands were banned from entering the rest of the hostel, unless escorted, and extra staff were on duty to make sure this didn't happen.

The routine was for us to go down and wait near the gate, meeting Dad and following him up to the hut. Any sort of holdup and we'd worry, though Dad always came in the end, often breathless and looking tired and flustered. Dad, we knew, spent Saturday mornings, and most evenings, looking for a home for his family.

And in this way our twelve weeks - punctuated with Dad's Saturday visits – were eaten up; my memories today are of door checks, and waits while sweets, comics and small gifts were emptied from bags, which were searched for contraband – alcohol mostly.

Then there are those other, weekday, memories; sights and sounds, tastes and smells, sensations which, once conjured, threaten, even now, to overwhelm, evoking as they do a summer spent running wild, with little parental control, living exclusively among women and children - dozens of other children, many of them babies and toddlers.

Who, for instance, could forget the sweet, addictive taste of gripe water? The bug bites, the itches and scratches, the boils, and the burns; or the antidote, that smooth, pink balm of calamine lotion?

As for the other sights and smells, well, taken at random, there were the long, seemingly endless rows of washing, the yeasty whiff of unchanged nappies, lines of filthy toilets, overflowing dustbins oozing their decaying contents onto warm tarmac. It was life in slow motion, with whole families waiting for something, anything, to happen - for a conclusion, for the end.

And while they waited, morning teams of women got down on their hands and knees, scrubbing and cleaning the long corridors of the huts. Why? Because the rules, unwritten but ruthlessly enforced, dictated that the women must work if they wanted to keep a roof over their heads.

And in the afternoons, with their chores completed, everyone, both mothers and children, went out hunting for fuel, for something, anything, that would burn, to feed the huts' ancient ranges, generating the heat needed to cook an evening meal.

Later came the queues, lines of inmates waiting with buckets, saucepans, and bowls, to collect water, or, before bed, and for the brave, to use the toilets and baths.

Finally, there were the nights, hot and stuffy, characterised by creaking wood, timbers cooling and contracting to the accompaniment of a barking fox or the screech of a nearby owl.

Sometimes, too, came the muted sounds of music, records played at 45 rpm by the women, our mothers, with a mixture of bitter defiance and rebellion - the smuggled-in sounds of Gene Pitney, Roy Orbison, Elvis, and Helen Shapiro, walking right back to happiness.

More memories. Recollections of the beginning of Ian's nightmares, the start of Malcolm's bed-wetting, the slow deterioration of a peripheral existence; of unwashed bodies, uncut hair, worn clothing, and worn-out women.

Little wonder that one of the first demands of the "Friends of King Hill" was "An acknowledgement of the fact that the constant threat of being parted from their children is making the mothers sick with worry, and an assurance that no family will be broken up."

Once a week Mum had to report to Mrs. Lynch, the welfare officer. All the women had to undertake this ordeal. As our stay went on, Mum's turn seemed to come around even more quickly. And that's what it was all about really. The clock is ticking, your hostel days are numbered. What is your husband, Mr. Terry, doing to find alternative accommodation?

The same questions were put to all the inmates. But Mum had limited options, as she was a former council tenant with outstanding arrears. As such, Mrs. Lynch had little to say to her. Instead, Mum was handed form N22, stamped to say she had attended, and was aware of the days she had left, her legal status, and the circumstances of her pending departure. The hostel rent must be paid, and accommodation left in good order. To this end, Mrs. Lynch sometimes returned with Mum for a hut inspection. If she were busy, she'd send a colleague.

Pat was different. She had a plan. 'When my time comes, I'm taking my boys fruit picking. And when that's finished, we'll go 'oppin' (hop-picking), over Paddock Wood way,' she said. 'It'll only be for three or four weeks but, well, it's something. After that we'll see. Take one day at a time, that's what I say. But they ain't taking my kids.'

*

Pat disappeared from King Hill during the night. It was August Bank Holiday weekend and she and her sons went quietly; no fuss, no bother, and without the indignity of other inmates staring at them as they left.

Pat left an empty hut, a note for Mum with an address in London, where she might, or might not, be later in the year. There was leftover food, and a list of grievances she promised to pass on to anyone who would listen.

And then came our turn. For us, the end or, as it turned out, the end of the beginning, came a fortnight later. It had elements of hope, of hopes dashed, of confusion, and farce. The official paperwork describes what happened as "a misunderstanding".

*

Plans for our departure began with a weekly visit to the office. Expecting a Notice to Quit, Mum came back instead with an envelope holding fifteen pounds. 'We're free, we're free,' she cried, dancing around the hut.

After weeks of delay, Uncle John, still based in Cyprus, had replied to one of Mum's letters. It wouldn't go far, he wrote, but it was the best he could do...

Fifteen pounds would buy all sorts of things, including new sandals and, more urgently, train tickets to Southampton; Mum's plan, such as it was, being to throw herself on the mercy of her mother, Gran Fuggle, the woman whom, I learned later, disowned her daughter when she became pregnant at sixteen, and whom we children had never met.

CHAPTER THREE

Not for the first time, I am indebted, in part at least, to my brothers, particularly Edward, for helping me reconstruct an account of the events that followed, from the whirlwind of arrangements put in place for getting the family out of King Hill, to the journey down to Southampton, and the scene awaiting us when we arrived.

For me, most memorable is Victoria and the Underground, where the tube took the family to Waterloo.

Travelling beneath the busy streets of London was an extraordinary experience, frightening and exhilarating at the same time. It was all such a rush: pandemonium at the ticket machines, the barriers, the escalators; a crush of people determined on a collective, lemming-like downward journey to a deep and dark destination, a buried world where, it seemed to me, a colony of giant moles might feel at home. It was like visiting another planet.

Down here, in this alien space, a different eco-system prevailed. Odd, warm winds came through the tunnels; peculiar oily smells rose from the tracks. A distant rumble suggested an oncoming train. Is that one ours? Together we moved forward, only to find that the noise was coming from another, hidden, burrow. Then, suddenly, a Waterloo-bound train came along. There was a rush, and a moment of panic as the doors opened and closed. Where's Ian, who's got Claire? It was a five-minute journey. But I've never forgotten it.

Arriving at Waterloo, it was to find the Southampton train coupled to a modern diesel locomotive: I'd hoped for a colourful steam engine with a name plate and was bitterly disappointed. Given what was waiting for us at the end of the line I should, I suppose, have been more concerned about the reception I might receive from my grandmother. But to be honest, the notion of rejection by family hardly crossed my mind. Mum had said the family's problems were solved, so I just focused on the trains.

The engine was modern but, as if by way of consolation, ours was a traditional corridor train; that is to say, it was made up of a chain of third-class carriages with, towards the rear, two or three coaches marked "First".

Walking through, Dad managed to find an empty compartment corresponding to his tickets. I went in and took a seat, but never one to sit still, was soon on the move, pacing the corridors, checking out the options. It didn't take long for me to discover first-class, and to decide that, for those demanding comfort, this upgrade, with its shiny dark wood decor and plush seating, was the place to be. Basically, it was like stepping back in time - the seating, the overhead string-framed luggage storage, the built-in ashtrays, the shaded reading lights, one high up in each corner, providing everything a crossword-addicted, cigar smoking gent might need for a comfortable journey. And for those posh people dreaming of adventure, a first-class compartment offered a series of framed, stylised, art-deco pictures of exotic destinations; Eastbourne, Brighton, and the Dorset Coast, all serviced by Southern Rail. In short, opportunities for exploration.

Wandering the corridors, swaying with the clickety-clack of the moving train, it was easy to imagine that I was on the run and that any moment, at the next stop perhaps, camp guards, sinister looking men in long leather coats, accompanied by Alsatian dogs, would climb aboard and, working their way down the corridors, start demanding passports and papers, their orders being to find the Terry family and return us to King Hill, to Mrs. Lipscombe, Mrs. Abbot and Nan Lynch.

When it came to my turn, the plan was to throw these pursuers off the scent by directing them to the corpse in carriage six.

At Fleet, or it may have been Hook or Micheldever – one of the more rural stations - a group of older boys, carrying satchels and sports equipment, came through the train. They wore green caps, green and white striped ties, blazers, and long trousers. One or two, less boisterous than their juniors, displayed metal shields on their lapels; they were prefects, honour-bound to be on their best behaviour, and to keep an eye on the plebs. It was a sharp reminder that the academic year was upon us and that we boys were playing truant, which was both worrying, and added to the excitement of the moment.

Hauled back to our compartment, Dad gave all of us strongly worded advice, telling us what to say, and not to say, when we reached Gran's house.

Firstly, we learned that Gran Fuggle wasn't Gran Fuggle anymore. Instead, she was Gran Yates, having remarried after Grandad John's death in 1947, shortly after the war. Grandad Yates would probably be at work when we arrived, but his absence didn't change anything. Basically, we boys had to be on our best behaviour: get off the train in an orderly fashion; help Dad with our suitcases and Claire's pushchair; stick together as we exited the busy station, be patient while Dad found a taxi, then sit quietly while the cab took us to Totton, a Southampton suburb, where we'd find Gran's house. And that is what we did.

I don't know what I expected - an older version of Mum, perhaps. But the woman who opened the door to us in Totton was small and thin, with a narrow, fox-like face. She wore butterfly glasses, which did nothing to hide an unwelcoming frown. I remember too that Gran had an apron on and carried a tea cloth, having come out from her kitchen.

'Well, here we are, we've made it!' Mum, with a winning smile, adopted the air of a long-lost child returning after an enforced absence; a grown-up daughter come back home for a holiday, expecting herself to be greeted with open arms.

Gran was not impressed. Producing Mum's crumpled King Hill letter from her apron pocket and, hardly stopping to catch her breath, she delivered what had, I suspect, been a carefully rehearsed response. It went something like this: How can you do this to me...I've got the neighbours to think of...You can't stay, we've only got two bedrooms...There's not enough room to swing a cat...The council would never allow it...I haven't told Reg; he'd have forty fits if he came home from work and found you here...

Gran was right, of course. She and Grandad Reg lived in a "prefab", one of hundreds of small square boxes put up to house families left homeless following wartime air raids on the city and docks. It was, the local authorities promised, temporary accommodation, provided on the understanding that council tenants would eventually be re-housed - typically in one of the high-rise blocks of flats we'd seen from our taxi, mushrooming up across a crane-filled city skyline.

Mum tried everything; she wheedled, she begged, she shed tears, she virtually shoved Claire into her mother's arms. But Gran was adamant; she wouldn't put us up, not even for the night. And no, we couldn't come in. If Malcolm needed a wee – and he did - he could go along the side of the house, she said, 'but he's not coming in to use the toilet.'

For Dad, Gran had nothing but contempt. 'Well, don't just stand there looking stupid,' she said, brushing Mum aside. 'There's nothing for you here. If you want help, you'd best get hold of the social services.'

While Dad went off in search of a telephone box, the rest of the family waited in front of Gran's house, where we sat, hot and thirsty, on a little square of lawn bordered by a low box hedge. Then Gran rapped on the window and mouthed the word "shift".

So, we wandered off, in search of Dad, praying he'd found a solution.

But it was to no avail. In a further echo of the old Poor Law, the response of Hampshire social services was to order Dad, a pauper, out of the county, refusing to offer any help and, despite his pleading, denying any responsibility. Dad had no history of settlement, and, since his in-laws were unable, or unwilling, to help, there was, in law, no recognised family connection. Move on, the rules said. We have our own poor; the taxpayers of Hampshire don't need any further burden on the rates. You're a family of scroungers. Get yourselves gone, back to your own parish. Go away.

*

Hours later, in the evening, we arrived back at Waterloo.

Escaping the train, a trickle of self-absorbed, determined passengers - those with homes to return to - headed for the ticket barrier and station exit. For our part, all we could do was watch them go. With no onward destination - the hour was too late for that - we spread ourselves out across a pair of benches, family belongings in a couple of battered suitcases beside us. Then we looked for Dad to tell us what to do, where to go, and what came next.

But nothing came next, or so it seemed. We just sat and waited, then waited some more. Soon Edward and Andy began to fidget and fight, and I joined in. Dad told the three of us to keep still, to sit up and stop larking about and "playing the giddy goat".

But we couldn't, or wouldn't, stay put, and instead began racing up and down the platform to the clock, the four-faced clock where lovers met. We'd just turned for the final furlong – Doug Smith (me) and Scobie Breasley (Andy) trailing Lescott Piggott (Edward) by half a length – when I noticed a man in a pin-striped suit. A real city gent, he'd stopped in front of our resting place and was leaning forward, talking to Mum.

Half a century or more later, I can still picture it. A cameo scene, Mum is wearing her mustard–coloured coat, the one with the butterfly collar and big buttons, her pale face half-hidden beneath a patterned headscarf. Dad, sitting at the other end of the bench, quickly moves up, closing the gap. From his pocket he produces a comb and rakes it through dark, Brylcreemed hair, casting sidelong glances at the smarter man, an imagined rival, as he does so.

Dad is dressed as he is always dressed. A man of two halves, his clothing is a jumble-sale mix; on top is a jacket, shirt, and wine-coloured waistcoat, set off by a bright red neckerchief; below, in marked contrast, workman's trousers, held up with a wide leather belt, and labourer's boots. Alan Bates meets Harold Steptoe.

'You look lost. Is everything all right?' A policeman came over, expressing concern at finding a family with young children out so late.

'I think I can help you there,' the constable said, in response to Dad's tale of woe. 'It's not ideal, but there is a place, a hostel, down at Newington. It's a bit of a trek but the beds are cheap, though they don't take men.'

Satisfied with this official intervention, the man in the pin-striped suit touched his bowler to Mum and, turning to us children, wished us goodnight and good luck.

Watching him striding down the platform, briefcase and umbrella in hand, I had an almost overwhelming urge to follow. He was a stranger, yet he'd given me a pat on the head, and each of us boys a shiny new sixpence. I expect that's why I remember him.

I didn't want to go to Newington Lodge. None of us wanted to go to Newington Lodge. But there was nowhere else. So that was that. Mum put Claire in her pushchair, Dad picked up Ian, and we set out, Edward, Andy and I taking turns to carry the suitcases.

This was the sixties, and, despite the lateness of the hour, the city that hit us, exiting the station, was very much alive and swinging. Buses ran, the cafes and bars remained open for business. Cars whizzed past our feet, their occupants calling out, to no one in particular, from wound down windows. Now and then a van or bus thundered past, vomiting tungsten-tinted fumes, throwing up warm dust, triggering the traffic lights, which changed, red, amber, then green, their signals urging us to "Go, go, go". Behind the lights, advertising stands, promoting everything from Pears Soap to Gordons Gin, flashed on and off; all of it, the shops, the bars, the buildings, and the bridges, brazenly promoting a city that had found a way of turning night into neon day.

As for the London streets, well, Dick Whittington, as he himself quickly discovered, was wrong. The city's roads weren't paved with gold; they were littered with rubbish; food wrappers, discarded newspapers, chewing gum and fag ends. My eyes went to the floor, and I thought of Pat. If only Pat was here! A nod from Pat, a couple of empty tobacco tins and I'd be rich!

Setting off, I dawdled along, slowed by the suitcase I was carrying, stopping to switch hands, worn fabric rubbing against my bare legs. Then I heard Dad, nerves frayed, calling me back. 'I'll bloody swing for you,' he said. If only I had a pound for every time Dad had used that expression...

But I wasn't listening. No, I was on a mission. 'Take the suitcase, it's your turn,' I told Edward. Then I was off.

The Waterloo policeman, giving directions, had said something about an elephant and a castle, and I was determined to be the first to find these exotic things. An adventure, an escape from reality, a way out beckoned; it was like a call to prayer.

Crossing a river, I negotiated shoals of black cab crocodiles, dodged a big red hippo – a London bus - and, having tackled a zebra crossing, made it to safety, the pavement of a distant shore.

A deep breath and I was off again, loitering at lamp posts, battling Belisha beacons. I had my seven league boots on now. Up ahead lay the future, behind me the past. And that was where I wanted to be; somewhere else, anywhere but in the here and now. I strode on, looking for clues, all the while expecting to come across an elephant or a castle, my search being a means of escape, the potential discovery a personal triumph.

Elephants – the African sort with big, floppy ears - triggered memories of a trip to the zoo, or an illustrated book, perhaps pictures celebrating Hannibal and the great days of Rome: cool alpine mountains, the Carthaginian general and his army waiting in the shivering cold, doomed to face a laurel-headed Roman consul commanding a cohort of crack Republican troops.

So that, in my imagination, was the elephant. But what about the castle? Centuries pass and I'm called to war, fighting alongside Richard Coeur de Lion in the Holy Land. It's the Cross versus the Crescent; Crusaders desperately defending crenelated citadels against the infidels.

'Bring up the battering rams and siege engines,' orders Saladin. We Christian knights respond, doing Christian things, pouring pitchers of boiling oil down upon the heads of the Saracens below. Serves them right.

An eight-year-old, if he thinks about it at all, judges the world to be ordered and rational. Grown-ups know what they're about, or so I'd been taught to believe. Adults thought before they acted, and had a back-up plan, just in case. And besides, everything would turn out right in the end, because the world was fundamentally fair and just. Then came our eviction and all that followed - a slow descent into a strange world where Mum and Dad had little influence over what happened to their offspring and where, indeed, Dad, and fathers in general, were, I'd learned, no longer welcome. No wonder, then, that I began to withdraw into a realm of my own, to create a place of refuge; an imaginary world, yes, but one ripe with possibilities. As for the elephant and castle, the least I'd expected was a circus tent. Dad said it was a public house.

*

A long night after that Waterloo trek I woke up, confronted with a startled, puzzling sense of being somewhere unexpected, adrift in a strange place. Through half-opened eyes, an arched window, and a white ceiling - which, it seemed to me, was much too far away – came slowly into focus. Unwelcome, vaguely familiar smells invaded my senses: the whiff of sour food, stale bodies and tobacco, a hint of carbolic and disinfectant. Odd sounds assailed my ears, telling me I wasn't alone. There were coughs and groans, callings out and, further off, footsteps, which, in that large, high-windowed place, seemed metallic and hollow, like the rattle of a set of marbles in a tin can.

For a second, I was back in King Hill. Then, suddenly, came the flash of knowing, a flood of adrenalin, the final phase of waking, the whoosh of coming back. A moment or two later and I was properly myself, able to think more clearly: I'd spent the night in emergency hostel accommodation. This was Newington Lodge.

Somewhere out there, lost in this massive building, Mum and my brothers and sister had been given beds; perhaps, like me, they had been placed in separate wards. If so, how would Mum ever find us again? And Dad. Where was Dad? Where had he spent the hours of darkness?

'Didn't you see the sign? This is T Block. Mothers and children only. No men allowed.'

The warden had been most insistent. No men. 'Make up your minds,' he'd shrugged, judging Mum and Dad's despairing embrace to have gone on long enough. 'I don't have all night. Are you signing in or not?'

'Go on, lovey,' Dad said. 'You'll be all right. I won't be far away.'

Turning to the warden, Dad asked about the gardens. 'I saw benches on the way in...'

'No chance mate,' came the response. 'That block is for the elderly, full-time residents.'

Dad's best bet, the warden said, was to go back to Waterloo, and return in the morning. He offered to ring for a taxi. Dad chose to walk.

All of this, and more, came back to me as I drifted in and out of consciousness, struggling with words and images from Doddington, King Hill, and Southampton - random pictures of negatives from a splintered past.

Dominating my thoughts was the massive presence that was Newington Lodge. Closing my eyes, it loomed before me just as it had the night before, dwarfing the surrounding area, a symbol of power and oppression. In the dark, against the city skyline, it might easily have been the crusader castle of my imagination. Like the castle, it spoke of control, the triumph of the strong over the weak.

The central stronghold was where, after a long search, I hoped to find my Mum. Should I set out on the quest, or stay put? I'd slept in my clothes so it should, I thought, be easy enough; all I had to do was to find my shoes and sneak out before the other inmates began to stir...

'What are you gawping at, kid?' Next to me, no more than three feet away, a young girl, seventeen or eighteen perhaps, had climbed out of her bed and was adjusting her clothing. Faced with a bulging belly - she must have been five or six months pregnant - I turned over; hers was a private moment, and I was an intruder.

But there was to be no escape. On my right, a tousle-haired blonde sat crossed-legged on a dirty mattress, applying her lipstick. As I watched, a young girl, four years old perhaps, crawled out from under a dirty grey blanket and began bouncing up and down, her mother's compact mirror rising and falling in a synchronized rhythm with this, her daughter's gymnastic display.

'I'm going to wet myself,' said the girl, throwing me a toothy grin. 'I'm going to wet myself,' she repeated, with renewed urgency. 'Mummy, I need to go. I need to wee... I'm going to do it, Mummy, I am.' Then she did, the warm yellow liquid hissing and running down her legs, dripping and dribbling and forming a little puddle on the floor. Her mother took no notice. I turned away.

Two beds down a young mother, stretching like a waking cat, reached under her mattress for a packet of cigarettes. Another woman, half-naked, sat scratching bug bites, while a third silenced her child with a sugared dummy and the promise of a soggy rusk. I felt increasingly like an interloper.

'You look like you've been dragged through a hedge backwards.'

A short, stocky woman came and introduced herself to the girl from the next bed.

'Shirley, 'ain't it? I'm Mo.'

Let me guess you came in last night? Don't look so surprised,' Mo smiled at the other girl, who looked surprised.

'There ain't no secrets in this place,' Mo said, casting a glance in my direction. 'Besides,' she went on, grabbing the girl's handbag, 'this is a sure give away, this is. You put your bag under you at night, see? Leave it on the floor and it'll walk, see? Same with your clothes, your cards, and your private papers. You must stick them under your mattress, and right in the middle too. Leave them out and you'll lose everything; your cash, your papers, everything. See?'

Mo offered other survival tips. 'You stick with your Auntie Mo; she'll see you right. You'll soon learn the ropes.' And with that she went into the girl's handbag, helping herself to a cigarette.

Mo had been in Newington for a week or more, living out of a suitcase. 'There's loads of places like this,' I heard her tell her new friend. 'But this is the worst. You do know where you are, don't you? Well, you're in the bleedin' workhouse, that's where you are. Reception centres they call them nowadays, and Newington's the worst. Place is *no-bloody-torious*. It's been in all the papers, on the radio, you name it. I was here last time when the telly came. We had ITV, Panorama, the whole lot. Not that they got in. Oh, no. Not a chance.

'The warden stopped all that. She made them talk to the girls outside, she did. Only one or two, mind. And little wonder. I mean, what's the point in complaining? *I* wouldn't speak up. Not me. No bleedin' chance. See no evil, speak no evil, that's my motto. Get kicked out of here and you'll find yourself barred from every kip on this side of the river. Permanent. No, you stick with me, girl. Auntie Mo will see you right. Now, come on, shake a leg. Finish dressing and I'll take you down to the mess hall...It's Bedlam down there when it's full.'

The queue for the mess hall was where, by following the increasingly vociferous Mo and her adopted protege towards a din of scraping furniture and cutlery, I finally met up with Mum and my siblings.

'Thank God. Now we're all together, we can go.' Mum wanted to leave, to get out, to find Dad. She seemed dazed, disorientated, unable to think straight, and admitted as much.

But we were hungry, and escaping was difficult. Leavers were sure to be noticed and, besides, there would be papers to sign. Behind us a line of bodies had built up, stretching down the corridor. It was policed by a uniformed attendant whose main job, it seemed, was to threaten anyone seen to be pushing or stepping out of line with a return to the back of the queue. Best to stay put.

Mum, increasingly agitated, glanced round at the lengthening line of bodies. A girl came past and tried to cadge a cigarette. Another woman, sensing that she was new to the game perhaps, wanted to know if Mum had any powdered milk or gripe water to spare - her youngest boy had a bellyache.

'I never thought it would come to this,' Mum said. Rejection by her mother, separation from Dad, a sleepless night in Newington and she'd had enough.

By her own admission, Mum was at her wits end, at the end of her tether. Yet there was more to it than that, I think. Mum, I'm sure, could see herself in these other young mothers, and recognised, if she hadn't done so already, just how far she had fallen. At least half of the Newington women were in their mid-to-late twenties but already looked old and beaten. And Mum too was tired, increasingly demoralised. 'I never thought it would come to this,' she repeated. It was what she'd said before our Doddington eviction, and again, on an almost daily basis, during the family's time in Malling. Well here, finally, in a former London workhouse, it had. And once again Dad found himself excluded, prevented from being there to support us, and comfort his wife.

Meanwhile, back in the queue, Mo was giving everyone in earshot the benefit of her experience of Newington, and its recent history. It wasn't helpful.

'I tell a lie. A news crew did get in once. But Matron was soon on to them. Caught the cameraman in a cupboard and a reporter trying to squeeze himself under a bed, she did. Can you picture it? Talk about Laurel and bleedin' Hardy. Got themselves arrested for trespass, the dopey pair did. They ended up spending a night in the cells and had their equipment and other stuff confiscated. A fat lot of good that did us!

'Complain? Don't make me larf,' snorted Mo, warming to her subject. 'Like I said, it's a bleedin' waste of time. Soon as one of the girls speaks out, the matron and her Welfare Committee scare some poor cow into coming forward to swear it's all lies. 'Newington's smashing,' she'll claim. 'A regular home from home.'

Mo was in her stride now – on her high horse, Mum said afterwards - and it would have taken a brave person to silence her, though her voice became quiet, more intimate in tone, whenever an attendant walked past.

'They'll always find someone,' she said. 'Either that or they'll name names. "You don't want to listen to so and so," they'll say. "She 'ain't really homeless. How can she be homeless when she's left her husband, going away voluntarily like that?"

'Of course they don't tell the whole story; how the old man likes the bottle, belts his missus, and beats the kids until they're black and blue. No, I tell you. These so-called Reception centres are terrible places.

'But Newington is the worst, especially for diseases,' Mo said. 'Well, it's packed to the rafters, so what can you expect? Dysentery is the worst. The ambulances come and go all day. You stand outside and watch, see if I ain't right. It's the muck they serve in here; that's what I reckon. It's bleedin' dangerous, it is. But what can you do? The kids get hungry, and they've got to eat, ain't they?'

And with that Mo's name was called and she was ushered into the dining room to collect a morning food ration.

Following on, I looked up at an enamelled sign over the door. "God's Blessing on this House", it read.

Breakfast was the same for everyone. Heads were counted and each woman given a corresponding number of meal tickets. When a space became available, volunteers, wearing either a red armband or a patch of red cloth pinned to their fronts, escorted the next waiting family to a table.

Mum's breakfast ration was tea, served in a tin mug, and two slices of bread and marge, while we children had a choice: a dole of porridge, or a fistful of cornflakes. When Edward asked for a drink, the attendant told him there was a jug of water on the table.

The dining hall was a massive, barn-like space, with three of its four walls half-tiled in ceramic off-white. Along the remaining side of the room ran the food counter, the space in front taken up by rows and rows of trestle tables and long bench seats, capacity enough to cater for three or four hundred. The noise of scraping furniture, the clash of cutlery and the echo of raised voices was overwhelming.

Volunteers were everywhere, their presence a reminder of something Mo, sitting a couple of tables away, had said about the Newington regime. Families, she advised, had to leave the building after breakfast and stay out until four-thirty. The only way to drag it out was for a woman to become a volunteer, to get herself a job scrubbing floors or working in the kitchens, washing up, or peeling vegetables for the evening meal. And, where necessary, to arrange a childminder.

One woman, different from the others, sat apart. Not for her the red armband or square of red cotton. Instead, she wore a starched blue and white uniform and a nursing matron's hat.

Matron Jones, a big, globular woman - her full title was Matron-in-Charge - sat quietly at a little round table which she'd had placed near the door, giving her a clear view of the morning's comings and goings. The table was covered by a crisp white cloth with, at its centre, a single red rose in a smoked glass vase. One of the inmates brought Matron toast and marmalade, while another carried tea on a silver tray. Mum told me not to stare.

But if Mum hoped the family might go unnoticed, she was to be disappointed. Matron had spotted us, a group of newcomers, almost at once and, having had enough of her breakfast, and with only a cursory attempt at an introduction, came and plonked herself down beside us.

'Terry family? Came in late last night, yes? Just one or two questions before you start your meal.'

One or two questions? Matron had a list. Where did we come from? Did Mum have any money? Was there a man or husband in tow? Mum was reluctant to respond. Pressed, she gave Matron the bare bones; King Hill, our abortive trip to Southampton, and the advice Dad had received from Hampshire County Council about taking his family back to Kent.

'And that's what we plan to do,' Mum said.

'I see,' Matron replied.

But I'm not sure that she did. Matron, you see, was for a moment distracted, obliged to concern herself with what was happening across the hall where, half-way through Mum's quiet confession, a squabble had started.

Satisfied that there was no need for her to intervene, Matron turned her attention to my sister. 'What a sweetie,' she cooed, taking Claire from Mum's arms. Her name? Mum, alarmed, quickly snatched Claire back.

'So, let's get things straight,' Matron said. 'You're saying you won't be staying. Is that right?'

'Yes, I've told you,' Mum replied.

Well, Mum had a choice: finish breakfast, pay for a night's lodging and leave, or report to the medical room for an examination, and a rectal swab.

'What's a rectal swab?' I asked.

Before Mum could answer, a small birdlike creature, all bonnet, flying ribbons and epaulettes, crash-landed amongst us, sliding along the bench, coming to rest against my shoulder. Matron took this interruption as her cue to withdraw.

'Good morning to you, sister,' chirped the new arrival, addressing Mum. 'My name's Agnes, Captain Agnes. I expect you spotted me doing my rounds?'

'Salvation Army,' whispered Mum, in response to my quizzical stare. As if reading her mind, Captain Agnes deposited copies of *War Cry* on the table.

'Are you really in the army,' I said, taken by surprise.

'Like a real soldier?' asked Edward, edging away from this strangely garbed intruder.

Captain Agnes explained. 'Well, I *am* a soldier. But not that kind,' she said, pre-empting my next question. 'I'm a soldier of

Christ, with five years' army service. See these two stars,' she raised a hand to her shoulder proudly, 'five years, which makes me a captain.'

'Yes, but if you're not a real soldier, what do you *do*?' I asked.

Mum, putting a finger to her lips, gave me a nudge.

'That's quite alright, dear,' said Captain Agnes. 'What do I do? Let me see. Well, my mission is to bring help, hope, and comfort to those in need, and that includes the residents of Newington Lodge. I'm here two or three times a week, working with families living in poverty, the homeless, that sort of thing.'

So, was Captain Agnes going to support us? It seemed not. Given the captain's remit, it soon became clear that there was little, or no chance of any help for Mum, practical or otherwise. After all, the Terry family were neither local, nor Londoners.

But what about hope? Well, maybe.

'Did you know, boys,' Captain Agnes said, 'that Charlie Chaplin was an inmate here? Yes, he was. I promise you. He really, really, was.'

The "little tramp" it happened, was something of a personal hero. Looking back, I suspect Captain Agnes had used him before; he was a handy role model, an example of someone who, despite his humble beginnings, had gone on to find fame and fortune.

'Yes, it's true. Charlie Chaplin, from the silent movies. You know, bowler hat and swinging cane, moustache, and baggy trousers. Kick up the pants, fall over. Get up, swing a punch, fall over again. Now wasn't he a funny man? Of course, it was a long time ago,' she said, acknowledging our blank faces. 'But it's all there, in the records, the admissions ledger: 1896, Charlie Chaplin, mother and siblings. And, well, look at him now. A millionaire, I shouldn't wonder. A millionaire and living in Switzerland. It makes you think, doesn't it? I say, it makes you think...'

I *was* thinking. I was thinking about Chaplin's money. I was thinking about Switzerland, America, and the movies (with a million pounds in my pocket I could go and live with Auntie Betty in Tennessee). Mostly, I was thinking about Dad and getting out, putting Newington Lodge far behind me.

First, though, there was the little matter of breakfast. Invited to give thanks for our cornflakes we, all of us, stopped eating and, hands clasped together, joined Captain Agnes in prayer. 'For what we are about to receive, may the Lord make us truly grateful.'

Amen.

CHAPTER FOUR

Leaving London on a Kent-bound train, my head echoed to the sights and sounds of the disappearing city. A brief, if colourful, relationship with the metropolis, relived, made a welcome diversion. A random shuffle of morning memories, central to which was our reunion with Dad, helped keep me in the moment, blocking out both Newington Lodge, and frightened imaginings of what was to come.

I can't say why, but many of those London sights and sounds, remembered years later, involved horses: Southwark and a team of brightly decked-out drays - a busy scene; an open cellar, a cart load of beer kegs and barked out orders to 'Walk round it, mate. Walk round it'; a mounted policeman exiting one of the parks; a single nag trotting a cart flicked along by a balding rag and bone man sitting atop four near-naked pneumatic tyres.

Finally, London "proper": Westminster Bridge, Big Ben, the Houses of Parliament, and Westminster Abbey; buildings, part of a collective psyche, central to national life, which, until Newington Lodge, had existed for me only in words and pictures. It was a child's view of England's island history: I could hardly fail to be impressed.

And there was more. At Grosvenor Bridge our train, made up of a dozen or so snaking coaches, sparking metal on metal, crossed the Thames. Now, coming out of Victoria, the vista broadened; everything in sight being bigger, and on a larger scale, than anything within my short and narrow experience. Vauxhall and Tower Bridges, a pageant of barges and boats and dipping cranes, a widening prospect set off by the flaming colours of autumn trees, lining the Embankment. And all of it, the boulevards, and the wide, watery thoroughfare, guarded by a chariot-mounted Boadicea, an ancient British queen co-opted to bear witness to the steady flow of time.

Soon came Battersea Power Station and, after that, as we picked up speed, the suburbs; the grand monuments of central London yielding to the workaday - mile upon mile of terraced houses, gardens and allotments, improvised sheds of every shape and size, grassy spaces running down to meet the railway.

At Borough Green, a man pushing a wheelbarrow stopped, looked up and waved. I waved back. This was a good omen, I decided.

But was it? Maidstone was still an hour away. Short of pulling the communication cord - bringing a temporary, if expensive, £5 delay to the journey - some sort of closure was coming, of that I was sure and certain. Claire was crying, Ian and Malcolm complained of hunger; we children were all tired and downhearted.

I sat gazing out of the window, praying for someone to lift me up and set me down somewhere else, in a place called home. And there *was* hope. After everything the family had gone through, a reprieve might yet come.

Or was the family really doomed to separation, cast to the four winds? I remembered hearing groups of women at King Hill discussing the horrors of separation; the idea that we could face the same fate was alarming and suddenly very real. Yet even now, at the last minute, might not a housing agreement be possible? Given time, Dad, I was sure, would be able to pay off his rent arrears.

It was desperate stuff, but I began to formulate a plan. Firstly, there was fruit and vegetable picking; the whole family could get involved with that. The work was seasonal, but lucrative; strawberries, apples and pears, carrots, and spuds; we'd done it before and could do it again. Soon it would be hop-picking time. Hop-picking was challenging work, but an experienced hand could make a tidy sum.

As well as fruit and hop-picking, there were other money-making opportunities. Car washing, clearing gardens; a dozen ways for us children to contribute. Edward, eleven years old now, might look for a paper round, or find a milkman who needed a Saturday boy.

And then there were the tricks and ruses learned at King Hill. I was just considering a return to tobacco trading – Mum to have first dibs, saving money on the price of cigarettes, when a guard came by, inspecting tickets, and announcing our imminent arrival at Maidstone East.

A short walk, two hundred yards perhaps, saw the family contemplating the commanding façade of County Hall, wherein was located the Social Services Department. This large imposing building, dating back to 1824, stood, and stands, almost opposite the railway station. All we had to do was cross the road, get past a peaked-capped doorman and present ourselves at the reception desk, where staff kindly agreed to look after our luggage, and Claire's pushchair.

Dad had directions, but they meant tackling a maze of corridors. Yes, there were signs on doors and walls – Personnel, Finance, Archives Department - then steps up, and steps down. But none of them helped.

At one point, we bumped into a woman pushing a trolley loaded with files; she sent us back the way we had just come. Eventually, after more twists and turns, we managed to find the office that Dad, phoning from Victoria, wanted - the office of a Mr. Borden. Two knocks on the door, a pause, and a distinctive voice uttered the single word: 'Come!'

Furnished in heavy oak, Mr. Borden's chambers were a cross between a court room and a registrar's office; it was the sort of space you will be familiar with if you have attended a civil wedding or gone to register a birth or death. There was certainly no mistaking it for anything other than a place where solemn, public business took place.

The contrast was striking. Outside, in the corridor, all was hustle and bustle; doors opened, doors closed; telephones rang, a bank of typewriters pecked away; the smell of stale tobacco, and the odour of the canteen, hung like a cloud. It was, all of it, evidence of the tireless, diligent work of the

Social Services Department – busy bodies going about other people's business.

Meanwhile, the closing of a heavy door away, the ambience was quite different. Here, amid a suite of dark wood furniture, grand looking books and weighty shelving, a mood of dignified, carpeted calm prevailed. Down one side of the room ran a series of high, sashed windows; on the other a lengthy line of glass cases, filled with leather bound volumes, dominated. The bust of a local worthy, a former mayor or alderman perhaps, sat on the central unit, while other red-robed officers, painted in oils, hung on the walls, quite literally looking down upon us. It was all very intimidating.

Two rows of chairs had been set out in front of Mr. Borden's desk, though whether they were there for our benefit, or represented a permanent arrangement, I couldn't say. I do remember an assistant. Her name was Mrs. Kay. It was Mrs. Kay, dressed in her workaday twinset, who stood to acknowledge our arrival, motioning the family to sit. Then she went back to her own seat and waited, as we all waited, for Mr. Borden to consider the evidence and pass judgement.

An awkward silence, during which time Mr. Borden ignored us, ensued. The telephone rang, and Mrs. Kay answered. 'He's busy right now,' she said, returning the receiver to its cradle. Mr. Borden, oblivious to the interruption, perused a file of papers, which I assumed pertained to us, the Terry family.

The pause gave me a chance to size him up, this man who was to decide our fate. What was there about Mr. Borden that might betray his character, or mood? Well, it was hard to tell. My immediate impression was that thinning, reddish hair aside, he was quite young (young was positive), in his late thirties, perhaps. But when Mr. Borden raised his head, it was to reveal heavy pouches under his eyes, bags that formed a natural resting place for the frames of a pair of round-rimmed glasses. He was probably older than I had at first imagined.

What did Mr. Borden's clothes say about him? Well, it was contradictory. His dress was formal, yet he'd removed his jacket, rolled up his sleeves and loosened his tie. Did this signify a relaxed approach to his work? Well, maybe. Then again, none of the office windows were open - perhaps they wouldn't open - and it was a warm day. Who could blame him for dressing down?

Next, came the office furniture. The state of Mr. Borden's desk, I decided, did not auger well for a positive outcome. It was heavy, and deep - so deep that a boy might build a den and camp out underneath, I thought. It was also tidy - too tidy, neat, and uncluttered. His in-tray was empty; the out-tray full, loaded with files and letters waiting for the afternoon post.

A wooden name plate, with K.G. Borden engraved in gold lettering, mirrored the plaque on the office door. And this was a worry too. Mrs. Kay didn't have a name plate, or a plaque. She shared the same desk, and there were two telephones, but, unlike Mr. Borden, she didn't have a leather office chair. She had to make do with a modern bucket looking affair.

Ultimately, there was no way of divining the family's fate from any of this. Yet the attempt, a reflex action almost, helped me cope with the intensity of feelings which washed over me as we waited. Perhaps things might go well for us, after all.

At last, Mr. Borden looked up. He smiled. He removed his glasses. Then, hands linked in a cat's cradle under his chin, he spoke. 'And what can we do for you this fine sunny afternoon?' he asked, addressing himself to Dad. It was the same kind of cheery, patronising attitude we'd come to expect when answering to officialdom.

Dad, asked to approach the desk, did his best to explain, but he spoke too quickly, stumbling over his words. Twice Mr. Borden interrupted, asking him to start again, from the beginning.

But where exactly was the beginning? Dad spoke quietly about his mother's death, the time he'd lost from work, the prolonged winter, the ice, and the snow. He explained, too, about Mum's mental health problems and the stress of coping with a large family.

Mr. Borden, it appeared, knew all about this, and was soon waving a large, fat file with our name on it. 'Yes, yes, but King Hill provides emergency accommodation, the maximum period of stay is twelve weeks. You knew this, didn't you Mr. Terry?'

'Yes.'

'Well, speak up, man, what have you been doing with yourself for the past three months?'

Dad paused and took a deep breath, choosing to address his response to Mrs. Kay - perhaps because, as a woman, he thought she might be a little more sympathetic. Maybe she was a mother herself. Was Dad a 'feckless ne'er do well?' This was his chance to prove otherwise.

'I found work labouring on a building site, at the bottom of Boxley Road, not far from the prison.'

'Ah, the new flats and houses. I know. Good money? Overtime?'

Dad said yes, he'd been on about £17 a week, sometimes a bit more, though often a little less. It all depended on the weather. Once or twice he and the other men had been rained off.

'And what have you done with your wages? Got any pay packets?'

Dad hadn't kept his payslips, and they wouldn't have helped if he had. The fact was that his earnings had gone out almost as soon as they'd come in. There was the rent for his digs, the hostel charges at King Hill, money for food, travel back and forth to see us, his family, five shillings a week to keep our furniture in storage...

'And housing? Can you tell us what you have done to find a suitable home for your family?' It was Mr. Borden's turn to intervene.

Dad had done his best, that's what he'd done. He'd spent the summer traipsing from agency to agency, checking notice boards, making phone calls, and following up newspaper ads. And it all cost money, especially when he had to ask for time off work. But it was hopeless. If Dad found a place the rent was too high. If the advertised rent seemed affordable, his hopes would be dashed on arrival at the property, the 'To Let" board at the gate directing prospective tenants to a further sign in the window, where a list of exclusions almost inevitably included children - to which most landlords, quite legally, added the categories: Irish, Blacks and dogs.

Mr. Borden, who must have known that, regardless of individual circumstances, finding private rented housing for a family of eight was nigh on impossible, held up his hand. Perhaps he thought Dad had suffered enough. More likely he'd heard it all a dozen times before. Whatever the reason, he'd shown little concern or sympathy for our predicament and, indeed, had at times barely seemed to be listening, occupying himself instead by producing a handkerchief and rubbing away at his glasses. Now he turned to Mrs. Kay. It was question time.

Mrs. Kay brought forward two empty chairs and, having invited Dad to sit, beckoned Mum to come and join him.

A weak smile, a clearing of the throat, and Mrs. Kay launched into a series of questions, reading from the sheet in front of her.

'Can you confirm that the children here today are yours, and that Mr. Terry is the father. Are all six legitimate?'

'Yes,' said Mum, taken quite off guard.

'Does anyone present suffer, or has suffered in the recent past, from a contagious disease?'

'No. I don't think so...'

'Answer the question please, Mrs. Terry. Yes, or no?'

'Well, no, then.'

'Thank you.'

'Has any member of your family ever spent time in a mental hospital, asylum or other institution?'

'I don't understand, why...'

'Is there any insanity?'

'No,' Mum said, in a "certainly not" tone of voice.

Did she have any other family who might help with accommodation?

Mum repeated the story of our trip to Southampton.

'Unfortunate,' said Mrs. Kay.

'Parents not interested,' said Mr. Borden, and Mrs. Kay marked the form accordingly.

'Siblings?'

'Yes,' said Mum, an older brother and sister, although both, she explained, lived abroad.

Mrs. Kay asked for details and Mum told her about Uncle John and Auntie Betty. 'My sister was a land girl during the war; she met and married a GI and moved to Tennessee. That was in 1946, I think.'

'Sister not interested,' said Mr. Borden, and Mrs. Kay marked the form with the letters "N.I."

'And the brother?'

Uncle John, Mum said, was a civil servant and worked for the War Office.

'Does he, now?' said Mr. Borden, raising an eyebrow.

'Yes, he's presently based in Cyprus.'

'Not interested,' said Mr. Borden, with a shake of the head.

'John *has* helped,' said Mum, interrupting the steady flow of questions. 'He sent me fifteen pounds.'

'And you spent it on?'

This, for Mum, was too much, the final straw. She didn't like Mr. Borden's tone and was quick to tell him so. 'I didn't come here to be treated like dirt,' she said. 'And before you ask, I have no intention of telling the likes of you what I've done with my brother's money. So, go ahead, put him down as not interested if you like. But the truth is always the truth and I'm not going to sign anything that says otherwise.'

There was a moment's silence. I wanted to cheer. Edward shouted out in open defiance. Mum burst into tears.

At this point, Mrs. Kay picked up her telephone and, in response, a younger woman came and took us children from the room. Mum kept Claire.

And that was that. While we boys sat in a small annex, drinking orange squash, and squabbling over a plate of biscuits, Dad signed form *CD24 (Children Act 1948) Application for the Reception of Children in to Care.* This, legally binding document formally handed us over to the council. We boys became "Looked after Children", in the care of the state. Years later I obtained a copy of the form, using the Data Protection Act. I have it in front of me as I write.

*

The social worker who came to take us away was a tall, kindly-looking man with untidy hair and a dark, bushy moustache. I remember he wore a tweed jacket and carried a leather briefcase. His polished brogues were of leather and, to complete the look, someone had sewn leather patches on to the elbows of his jacket. He introduced himself as Mr. Waller. If I close my eyes and summon him now, a fortyish, rather scruffy George Orwell appears.

'You must be Edward - the eldest?' asked a slightly hesitant Mr. Waller, holding out his hand.

'Where's my mum and dad?' said Edward in response.

'And our sister, Claire,' I said. 'What have you done with her?'

'I'm afraid Mum and Dad have gone,' replied Mr. Waller, by way of explanation. 'We - that is Mum and Dad - thought it would be better this way,' he said. 'After all we don't want a fuss now, do we? Best if we are all brave soldiers and try to avoid any upset, don't you think?'

Mr. Waller did his best to soften the blow. 'Look, the news is not all bad. Mum and Dad can visit your new home at weekends and write letters.' Then he told us about Eastry, and the journey, and the distance: forty miles. And we reacted, each brother in his own way. Edward jumped to his feet and made a dash for the door, but Mr. Waller got there first and held on to the handle. Andrew called Mr. Waller a liar; Mum and Dad would never abandon us like this. Malcolm and Ian cried. I was too shocked to react.

As it happened, we boys had much to do with Mr. Waller, both during our time in Eastry, and afterwards. It turned out that he was a Senior Child Care Officer, a position of great responsibility. However, his duty of care didn't seem to include driving, since he handled his Morris Traveller like he was Stirling Moss. If for nothing else the journey down to Eastry would have been memorable for Mr. Waller's driving; Edward, white knuckled, sitting in the front, clutching Ian's teddy, Archie; the rest of us in the back, bouncing around like four peas in a rattle. It was the first time I'd been in a motor car. I remember it smelled of pipe tobacco.

I was not a good passenger. I hated the lack of space, and the smell and even the feel of the leather upholstery made me feel sick. And there was that other pain; the pain of enforced separation, which increased with every passing mile. It was an ache that was to return repeatedly over the coming months and years, and always with the same sharp intensity. I felt it at the end of every parental visit, at the approach of every goodbye. I didn't have a name for it then: it was not until adulthood, when death became something real, that I recognised it for what it undoubtedly was; the grief of separation and loss, and the fear of never being together again.

Ten miles out of Maidstone, along the A20, Mr. Waller's car passed a sign for Doddington and Andy and I whispered about village life and our old home. Another family would have moved in by now. What changes had they made, if any? Their own furniture, yes. And if they had any money, and any sense, new wallpaper in the sitting room.

There would be children, of course. And those children would have our bedrooms. Outside, on the landing, they'd find rows of marks climbing a doorframe; Dad's idea – a birthday ritual, once a year, as we sprouted. How would the new kids measure up? And the last minute, pencil scrawled autographs on the bedroom walls; would the incomers speak our names, even as they rubbed us out? At this very moment, they might be playing where we played, discovering our secret places. And all this as we whizzed past four miles - and an entire world, away. It made our eviction seem even more poignant, and surreal.

The family had been gone from Doddington for three months; three long months of summer. Now events were gathering pace and decisions, life changing decisions had been made, with hardly a glance in our direction. I felt like I was looking in at it all from the outside, that I'd become a bystander in my own life.

What I would have given to be back in our old house, waking up in my own bed to discover, with massive relief, that nothing was amiss, that it had all been a bad dream.

I pictured myself going downstairs for breakfast and, afterwards, being free to go and play outside. Dad's garden would be much the same, full now of flowering hollyhocks, delphiniums and creeping nasturtiums, his vegetable plot ripe with peas, runner beans and marrows. Then it struck me: soon all this would be gone; the season's crop harvested, fruit and vegetables devoured, and, in a final act of mundane desecration, the garden tidied for winter. Then all trace of the Terry family would be gone. Forever.

And then there was our education. We were a week or more into a new academic year; if they hadn't realised before, the whole of Doddington school would, by now, know that the Terrys had gone, and wouldn't be coming back.

I thought of Mr. Morris, the headmaster, at his first assembly, welcoming the new intake, seizing the opportunity to use us as an example. 'Does anyone know what the word *eviction* means?' he would ask from his rostrum. 'Well, the Terrys owed money. It seems Mr. Terry didn't budget properly, and so the family had to leave their home, and the village...Now, who can define *prudence* for me?'

It wouldn't have happened like this, of course. But there was bound to be talk, in the playground and, among the adults, in the staff room. It was only natural that I should care about the opinion of my teachers. Indeed, I'd spent weeks speculating, fretting about how they would react to my sudden disappearance.

Mostly I worried about Mrs. Gates. It was Mrs. Gates, my reception class teacher, who'd rescued me from the school pond, three years since, way back on day one. 'Was it the fish?' she'd asked. 'I expect it was the movement and the colours, the flashing silver and gold that tempted you in. Look closely and you can see all the colours of the rainbow. But you must stay on the grass. Understood?' This while she stripped me naked, replacing my sodden clothing with an oversized pair of girl's navy-blue knickers and a large singlet, my uniform placed on a radiator to dry.

By term's end, with Christmas looming, Mrs. Gates had me worked out. 'Douglas, you are a romantic and a dreamer,' she said, then relegated me to the position of second sheep in the nativity play- a lack of judgement and imagination long since forgiven.

It was Mrs. Gates who arranged for me to move from my house team, the Vikings, to the Normans, so that I could join with Edward and Andy in amassing merit points in class work, games, and sports. We won the school trophy two years running.

It wasn't rational, but I was sure I'd let them all down – Mr. Morris, Mrs. Gates, the whole school. In retrospect, I'm sure that it was now, on the road to Eastry, that the shame of the family's eviction finally hit home; now that I began the long struggle with the idea that I must be to blame.

On one level this was nonsense, of course; I was a child and, as such, had no say or influence on what had happened over the previous weeks and months. Nor was I responsible for instigating this long journey into the unknown.

But deep down I knew I was guilty. I'd been *taken into care.* The very words had a ring of doom about them. *Taken* into care. I didn't know it, but I was about to find myself in the clutches of a group of adults skilled in playing on these feelings of guilt, and in convincing me that I was deserving of punishment.

An hour or so out of Maidstone, and the heavy autumnal orchards, the oast-houses and the flashing, hypnotic lines of familiar hop poles fell behind. The Morris began to climb, following the A28, where solid wooden signposts invited detours to Chartham Hatch, Nackington and the romantically named Old Wives Lees (where even now, I imagined, some old wives might well be hard at work gathering in the lees, the residue of the summer harvest).

Up here growth was sparser; there was more chalk, and even the buses, blushing at a visible decline in the soil's fertility, changed colour, rural green giving way to the deep purple of bruised plums – Maidstone and District yielding to the East Kent Omnibus Co Ltd.

Soon Canterbury was upon us, and Mr. Waller was pointing out the cathedral, and talking cricket. He'd been a good opening bowler in his day, he boasted. Now he kept active by playing tennis and golf when time allowed. In fact, when it came to sports, Mr. Waller, it seemed, was something of an all-rounder and, as such, keen to promote Eastry's reputation for physical activity.

There was cricket, football, badminton, and table tennis. Did we play football? Yes, of course we did. All young boys played football. Well, we would be pleased to know that sides from Eastry were both competitive and successful. Teams had been known to travel as far as the other side of the county, to Tonbridge or Sevenoaks, for a match: Kentish Men versus the Men of Kent. But, continued Mr. Waller, there was more to Eastry than sport. There were other opportunities - Cubs, Scouts, Boys Brigade, Sea Scouts...

Soon came Eastry village, groups of detached houses, shops, a garage. I began counting the High Street pubs – *The Bull*, *The Five Bells* - saw a sign for a school, and caught a glimpse of the church, its tower casting a shadow across a patch of summer-faded village green.

Then, almost as quickly as they had appeared, these man-made things were left behind, the Morris flying downhill with, ahead of us, it appeared, nothing but open countryside, a cornfield, and a stand of firs. It was here, at the trees, that Mr. Waller braked, swinging his car sharply to the left, on to a short, gravelled driveway, where it came to a halt.

Facing us, facing the Austin, basking in the evening sun, sat a large, complacent gatehouse, while further along, running away towards the middle distance, marched a row of ugly, semi-detached houses. Beyond these I caught a brief glimpse of a playing field.

'Here we are, boys, the Cottage Homes,' said Mr. Waller, opening the passenger door. I fell out first and was sick all over his shoes.

CHAPTER FIVE

A small bony woman with a face like a wrinkled apple came out to greet us. This was Mrs. Adams, the home's matron. It was clear from her demeanour that she'd met Mr. Waller before.

Mrs. Adams welcomed Mr. Waller by fetching a rag out of her housecoat pocket and commanding him to clean the vomit from his shoes. I received a Medusa-like stare. As well as Eastry's administrative centre (it also served as a store, a sewing room and laundry) the gatehouse was Mrs. Adam's home, and not even a Senior Child Care Officer entered with dirty footwear.

Mr. Waller's shoes having passed inspection, Mrs. Adams marshalled our group into the building and through to a stuffy, smoke-filled rear office, where her husband, the superintendent, sat drinking tea in the company of two other women. Mr. Waller said we were to call Mr. Adams "Super." The two women were Auntie Harris and Auntie Fitzgerald. I distinguished between them thus: Auntie Fitzgerald was old (mid-fifties as it turned out) and had grey hair. Auntie Harris was ancient and smelled of fish.

Completing the reception committee was a younger looking man, Dr. Brocklehurst. The good doctor had come along, he explained, in his role as local County Medical Officer.

Dr. Brocklehurst, like Mr. Waller, worked for the council, his Eastry job being to examine individual boys and girls, both on arrival and departure, to make sure they were fit and healthy. Later Mr. Adams would register the new intake with Dr. Rose, at the village surgery.

Almost at once, we boys faced our first inspection. It went like this. Taking her cue from Dr. Brocklehurst, Mrs. Adams ordered the five of us to strip and line up against the office wall, youngest to eldest, facing away from the window. We weren't to speak, but to put up a hand if we needed help. Malcolm raised his hand, and Ian copied him. None of us protested. As we removed our clothes, Auntie Harris collected them up and tossed them into a corner. It was to be two years before they resurfaced.

Once we were naked, Dr. Brocklehurst came over and began prodding and poking his way down the line. He looked in our hair and ears; he searched under our arms and between our legs. Then, as if to make sure, he repeated the exercise, retracing his steps. As he moved, he leant forward and tapped a pencil on the tops of our heads, each in turn, as though striking the keys of a xylophone. 'Nits, nits, nits, and fleas,' he declared. Then, when he reached Malcolm, 'Nits, boils and eczema.' I too was found to have boils, on my arms and back. Mr. Adams promised they would be cut out the very next day. I still have the scars.

Dr. Brocklehurst, having performed his statutory duty, and judging the teapot to be empty, clicked his bag shut and picked up his hat and coat. Shortly afterwards Mr. Waller also got ready to leave. He said his quiet goodbyes, promised to come the following week and told us, for the umpteenth time, not to worry.

With Mr. Waller's departure went our last link to Maidstone, and Mum and Dad. We'd shared a long car journey; nearly two hours. It seemed like half a lifetime.

The medical inspection completed, all that remained, for now at least, was for new clothes to be issued and house parents to be agreed upon. Not for the first, or indeed the last time, we children were discussed as though we were invisible.

Auntie Fitzgerald began the bidding. She wanted Ian, because he was the youngest: a younger child, she said, would be less trouble than the "delinquents" she was often saddled with.

Auntie Harris countered by reminding her that under-fives should go to Auntie Cornish in May Cottage, or Auntie Ireland in Rose: that was the usual way younger arrivals were shared out. But Auntie Fitzgerald, expecting this line of argument, was one step ahead. Under normal circumstances, Ian would go to Rose or May, yes. And earlier in the day, there were empty beds, one in each cottage. However, these were filled during the afternoon, when Mrs. Adams agreed to take two young girls from Ashurst Place, a local nursery. So, Ian would have to be put in with a group of older boys after all, and Auntie Fitzgerald saw no reason why she shouldn't have first dibs.

Mr. Adams, glancing at his wife, shook his head. He wanted Ian placed with Edward, eldest and youngest together, the elder brother helping to keep an eye on his younger sibling. Auntie Fitzgerald was asked to take them both, but she refused; she didn't want another, older boy.

The debate went back and forth, Mr. Adams suggesting one combination, and Auntie Fitzgerald coming back with an arrangement of her own.

Suddenly, Auntie Harris, impatient and tired of this verbal tug of war and its "what ifs" and "how abouts" changed tack. It was time for a direct approach. Slamming down her empty teacup, she came over to inspect the line of naked young bodies displayed before her, strutting about, mimicking Dr. Brocklehurst. If anything, she was even more thorough, making us open our mouths, focusing on our teeth. I remember too that she made me move my hands from in front of my genitals, ordering me to stand rod straight with my arms at my side. 'This one's pale and sickly,' she said. Then she asked me if I was a bed wetter.

It was Mrs. Adams who settled matters. But not before we boys had been issued with new clothes. There were Aertex shirts and grey tank tops, along with grey shorts, grey socks, and elastic garters. As for our trousers, well it was a case of once worn, never forgotten. They were made of a sort of cheap serge material which, until you got used to them, rubbed, and chafed, and made you itch. The only concession to colour or individuality was a striped snake-clasp belt. Mine was blue and white.

Stripy, Proban pyjamas – labelled "Fire Resistant" - and dressing gowns completed the kit. The dressing gowns were almost as coarse as the short trousers, and came with belts sporting braided, coloured tassels. Before the week was out each one of these items of clothing would be labelled. Twice. One tag, its lettering picked out in red, gave the surname of the wearer and cottage; the other read *KCC: Eastry Children's Home.*

Auntie Harris said that the labels were there to let the police know where to return us if we ran away. But in truth the uniform itself was enough for identification purposes; a child wearing Eastry clothing stood out like a sore thumb.

After we'd been weighed and measured, and helped to put on our new clothing, Mrs. Adams directed Auntie Harris to take Edward and Ian. Auntie Fitzgerald was stuck with Andrew and Malcolm; it was her reward for making a fuss.

And that was how things were decided; two brothers went to Thorn Cottage – all the houses bore the names of trees - with Auntie Harris, while the other pair went to Lime with Auntie Fitzgerald.

As for me, I was left standing in the office, my back quite literally against the wall. Abandoned, and still nauseous, I felt more naked in my new clothes than I did when I undressed for Dr. Brocklehurst. It was, I think, the first time in my life that I had been truly alone. Even Archie, left sitting propped up on Mr. Adam's desk, looked forlorn and forgotten. Who was coming for me?

Auntie Joyce was coming for me when she could be found. It seemed Auntie had taken a half-day holiday, and no one was sure when she would be back. So, while Mrs. Adams walked up to Almond Cottage to track her down, the "Super" closed the office curtains, lit his pipe and, picking up a pen, settled down to complete his paperwork. I was ignored.

Mr. Adam's pulling the office curtains was, of course, a natural, and routine, response to the fading September light, one which, for him, held no significance at all. But for me it was a great symbolic moment. With the closing of the curtains, I felt again an acute spasm of loss. Outside, beyond the window and the driveway ran the road that had brought me to this place, a road that led back to a world, the real world, where other children, the lucky ones, lived fortunate, ordinary lives. From now on, I knew, this was to be my lot: the boy on the inside, forever looking out.

Who was this Auntie Joyce? When would I see my brothers again?

Overwhelmed, and fearful, my head full of unanswered questions, and desperate to find an escape, I turned my attention to the room itself.

On one wall hung framed photographs of sports teams. And, in the corner, where my discarded clothes still lay, stood a long, narrow table covered in green baize, heavy with trophies won at football and cricket. There were certificates for swimming. Someone had come out on top at boxing.

Hard against the opposite wall stood a large fish tank. Remembering Doddington school, and Mrs. Gates, I screwed up my eyes in an attempt at self-hypnosis, focusing on the shifting colours and the movement of the angel fish, guppies, and minnows. But I couldn't make it last.

Next, I turned to the large railway-style clock that hung on the wall behind Mr. Adam's desk. I stared and stared at it, trying to synchronize first my breathing, and then my heartbeat, with the sound of its movement. That way, I thought, I might disappear, become invisible.

I didn't disappear, of course. I couldn't escape the present, any more than I could return to the past. But at that moment all I wanted was to be gone. I wanted to close my eyes and open them again to find myself back in Doddington, home amongst familiar hedgerows and cornfields.

I thought again about school. It had been three months, but if I went back, maybe, just maybe, I could find a convincing way to explain my absence. Tomorrow I would race Edward and Andy between the humming telegraph poles, just as we'd always done, to see who would be first to reach the schoolyard. Even the confinement of the classroom, with its rusty radiators, aroma of chalk and steaming clothes seemed like a kind of heaven when faced with Eastry, and the unknown.

Worse was to come. Mr. Adams, glancing up, noticed me staring at the wall behind him. There, below the clock, a cane lay proud across two large hooks, yet another trophy.

I recognised this cane. It was a Greyfriars model, shaped like a shepherd's crook, identical to the ones used to beat Billy Bunter, Denis the Menace, and a whole gang of other comic book characters. The difference was that this one was real. You could touch and feel it.

Mr. Adams took down the cane, tapped it across his palm and swished it about a bit, bending the bamboo back and forth. Then, suddenly, he did the most extraordinary thing. Coming out from behind his desk, he waved the cane under my nose, then began dancing around the room, using the weapon as a sword, slashing, and thrusting at invisible enemies. 'Ever seen Robin Hood?' I had, of course. Watching Richard Greene in his weekly fight to the death with the Sheriff of Nottingham had been a regular treat when we visited Gran. Mr. Adams, it seemed to me, would have made a better Friar Tuck.

'Take that, and that,' Mr. Adams cried, attacking his own empty chair. Next, he had a go at the curtains. 'Come out, come out; I know you're behind there; show yourself, you Saxon dog.'

Exhilarated, he continued round the room, looking for targets until, all at once, he lost interest, the fight went out of him, and he collapsed, perspiring, back into his chair.

'Phew,' Mr. Adams said. 'Let me get my breath. I'm getting too old for this swashbuckling lark.' Then he took a handkerchief from his pocket and wiped it across his brow, before picking up the cane from his desk, examining the weapon more closely. 'It's a beautiful piece, don't you think?' he asked. I said nothing.

The Eastry cane wasn't just any old cane. It was, Mr. Adams wheezed, a regulation cane, council sanctioned. Made to precise specifications, neither too thick nor too thin, and of an agreed length (three feet I've since discovered), the weapon was supposed to be a deterrent of the last resort; it was to be used sparingly, the reason for its deployment required to be logged, along with the number of strokes, in a Punishment Book. On these occasions a second staff member was supposed to be present as a witness. But, as I was to learn, this wasn't always possible, nor, indeed, desirable; so long as a child's skin wasn't broken, and no scars of a permanent nature were inflicted...

Mr. Adams, seeing my reaction, laughed. I wasn't in for a caning, he promised. Not tonight, nor any other night. Indeed, barring a serious transgression (the worst of which was running away; it drew attention to the home, and suggested ingratitude), or a sadistic desire on his part to inflict pain, he would never again need to punish any child. Indeed, in a week or two, he and the matron would be no more. The superintendent had reached retirement age, and he was to be superannuated. Mr. and Mrs. Adams were leaving the service for good.

It had all been agreed months ago. Mr. Baker, supported by his wife, were to be the new management team. Their imminent arrival, from Grosvenor House, a small home in nearby Herne Bay, would allow Mr. and Mrs. Adams to retire to Dover. There, Mr. Adams confided, the two of them planned to live out their days in a little flat Mrs. Adams had found, overlooking the English Channel. Finally, after a lifetime of hard work and sacrifice, the couple could put their feet up, sitting together on a balcony overlooking the sea, sipping tea, reminiscing about the good old days, counting the waves, and numbering the gulls that bothered the ferries sailing back and forth to France. It was, said Mr. Adams, no more than he deserved. And I'm not sure that he was wrong.

I didn't know it at the time, but Mr. Adams taking me into his confidence like this was, as I was soon to learn, an exception, self-disclosure of this sort – of any sort – being unheard of, especially among the permanent, live-in Eastry staff. "Don't ask" was the rule, and you didn't need to be told twice. Simply to show an interest in where Auntie was off to, or when she might be back, for example, was to risk a clip round the ear, or worse. For my part, I'd have hesitated to ask Auntie her favourite colour. "Ask no questions, hear no lies," was the advice. Little boys should be seen and not heard.

But this was different. Mr. Adams was leaving, going for good. And his wife, absent from the room, wasn't there to keep his tongue in check. Besides, as he said himself, with the arrival of the Terrys the home was full, as it was on the day he started out.

How long had it been? Twenty-nine years? Yes, it must be. Twenty-nine long years ago, in the summer of 1934, Mr. Adams, sitting on this very same chair had made his first entry in the admissions and discharges register. That, as he reminded me, was before the Second World War. 'Who knows where the time goes?' he said, after a moment or two of reflection.

Mr. Adam's first child was lost to the archives, but he'd remember me, he promised. And with good reason. With any luck, I'd be the last. Mine would be the last name he'd write in the register, the last boy whose height and weight he'd record in the medical book, and the last boy he'd send off to Auntie Joyce in Almond Cottage. Mr. Adams saw this as a cause for celebration. I closed my eyes, determined not to cry.

How many children had come through the gates of Eastry since Mr. Adams took over in 1934? Well, when full, the home held a little over a hundred boys and girls, so it must have been thousands. Some children came for weeks, days even. Others arrived as infants and stayed until leaving school, often, in the case of the boys, joining the armed forces. A sizeable number returned more than once, depending on family circumstances, or the season of the year.

As for the work that September evening, Mr. Adams concluded with some well-practiced words of encouragement and guidance. His advice was for me to forget the past and the circumstances that had brought me to Eastry. If I worked hard and obeyed the rules, I might yet make something of myself.

Only last week, Mr. Adams boasted, a boy named Robert, in which his staff had invested years of time and effort, had graduated from Thorn Cottage. 'Been here since he was about your age, he had. Now he's a big strapping lad of fifteen, all grown up and gone for a soldier.' Robert, he explained, had transferred from Eastry to the nearby seaside town of Deal, joining the Marines as a bandsman. What did I think of that then?

It was a good attempt, but I wasn't taken in and, looking back, I doubt if Mr. Adams believed half of it himself. The bonhomie, the picture he painted of a future I should aspire to - one that seemed already decided - coming on top of all those euphemistic references to Aunties and Uncles, Housemothers and Homes left me feeling frightened, frustrated, and confused. I had a mother already, why would I want to swap her? And I'd had a home too, until it was taken away. Then there were the so-called "cottages." I'd glanced along a row of these awful-looking buildings from the gate when we arrived; it was where Edward and Ian, Malcolm and Andrew had been taken, and where I too was about to be incarcerated. These weren't cottages: I'd lived in a cottage, and I knew the difference. So, I waited until Mr. Adams was in full flow; then I spoiled things by interrupting, asking what was going to happen to Archie, Ian's Teddy, still propped up on the office desk. I suspect that the "Super" was relieved when, finally, Auntie Joyce came to take me away.

CHAPTER SIX

The day began when Auntie Joyce said it began. Sometimes, if she was in an especially evil mood, morning came as early as six-thirty, often accompanied by a fire drill. Most days, however, she was content to leave us in our beds until seven. In the end I don't suppose it was much of a contest, since the longer "her" boys went undisturbed, the more time Auntie had to sit in the kitchen drinking a second or third cup of tea, before lighting up another Park Drive. It also increased the chances of the papers arriving before she made her way up to the dorm.

Auntie didn't really get going in the mornings until she'd read the news. Thinking about it now, I'm sure that all those tales of scandal and woe must have given her a kick. Certainly, they seemed to feed and excite in her a very particular kind of *schadenfreude*. A bleary-eyed browse through the Daily Mail, a vicarious delight in the pain and suffering of others, was just the ticket. Give her a natural disaster or, better still, a gruesome murder - with all the grisly bits left in - and Auntie was reinvigorated. Indeed, stories of violence and mayhem were seized upon as a vindication and were repeated as such – scandalous, or shocking news from any quarter being trumpeted as proof positive that we were all, individually and collectively, *going to the dogs*. Sputniks and spies, Khruschev, Keeler and Kennedy; we boys understood little of it. Yet there were times when, primed by her own muddled and jaundiced view of the world, Auntie had us convinced that we were all, well, doomed; that it was only a matter of time before the bomb dropped, and that being blown to kingdom come was *no more than we deserved*.

Ironically, a new arrival - that is to say, a boy waking from his first night in Almond – might have been forgiven for seeing Auntie Joyce in a more sympathetic light, especially given her liking for a ditty or two. The tune on my first morning was a simple one; *Clementine*, as I recall. Auntie, I soon learned, owned a large, head-filled library of similar, traditional songs. They were catchy, infectious even, their simple structures and choruses ripe for improvisation and, coming from Auntie, smut, and innuendo. *Waltzing Matilda*; *She'll be Coming Round the Mountain*; it seemed there was hardly any tune which couldn't be adapted to include references to bodily functions, or exhortations for us boys to "plink our plonkers" and "keep our peckers up". Auntie, it was obvious, thought this *Carry-on* style of humour amusing. For me, the novelty soon wore off.

But at least Auntie gave the dorm fair warning that she was on her way. And we knew what to expect. For if her singing was part of the daily ritual, so was what followed.

Having climbed the stairs, Auntie's routine was to stop and stand against the door frame for a moment or two to get her breath back (staff left the double doors open at night in case of disturbance). Then, following this pause, an odd clicking noise would start up. It was Auntie indulging in her habit – disgusting even to my young ears – of rolling her tongue around her mouth, lifting, and dropping her lower dentures. Auntie did this when she was "on the warpath". She also liked to jangle the set of keys she kept in her housecoat pocket- another sign that she was not to be crossed.

Having got her second wind, Auntie would step into the room and, ambling down between two rows of beds, six on each side, make her way towards the disused fireplace at the far end. This was the first inspection of the day, a straightforward body count, making sure her charges were all present and correct, Auntie's head turning from side to side, back and forth, like an umpire at a tennis match.

Almost at once the singing would start up again, only to stutter and trail away so that, by the time she reached my bed, it was little more than an asthmatic wheeze.

But that signal was enough. With Auntie almost on top of me, my body made its instinctive response. I couldn't stop it; it was the same every morning. The adrenaline flowed, muscles tensed, and my heart began to pound. I had to remember to breathe. A coiled spring, a runner at the blocks, I was ready and waiting – waiting for the silence. Then, I knew the countdown would begin.

Meanwhile, Auntie, leaning against the mantelpiece, sipped her tea, played with her keys, strung things out a little. She was the boss, and we boys would do well not to forget it.

And I suppose that's how I best remember her – a big saggy-faced woman of about fifty or so, wearing her trademark nylon housecoat and slippers, juggling a set of keys, clicking her false teeth. If I close my eyes, I see heavy, dark-rimmed glasses and unkempt greasy hair. It's Dandy Nichols in *Till Death Do Us Part*. Or Ronnie Barker in drag.

Remove a group of reluctant, and bewildered, young children from their parents, and deposit them in a strange place – filled with even stranger faces – and the likelihood is that a number will develop the symptoms associated with *enuresis*, the medical term for an inability to control the bladder. In short, every institution has its share of bedwetters, and Eastry was no exception. Precautions were taken as you might expect. Each boy was issued with a rubber undersheet, and instances of wetting, or soiling, were supposed to be recorded and reported for further investigation. Auntie, though, wasn't interested in the medical or psychological side of things. As far as she was concerned, bed-wetting was a personal affront and, as such, not to be tolerated. Known offenders were the first to be targeted when the countdown stopped - ten down to zero, by which time we boys were expected to be up and standing next to our beds, counterpanes, blankets, and sheets pulled back ready for inspection. Any boy not responding quickly enough would be turned off his mattress onto the bare floorboards.

I was a witness to this violence from day one. After a restless night, I woke to what was now a familiar disorientation – this was my third bed in three days – and lay as still as I could, praying that I might remain unnoticed.

But the world refused to go away and slowly, inevitably, a new day began to intrude. Distant sounds and rising smells told me that downstairs someone was moving about in the kitchen, preparing breakfast. Across the long, whitewashed dorm one or two bodies had begun to stir, while somewhere in the distance, in the cottage next door perhaps, a radio station played "She Loves You". Out in the fields, a panel of seagulls responded, squabbling over the very same song. Were the Beatles a hit, or a miss?

Suddenly, Auntie Joyce was in the room. But I didn't move. 10... 9... 8...7...6; the countdown began. Still, I didn't move. An internal debate got no further than the fact that, out there, beyond the safety of my bedclothes, a room full of strangers waited. So, I stayed where I was, warm and snug in my little bubble, mind floating halfway between waking and dreamland, body pleasantly paralysed.

I was an Eskimo hibernating in my igloo, then Scott of the Antarctic huddled in his tent, nonchalantly singing Lennon and McCartney songs, calmly waiting not to be rescued. I'd just completed a final frost-bitten diary entry when the screaming began.

'Keith, Keith, get up Keith. Have you pissed yourself again, Keith? You bloody well have, haven't you? Get out. Get *out.*'

I sat up just in time to see the boy from the next bed hit the floor.

My first reveille: I can think of no better word for it. I'd never been so close, nor so curiously, and helplessly, detached from such a scene of violence. Indeed, I'd never seen anything like it: little wonder that I remember every moment. I can still see Keith, a small tubby boy, ripe for bullying, standing at attention, near enough to touch. And I can see Auntie facing him, arms crossed, wanting to know *why*. 'Well Keith,' she said. 'I'm waiting.'

Then the whole dorm waited, while Keith stood and squirmed, his eyes cast down, face red with shame and embarrassment.

The ensuing silence was painful; the scene like a game of statues, its participants frozen in time. And it wasn't a quiet silence. Rather, it was the kind of silence that rings out. It was a silence of the sort you experience following a rifle shot or an avalanche, or at the end of a Remembrance Day service, when the singing ends and the poppies begin to fall: the response, when it came, was bound to be anticlimactic. And, sure enough, on this occasion at least, there was no grand gesture, no violent outburst or act of defiance. Instead, the moment passed, Keith putting his peers out of their misery with an attempt at an explanation. 'I couldn't help it, Auntie,' he mumbled. 'It just happened.'

But Auntie wasn't prepared to let it go. Keith had gone to bed wearing his favourite Davy Crockett hat – a tatty synthetic thing that pretended to be raccoon, with a tail hanging down at the back. Auntie picked it up from the floor and hit him with it. 'I couldn't help it, I couldn't help it,' echoed Auntie, throwing Keith's words back in his face. Then she hit him again. 'What do I think of your excuses, Keith? They're pathetic. That's what they are. And you, Keith? You're pathetic too. You're a great big, moon-faced, gormless lummox, that's what you are.'

Of course, Keith had to apologise.

'Say sorry to me,' Auntie said, coming menacingly close once again.

And Keith said sorry.

'Say sorry to the other boys.'

More apologies.

'Say sorry that they've got to wait for breakfast, while I'm left to deal with *you.*'

And so, it went on. Quietly, humbly, and repetitively, Keith said sorry. He said sorry to Auntie. He said sorry to the rest of the room. He apologised for being born. Then Auntie ordered Keith to strip naked, clear his bed and wipe down his pink rubber under-sheet, before being marched off to the bathroom.

'Keith's off to join the Red Hand gang,' was Auntie's parting shot. And sure enough, when he came to the breakfast table, Keith carried the outline of Auntie's hand on his leg. She'd hit him hard – hard enough to hurt, but not hard enough to bruise. And the mark would be gone before Keith arrived at school.

*

The bedside inspection, I soon learned, was just the start of things. Between breakfast and school, each boy was obliged to report to Auntie for an examination. Had we dressed tidily? What about our teeth, our hands, and our faces? Fortunately, this was one of the busiest times of the day, so there was always a chance of sneaking out without Auntie noticing.

But it was a risky business. Any boy trying to leave the cottage without Auntie giving him the all-clear, was likely to face a severe mauling.

And it wasn't easy. For a start, there were almost always added staff employed for the morning shift – usually Mrs. Flowers or Mrs. Bean, from the village. The day staff may not have been as harsh as Auntie, but they couldn't be relied upon to turn a blind eye.

Then there was the building itself, designed, it appeared, with potential escapees in mind.

Leaving the dorm, the first obstacle was Auntie's bedroom, set slightly back to the right of the corridor. Opposite, on the left, was the staff toilet. As it happened, we boys used this too, but only at night. It was a concession aimed at removing the only legitimate reason an inmate might have for going downstairs. Headaches, belly ache, visits from vampires and sightings of ghosts and ghouls didn't count.

The stairs presented a challenge of their own. Constructed of dark mahogany, they were at least five or six feet wide and dominated the house. Descending, you walked on a flower patterned, threadbare carpet, the boards beneath creaking and groaning, threatening to snitch on you with every step. It took experience to find a quiet way down; it was like negotiating a minefield.

There was an alternative, and quicker, route: via the banister. But its woodwork was chipped and uneven and a large newel cap, in the shape of a pineapple, waited at the bottom. Sliding down this way was almost a rite of passage. We boys were all, in our turn, dared to have a go. Few tried it a second time.

Opposite the stairs, on the right of the ground floor hallway, was the staff room, or study. This is where we boys lined up to be inspected, to receive private punishment, or to collect our pocket money on a Thursday evening. Auntie said that the only other occasion we should knock on her door was if the house were on fire – which, ironically, is precisely when we would have chosen to stay away.

Inside, Auntie had done her best to make things homely, the room being furnished with a chintz-covered sofa and two chairs, a low coffee table and a magazine rack stuffed with old newspapers and knitting patterns. These bits and pieces, arranged around a semi-circular hearth rug, faced a TV set and a two-bar electric fire. One wall displayed a framed seaside scene, another a set of flying ducks.

To one side, facing the window, was Auntie's desk, where she wrote up her daily events diary, menus, staff rotas and other logs. This was the business side of the room. A free-standing bookcase held individual records, stored in a row of grey lever arch files; one for each resident, twelve junior schoolboys aged seven to eleven years. Oh, and there was also a medical cabinet, a wall-mounted key rack, and a black telephone. But the telephone seldom rang. And never for me.

To the left of the study was the front door, though this, in common with the staff room itself, was out of bounds, unless a visitor or social worker came calling. Otherwise, we boys only went to that end of the corridor to collect our caps and coats. There was certainly no chance of creeping out that way; Auntie kept the door firmly locked and bolted.

Opposite the study was the Day Room, which, excluding the dorm, was the largest room in the house. At one end, stood a large rectangular dining table, used for meals and, in the early evenings, for homework. There was also a settee and two easy chairs.

Since most, if not all, of the residents used the Day Room during the evening, there was invariably a race to see who could finish their chores first and so get a seat. Arriving late, you would have to watch the TV sitting cross-legged on the parquet floor, waiting to move up when a chair or place on the settee became available.

Most evenings, Auntie would sit at the table behind us, making repairs to clothing, sewing name tags, or knitting. She didn't say much, but drifting clouds of cigarette smoke, accompanied by the noise of her dentures competing with the sound of knitting needles, were all reminders of her presence, preventing us from relaxing.

And we had to keep quiet, Auntie alone commenting on what was happening on the screen. If she spoke at all it was to tell us to hush up, or to ask someone to adjust the vertical hold: 'No, not like that, hit it harder,' she'd say. 'Now sit down, or am I supposed to see through you?'

Often, it was a relief when bedtime came. Every half an hour Auntie would call out a name. Seven-year-olds went to bed at 7.30 p.m., eight-year-olds at eight, and so on. Everyone had to be in bed by half-nine, regardless of age, or what was on TV.

On Saturday and Sunday afternoons the Day Room remained open, but only if it was too wet to be outside. It was now that we had access to our personal belongings; presents and pocket money purchases, kept in labelled cube-shaped boxes, stacked along one wall. These plywood containers Auntie labelled "lockers", a misnomer since there were no locks or keys. Anything a boy particularly valued, such as penknives, torches, and Airfix models, must be hidden elsewhere.

Piled on top of the lockers were toys and games intended to encourage participation and sharing, including a collection of second-hand board games - Ludo, Snakes and Ladders, and Tiddlywinks. These donated items almost always came into the home with pieces missing, while those that were complete quickly lost parts or counters to squabbles and fights. If you wanted to play Draughts you had first to raid Auntie's button tin; Mayfair or Park Lane could only be bought – and mortgaged – after producing an improvised card of your own, while Cluedo's Professor Plum had long since disappeared, eloping with Mrs. Bun the Baker's Wife, taking the candlestick and lead pipe with them.

Almond was home to boxes and boxes of incomplete jigsaw puzzles – a windmill with one sail, a Horse Guard minus sword and half his plume – and there was also a sorry-looking library of tattered paperbacks and annuals. For me, the most interesting thing about these books, and, indeed, the board games, was their provenance, five or six of them carrying the names of their earlier owners: *To Jane on her tenth birthday; To Brian, with love from Uncle Bill and Auntie Joan, Christmas 1957.* I was fascinated by these dedications and would run my hands over the lettering, as an archaeologist might in examining an undeciphered stone tablet. Who were these privileged children? Where did they come from, and where were they now?

Waste not want not. Piles of these once-treasured items, I learned, made their way, anonymously, to the home via the main gate; others were dropped off by local charities at the office. Here they were sorted, with the better toys and games being held back until Christmas, before being distributed, wrapped, and labelled, to individual cottages, at the superintendent's discretion. Should I have been grateful, or should I have despised the donors for dumping their unwanted clutter on us? I was never quite sure.

The Day Room was closed during the day, at least during term time. There was breakfast of course, but afterwards the room was quickly vacated, as we boys went about our chores, or prepared for school. By eight o'clock two or three of us would be helping with clearing the table or washing up, while the rest queued to use the outside toilet, or fought to get into the bathroom, one sink for twelve boys.

The busiest room in the mornings was the kitchen. Looking back, I'm tempted to compare this, the scullery, to the galley of a ship – the MS Almond, a battered Edwardian steamer, if you like. Long past her best, an anachronism even, here she is, still in service, being prepared for yet another voyage. Down below dried food, cereals, sugar, and other supplies, are hastily stowed, locked away in the pantry. Pots and pans are scrubbed, and scoured, and the window hatch (through which an evening cocoa ration goes out to the crew) is raised to release a fog bank of steam which rolls across the kitchen from the direction of two large, foaming sinks.

Keep watching and you'll see a wooden drier, rigged out with flags of KCC embroidered tea towels and cleaning rags, shoot upwards, hoisted aloft by older hands, while below, the juniors wash down the stone flags of the decks. And there, to continue the analogy, stands our captain, in the person of Auntie Joyce, supervising proceedings, ensuring the work party doesn't mutiny, or pilfer food.

This, with Auntie thus occupied, was as good a time as any to jump ship. The best way was to slide along the wall, on the right of the passageway. Then if you were spotted you could pretend to be examining the notice board, digesting instructions to "walk, don't run", studying the fire-drill or reading advice aimed at imaginary visitors, informing them that they were welcome at any time "by arrangement with the management". Get past the noticeboard and you must decide whether to make a run for it. Then you might, or might not, make it out.

It was cat and mouse really. Some days you'd escape unnoticed, other mornings you'd make it as far as the back door, only for a triumphant Auntie to appear, as if from nowhere. Then you knew you were in trouble.

Caught out like this, the best thing to do was to freeze, and accept what was coming to you; namely, a thorough seeing too. It was what you were trying to avoid in the first place, of course, only now it was ten times worse; often it meant being manhandled to the point of giddiness. Clothing was clawed, the lapels of your blazer or the belt of your coat (we wore black Bogart-style mackintoshes with buttons and pockets all over the place) twisted and tugged as Auntie fought to haul her captive to one side. Struggle and she'd push and pull, shake, and spin you around until the teeth rattled in your head and a universe of stars fizzed before your eyes.

It was pointless anyway; Auntie was far too strong and would soon get you where she wanted – pinned up against the wall. Then, bending, she would come in for the kill – you could feel the rims of her glasses up against your nose – and, breathing all over you, splatter you with a volley of platitudes; stock phrases all of them, and all delivered in the same tone of feigned surprise, or injured disappointment. 'What do you call this?' she'd say, pulling at a belt. 'You're done up like a sack of potatoes.' Or, after checking behind your ears, 'Call that a wash? You must think I came in on the last banana boat!'

Sometimes she'd send you back inside, but for the most part it was enough for Auntie to have caught a boy out. She was busy – and there was always tonight. So, with a final twist of a cap or tie, and dire warnings about coming back from school "in a state", you'd find yourself pushed out of the door and on to the yard. Then you were away and free.

But not for long. At the other end of the day came more inspections. These began at once upon return from school, when you had to report and say "Good afternoon" to Auntie, have your clothes and shoes examined –

again – and give an account of the day. Afterwards, Auntie would dish out evening chores - anything from cleaning shoes in the boot room to litter picking around the grounds. These jobs must be completed and checked before five, when we lined up to have our hands inspected ready for the evening meal. Afterwards there was clearing the table, washing, and drying.

Wednesdays and Saturdays were bath nights. There was a rota and rationing – one bath of water for two or three boys, with a better than even chance that an earlier occupant had peed in it. We were each allowed ten minutes, then afterwards stood outside the staffroom door in pyjamas and dressing gowns, carrying our clothes, ready to offer them up for exchange and examination.

This, nominally at least, was a general inspection, most items of clothing Auntie gave no more than a cursory glance - a torn pocket here, a missing button there – before being put to one side or thrown into a large, wicker laundry basket marked KCC.

It was our underpants that Auntie was after. Underpants came in for special attention, being scrutinised last of all. 'Pants,' Auntie would demand, and you had to hold them out, stretched at the waist for her to have a good root around, searching for tell-tale stains or skid marks. Sometimes, if she suspected an attempt had been made to wash away the evidence, she'd snatch the pants from you and put them up to her face, sniffing to see if they were damp, or smelled of soap.

There were only two possible outcomes. Either your pants passed muster, or they didn't. If they did, Auntie would invite you to take a sweet from the tin she kept open on the desk for the occasion. If they didn't then *whack*, she'd hit you across the knuckles with a long wooden ruler.

So how to keep a pair of Y-fronts spotless for three or four days? I struggled back then, and I'm sure I couldn't do it now. Auntie said I had a "problem bottom," but was I the only boy who soiled himself? It was two or three weeks before the penny dropped.

Meanwhile, I took to stuffing my pants with toilet paper. Unfortunately, the paper we were issued with was that Izel-type stuff; hard, crinkly, and guaranteed to start working its way down a trouser leg: I had visions of walking into school trailing half a loo roll.

The solution I eventually arrived at was not to wear my pants at all; or rather, to hide and retrieve them on changeover nights. It meant my trousers rubbed and chafed even more than usual; I had to get used to wearing them lower - I was forever being told to pull my trousers up – but the alternative proved more than enough of an incentive to make the discomfort bearable.

Of course, I had to remember where I'd hidden my pants. Mostly, I kept them in my school satchel, beneath an atlas and my plimsolls. Other boys, I discovered, adopted strategies of their own, and had their own hiding places.

But all of this came later. In the meantime, I had to suffer the ruler, though not before being given a stern, verbal warning. The first time, because I was new, Auntie let it go. I'd finished my bath, got into my pyjamas and dressing gown, and reported to the staff room, as instructed.

'Enter,' came the impatient response to my knock on the door. 'Pants,' Auntie demanded, hardly giving me time to get into the room. I was shocked and fumbled before doing as ordered.

'Come on, come on,' Auntie said. 'I haven't got all night.'

So, I stood and watched as Auntie stretched my underwear open for a good look, and a sniff.

The shame was humiliating. I'd gone to the study expecting a simple swap, to be issued with a fresh set of clothing before being sent on my way. Instead, I received a lecture, being warned about my future toileting habits. Boys who soiled themselves were lazy and disgusting; they faced dire consequences.

As it happened, I survived the next few inspections, though once or twice it was, I think, a near thing. Then, inevitably, Auntie spotted a small brown streak. 'No, no, no,' she said, with a vigorous shake of the head. 'This simply won't do.'

I raised my eyes from the floor – I always found it difficult to look Auntie in the face – to meet a wide-eyed gaze of shock and outrage.

'Hand' Auntie said, in a tone of "here we go again" weariness. Then I waited. And waited. I waited for what seemed like an eternity until, finally, Auntie reached across and picked up the ruler from her desk. Then she hit me across the knuckles: one, two, three. 'And don't let there be a next time, or it'll be four.'

While I stood there puffing and blowing, my right hand buried beneath my left armpit, Auntie, replacing her ruler, raised a half-finished cup of tea to her lips. 'Now look what you've done,' she said. 'It's gone cold.'

And so, it went on. Within a fortnight, I was taking the ruler across both hands; because I refused to say sorry, to show remorse, or cry.

I tried my best but seldom reached the required standard. On one occasion, Auntie caught me out before I'd gone beyond the bathroom. Taking a bar of soap and applying a splash of water, I'd rubbed away at my underpants for minutes on end. Then I sat down on the toilet seat and tucked them beneath me. For some reason I'd got it into my head that if I counted, up to a hundred say, they would be dry. I reached about fifty when Auntie came looking for me. My pants fell into the toilet bowl when I stood to attention.

I don't know how long I spent locked in the bathroom that first time. Probably my memory has confused and conflated all the other nights I was punished in this way, so that now I find it difficult to distinguish one stint from another.

In any case, the routine was much the same, and I wasn't the only one to suffer. Depending on the enormity of the crime, Auntie would either make you stand naked with your nose against the wall for an hour or so, checking up from time to time, or she would simply lock the bathroom door, leaving you alone - sometimes, if there was no school the next day, for most of the night. At the same time, she'd remove the bathmat and towels, denying her victim an opportunity to improvise, finding a way to keep warm.

That first time, I told myself I didn't care, and I meant it. I was stubborn, seething with anger and resentment. Then, slowly, as the temperature dropped, and the building fell quiet, my feelings of rebellion and disdain began to slip away.

The bathroom didn't stay quiet for long. Nor I discovered, was I alone. Soon came the army of the night, marching back, reclaiming surrendered territory.

A herd of two woodlice grazed at the skirting boards; something monstrous knocked about in the pipes and plumbing; a tap dripped with the noise of a cascading waterfall; moths hammered at the outside light.

A captive audience of one, I watched a renegade ant struggle under the door, dragging a boulder of sugar; looked on as a suicidal spider flung itself from the ceiling into the bath.

At the same time, over in the village a dog began barking, and another dog barked in response. Every sound, every rustle, creak, and movement became exaggerated, the night air vibrating to the slightest disturbance.

And it was cold, bone achingly cold. My instinct, always, was to make myself as small as possible. I'd start by sitting on the toilet seat with my head down on my knees, rubbing my arms and legs. When that didn't work, the thing to do, I decided, was to curl up like a ball, on the floor.

But I couldn't remain motionless for long; the ground was uncomfortable, hard, and cold. Getting up and moving about, flapping my arms for warmth, I'd look round for other distractions.

One time, I remember, I climbed up on the bath, stretching to write on the frosted glass window - my own name and those of my brothers and sister. Then I added our address, our Doddington address, which, for want of something better to do, I extended to include:

ENGLAND, GREAT BRITAIN, EUROPE, THE WORLD, PLANET EARTH and *THE UNIVERSE.*

But the condensation soon melted the words away, leaving an indecipherable mess. So, I gave up and, climbing down, took to muddling up the toothbrushes instead, taking them from their rack and flicking them into the sink. If Auntie had come in carrying a rag and a bottle of Ajax, I'd have gladly cleaned the basin and the bath and scrubbed the taps until they shone; I was that cold, and bored.

Where was Auntie? Was she coming for me, or had she gone to bed? There was no way of knowing. So round and round I went, counting the floor tiles, trying not to step on the cracks.

Next, looking upwards, I started a new game, interpreting the marks and stains on the bathroom ceiling. Up there, I discovered strange, fantastic landscapes, whole new countries, and continents, which my imagination populated, Gulliver-style, with tribes and nations of warring pigmies and giants.

One of these shapes, the biggest, formed a familiar pattern: an outline map of Australia. Or did it? I wasn't sure, so I closed my eyes tight, then opened them again. But it was still there, and, yes, I was staring at a map of Australia.

It was uncanny: there was the Great Australian Bight and the long, pointed tip of Queensland and, underneath, the separate, smaller smudge of Tasmania. Something liquid must have leaked through from the upstairs toilet, staining the plaster.

It's warm in Australia, I reminded myself. If I dug down from the bathroom, I'd probably come out in Sydney, or, if I were unlucky, in New Zealand. Australia had kangaroos and koalas, and the spiders went down the plughole in the opposite direction.

My best friend Mark was going to live in Australia, and he'd asked me to join him. We made whispered plans in the dorm at night. The idea was to get hold of a Dormobile, then just take off. We'd go travelling, taking in places like Bondi Beach, Ayres Rock, and Surfers Paradise, earning money fruit picking, moving on with the seasons, using the sun as our clock.

Apparently, it was easy. The Aussies, Mark said, were crying out for people, letting anyone in. Whole families – Mum, Dad, and kids, could go, and all for £10. You travelled by ship on something called "an assisted passage".

It was a long journey, across twelve thousand miles. But those weeks on board would be like a cruise, a holiday. Quite a bonus, eh?

Mark had already saved £2 in his Post Office account and showed me his savings book. It was his future, and he wanted me to share it.

I was both flattered, and doubtful; it all seemed too good to be true. Mark, though, had done his homework, got it all sorted out. He'd even obtained a map and a booklet, *Facts about Australia*, from the Chief Migration Officer in Australia House in London, after filling out a coupon published in the *Eagle* comic. "Ask your father first" was the advice.

Australia was not without its dangers. Far from it. Six of the world's most lethal spiders lived down under. Then there were the snakes, crocs, and the deadly box jellyfish. Not all creatures were as appealing as the wombat, the kookaburra, or the duck-billed platypus. A bite from a red-backed spider or a taipan snake meant almost instant death, especially if you happened to be far away from a hospital, which, studying our maps, seemed more than likely.

A large part of the island continent consisted of deserts, tens of them: the Simpson, the Victoria, the Great Sandy, it was hard to count. Vast distances, often hundreds of miles, separated each town or city, with more than half the population having chosen to settle in the South and East. In seven or eight years, Mark promised we too would be eastward bound; our ship, following Cook's *Endeavour*, being destined to make land at Botany Bay. The dangers, real or otherwise, only served to fuel our imaginations; planning and waiting made the whole scheme seem more of an adventure.

So how to get rich and live happily ever after? Bumming around picking fruit was okay, but the real money was to be made prospecting for silver or gold, we concluded. A good place to head for was Broken Hill in New South Wales, where silver and lead, along with other valuable ores were mined.

Then Mark, having read about the gold fields of Kanowna in an old *Boys Own Adventure* annual, decided that Western Australia was a better prospect.

We'd have to be careful though, on our guard. Once, in 1898, thousands of miners had stormed out of Kanowna to nearby hills, where a massive 100 lb gold nugget had been found. The only man to see it, a young priest named Father Long, had kept his secret for years, but at last revealed the exact spot.

Diggers moved tons of rock and earth, but none struck gold. It turned out, Mark explained, that two local men had covered a piece of iron with gold paint to fool the gullible priest. The villains responsible for this trickery were run out of town by an angry mob and the prospectors left disappointed. Yet who was to say that we, for our part, might not be lucky and find gold for real? No harm in looking. Yes?

'But what about Eastry,' I asked? 'Won't the Aussies know we've been in a Home?' Anyone in authority, I thought, would spot us a mile off. A care leaver might just as well have his former status tattooed across his head; it would certainly be stamped on his passport.

But no, apparently not. The Australian government, Mark promised, had experience when it came to dealing with people like us; desperate for numbers, they even took convicts – criminals, *people who'd been in prison*. And if it turned out he was wrong, or the Australians had changed the rules, well, there was always Canada.

Escape. I *could* get out of the bathroom, if only in my head. Tired, cold, and increasingly disconnected from my surroundings, I simply stepped through the wall, taking on the persona of heroes like Dan Dare or Braddock VC, square jawed, determined, and known for "playing with a straight bat". Or I was Captain Hurricane, a comic book Commando who, when the red mist descended (which was every Thursday) bent the turret of a German tank single-handed.

And if I was still in character when Auntie returned, well, so much the better. Now nothing she said or did could penetrate my defences; she simply couldn't reach me. Lacking the gift of imagination, Auntie was blind to the change, unable to see that the boy standing in front of her was anyone other than the recalcitrant child she'd locked up earlier in the evening.

But I knew better. Transfigured, I was a hero, a superman, somebody good. Steve MacQueen, the "Cooler King" from *The Great Escape*, was a favourite. It was Steve MacQueen who snatched the clean stripy prison-style pyjamas Auntie thrust at him, just as, moments later, and with a sneering lip, it was Steve MacQueen who stepped out of the "cooler" into the blinding light of the hallway. Was I ready to say sorry...

Once, I remember, Auntie chose Saturday lunchtime to make an example of me. 'Stand,' she commanded. It was my turn to say Grace. 'Now I don't want to hear another peep out of you,' she said waiting for me to thank the Lord for what I was about to receive. Not only was I to keep my mouth shut, but Auntie instructed the other boys not to speak to me in turn. I was to suffer the silent treatment, which was to last through to Monday morning. Auntie said I was being "sent to Coventry". Sadly, this turned out to be a figure of speech. Within a week I was back in the bathroom.

CHAPTER SEVEN

One of the few legitimate ways out of the home, to get away from Auntie, was for a boy to become involved with sports – football, cricket, or athletics. Once a week, on a Tuesday evening, there was an opportunity for the junior boys to go swimming, to the baths in Dover, with Uncle Ken. I went. Once.

My problem was that I couldn't swim. I'd never been near a swimming pool and, indeed, before Eastry, had never seen the sea. But Auntie insisted on putting my name forward, leaving me a whole week to worry about it.

So why didn't I speak up? Loss of face, I suppose; fear of being the odd one out, of letting people down. A newcomer, I was desperate to fit in, to be one of the team. The other boys had been going to Dover for three or four years; a short trip by minibus, an hour in the pool, and newspaper-wrapped chips on the way home. It all made for a fun evening.

Salvation, a way out, came to me in the changing rooms. Trunks! I didn't have any bathing trunks.

But I was clutching at straws, my hopes of avoidance at once dashed.

No trunks? 'Don't worry,' said Uncle Ken, throwing me a pair from his duffle bag. 'Oh, and I've got towels for afterwards, too,' he added. Then he showed me the plunge pool: 'Get in there first,' he said, 'and make sure you're clean.'

By the time I got to the main pool, hunched and shivering, the other boys were in the water. I looked on, watching Mark, close by, bobbing up and down, then dipping under, hand on nose, hair floating on the surface like a jellyfish, showing off. And John Norley too, swimming just beneath the translucent surface, seemed born to it, like a fish with a tail and fins. Even Keith, doing the backstroke, seemed to be enjoying himself. Surely swimming couldn't be that difficult.

'Go on then, young Terry.' It was time, Ken had decided, pushing me forwards. Taken by surprise, I took one or two involuntary steps towards the edge of the pool, and the water. For a split second I managed to steady myself. Then, suddenly, I fell forward. Unbalanced, with just one foot on the tiled floor, I reached out but found only empty space. I was grabbing at thin air, at nothing, my arms spinning in slow motion, like the sails on a windmill. I opened my mouth to yell out a confession: *I can't swim*. But it was too late. I'd kept quiet, and now I was going to pay the price.

Suddenly, it didn't matter anymore. My world, the known world, disappeared as I hit the water, which welcomed and swallowed me like a shark or a crocodile, dragging its quarry down and down. All I cared about now was survival.

Instinctively, I struggled, gasping for breath, making things worse. There were other bodies in the water, and I flailed about, desperately trying to find someone to hang on to. It was my only chance.

Where was Uncle Ken? I went under and came back up again. The surface noise was tremendous. Muffled voices and sounds, indistinguishable, echoed round the dome of the pool, way up above. Diamonds of light sparkled on the surface, blinding me; water ran from my ears and from my nose. I coughed liquid from my lungs, smelling and tasting chlorine.

Nearby, a body hit the water; out of control, I found myself swept away by a huge wave. Then I went under again. *Find something...don't swallow...don't swallow.* Disorientated, lost in an ocean of water, I felt in vain for the poolside rail.

The next thing I knew I was lying on my side, head resting on the tiled floor. Inches away, my focus fell on Uncle Ken's feet, a spray of dark hairs springing from his toes.

'What's wrong, Terry? Can't you swim?' Ken hauled me up, affecting concern. 'Why didn't you say? You'll have to come on Fridays, with the under-fives.' Then he told me, with a sneer, that I had snot on my cheek.

I never went back to Dover. And I haven't been near a swimming pool since.

*

Tall, lithe, well-toned, and in his late twenties, Uncle Ken was a fitness fanatic, insisting that all older boys sign up for his physical exercise regime.

The football season had kicked off; if swimming were too much, then maybe I could do something with a ball? So, I went up to the playing field for Wednesday evening training, meeting up with a team of other junior boys, Edward, and Andy among them. It was a rare chance for us to be together.

For Uncle Ken, winning was everything, his coaching sessions consisting of sprints, cross-country runs, push-ups, leapfrog - a whole regime of punishing exercises. Only after a thorough work-out did a ball appear. 'I'll make a sportsman of you yet,' Ken said when I collapsed in a heap.

I needed to toughen up; we all needed to toughen up, ready for the challenges to come. 'Pain is all in the mind,' Uncle Ken said. 'You boys are "looked-after kids", so you're going to get pushed, kicked, elbowed, maybe even spat at. You'll have to learn to give as good as you get. Go on, get stuck in, show the world you're not afraid,' he told me before my first game. Too competitive? The team motto was *Do or Die*.

I remember that first match well. And with good reason. A scrappy affair, a repetition of long balls, it was a game of kick and chase. Our defence was sound, but it was hard to see where a goal was coming from.

Then, towards half-time, Eastry won a corner. 'Mine' I shouted as the cross came over. I closed my eyes and jumped, hoping for a clean connection. Suddenly, with a whoosh and a whack, a heavy weight of leather and lace, of mud, water, and spray, hit me full in the face, knocking me to the ground. My timing had been out; I'd gone up a fraction too soon.

Looking up, I watched the opposition's keeper run away, disappearing down the slope behind their goal; in his wake, gaining ground, was Uncle Ken, the two of them racing to get a foot on the ball before it was lost in a sea of nettles.

Distant cheers told me I'd scored! I rubbed the sleeve of my shirt across my face, and wished we had nets.

Almost at once, Uncle Ken blew for half-time, and the team gathered round to listen to his instructions. More second half goals, I thought. Maybe even a hat trick.

But Uncle Ken had other ideas and told me I had to come off. Ten minutes into the second half I was to feign an injury. No backchat. No arguments. 'Fall over and roll about a bit,' came the order. 'I'll let you know when.' Substitutions, except for injuries, weren't allowed and Ken wanted to give another boy a chance.

I was devastated; being taken off was worse than a slap round the head. Why me? I'd been selected as centre-forward; I'd scored, and I was playing well. I opened my mouth to protest. 'Like it or lump it,' said Ken, turning away.

What to do? I didn't want to fall over because I didn't want to cheat or be labelled as a cheat. Besides, I couldn't act; I couldn't pretend like that. Why, oh why, didn't Uncle Ken pick on somebody else? Someone like John Norley.

John would do it; I knew he would. Give him an audience and John would go down like he'd been pole axed. He'd ham it up, writhe about and scream for a stretcher; anything for a laugh.

But it was useless. Uncle Ken had made up his mind. I sucked on my half-time orange, which tasted of bitter lemons.

The second half began and, quickly caught up in the game, I forgot all about going down. If Uncle Ken gave me a sign, I certainly didn't see it; my mind was on the opposition.

We were playing Bettshanger, a team of rough lads from the East Kent coalfield. They were an even harder side than Tilmanstone, another local mining team. Soon we would take them on as well, but mostly we played against other institutions. Ken would drive us thirty miles or more for a game of football.

It was only when Uncle Ken shouted 'five minutes' that I remembered his instructions.

Immediately a wave of fear washed over me. I could hear his words 'You've let me down...You've let the side down...'

But then, miraculously, came the chance for a second goal. Redemption! I could score and send Uncle Ken a message about my place in the starting eleven at the same time.

A free kick, a long punt up field, and the ball dropped right at my feet. I went past one defender and into the opposition's area, with just the keeper to beat. I had time - lots of time. Too much time, in fact.

Have a crack or place it? At the last moment, a tackle came flying in; I fluffed my shot, and the ball trickled harmlessly wide. Uncle Ken whistled, signifying full-time, before our opponents could take a goal kick and gain an advantage.

'You should have passed the ball,' said George Norley as we left the pitch.

'Three cheers for Bettshanger,' called Uncle Ken.

Afterwards, both teams trudged back to the "Rec", the Recreation Hall, a wooden hut used for Scouts and Cubs, sports, and social occasions, where Uncle Ken looked on as we changed.

I didn't like undressing in front of him; it made me feel uncomfortable. But Uncle Ken had a habit of hanging about. He approached me as I was getting ready to leave and, coming close, put an arm round my shoulder and squeezed. 'What's wrong with you, Terry, have you got cloth ears? You a spastic, or what?' He squeezed again, even harder this time, telling me not to bother turning up for next week's training; I was suspended, dropped for three matches.

I have a photograph of the Eastry junior football team. It dates from 1964, though I had to wait twenty years or more to get hold of a copy. The picture was one of a whole series of images of young boys, of which Uncle Ken had quite a hoard. Mine is the only picture I have of Edward, Andrew, and myself together.

Two things strike me about this photo. First, the kit. We played in Southampton (or, if you prefer, Stoke City) colours; red and white striped shirts (black and white in the photo, of course) with buttoned collars and long sleeves. That, at least, was the idea. In fact, our strip was an approximation, a confusion of ancient cast offs, with the first boy to the kit bag getting the best pick. You can see this from the picture. Fashion wise, most of the boots look pre-war, while our shorts are a gradation – white, followed by three or four shades of grey, through to black. Standing at the front, one boy, George Norley, seems decidedly odd. Look closely and you can clearly see that George has five hoops on his right sock, but only one on the left. Poor George must have been the last to turn up that day.

The second thing that impresses me about this picture is how enthusiastic the team all appear. Unwanted, abandoned or given up we may have been. Yet despite this, and despite Uncle Ken's bullying – or perhaps because of it – we look grittily determined, eager to go out and get stuck in. And why not? We were young and fit, with energy to burn and heroes to emulate. Football, and the team, gave us a chance to forget about so-called care, the cold, and the kit, and put our troubles on one side. For an hour or so we were just another gang of mop-tops, enjoying the beautiful game.

Enthusiasm is one thing, ability quite another. Of my two eligible brothers, Andrew was undoubtedly the better player. Andy, at barely seven years old, was the youngest boy in the team, but soon learned to use his lack of height and lower centre of gravity to gain an advantage. I can see him now, picking up the ball in midfield, twisting and turning, snaking his way through the opposition, leaving defenders flailing in his wake.

The bigger boys thought Andy a soft touch and gave him the nickname "Titch", but he was dogged and determined and would run half the length of the pitch to get the ball back. His hero was Dennis Law.

Edward's problem was that he lacked concentration. Also, he was left-footed, which led Uncle Ken to stick him out on the wing. With nearly all the play going down the middle of the pitch, Edward, inevitably, spent much of the game on his own, and got into the habit of wandering off. Where was he when the ball went out to the left? Usually half-way across the field, attacking a mole hill, or picking buttercups, depending on the time of year. And if he had nothing else to distract him, he'd go and hang around our goal, making mud pies with Keith. Uncle Ken was not amused.

Edward and Andy are easily accounted for; siblings, they stand out even after five decades. Returning to the picture today, other boys, housemates from Almond, also step out of the frame. Keith, a rosy cheeked rustic, is easily found, since he is wearing the goalkeeper's jersey; he was too heavy to play anywhere else. And close to Keith, two places to his right, is Geoffrey, another big, wide-faced Almond lad. He too stands at the back, which, fittingly, is where Uncle Ken chose to play him. 'If in doubt, put it out,' was the instruction. But Uncle Ken, who refereed our home games, soon came to regret the tactic. 'Not every time you get the bloody ball,' he'd bellow, blowing up for yet another throw-in or corner to the opposition.

At the front, on the left, comes Mark; shorts riding high, collar up, top shirt buttons pulled open. Mark's is a nonchalant pose; an arm – my arm – on his shoulder, right foot crossed over left, toe to the ground. 'Look' he seems to be saying, 'they smashed the £100,000 British transfer record to sign me!' Mark was the best player in the team, and he knew it.

Further along the front row stand the Norley brothers; curly-haired John, the same age as me, and George, from Lime, a year older. George looks decidedly unhappy, cross perhaps at having to wear a mismatched kit. And John, on the far right; he too strikes an aggressive pose. His head is down and pushed forward, and his mouth has dropped open; you can see the whites of his eyes. And his arms; they dangle at his sides and look far too long for his body. Back then John was the team clown and, within Almond, fancied himself as leader of the pack. Looking at him today he seems innocuous enough, just another angry little monkey.

Three or four of the boys pictured are, I'm afraid, still unidentified. It's frustrating. Their names, I know, are filed away somewhere in my head, but I can't remember what I've done with the key.

Yet the faces are not empty. Even now, if I stare and stare, my interest provokes a reaction; the boys seem to gaze back, considering me in turn, wondering how things have worked out.

One lad wears a look of exasperation. How can I have forgotten? Come on, I'm so-and-so, from Thorn. You know, I had a thing about fire engines. Surely, you remember the smoke, the blazing mattress, the evacuation. Ask your brother Edward (I did; he recalls the incident, but not the name).

Another boy, at the back, holds a familiar, unhurried pose, yet try as I may, the name still escapes me. Could it be Robert Lee, from Lime? Robert, given a magic set for Christmas, achieved notoriety after trying to conjure the tablecloth out from under a fully laden breakfast table – a tyro Tommy Cooper, without the laughs.

A third boy is, I think, Gary Luck from Cherry, who became an overnight hero after stealing a penknife from a boy in the village;

a theft for which he was sternly punished. But I could be wrong.

It's difficult after all this time. And strange, too, to think that we were the healthy ones, a sporting elite.

We were lucky. Not everyone made the team; indeed, dozens of boys were excluded, full stop. These were the ones with sticky-out teeth, birth-marked faces, and cauliflower ears; lads who stuttered and stammered; polio victims who wore special boots to give them the appearance of owning legs of equal length; or, in the case of Simon Wragg, callipers to help correct the effects of Perthes disease.

Some of these boys I remember well – in one or two cases, I must admit, because of the effort I put in to avoiding them. But it is the residents with behavioural problems who loom largest in the memory.

Take Barry Springer, for example. Barry was thirteen years old, and attended the Secondary Modern school in Sandwich, though, the records show, he could barely read or write. Mostly, I remember him for his National Health Service glasses, round-rimmed and pink as an artificial limb.

Barry's glasses, broken in the middle, were, I recall, permanently held together with a strip of sticking plaster. He had a habit of sneaking up on you when you least expected him - sometimes even managing to invade my sleep, a scary Norman knight boasting a plastic protective nose guard.

Barry, in common with the rest of us, was a collector. Collecting was something we all felt compelled to do, and for all the usual, jackdaw reasons. There was, I think, a sort of security in owning a group or a set; it was an expression of individuality, and bestowed a certain status, as well as offering an opportunity for bargaining and trade.

There were comics, tea cards and conkers, coins, and plastic soldiers too. There was also an informal tariff agreement; unwritten, but a useful starting point for negotiation. Thus, two conkers, provided they were "Sixers", equalled one Beano (recent edition, not torn or defaced), while a Mars bar might get you a packet of stamps (British or Commonwealth). Only Barry's collection presented any sort of problem assessment wise; how to value a box of bogies?

Barry's bogie collection – a compilation of his own and other boys' better efforts – lived in a match box, which Barry kept in his trouser pocket. He had a habit of taking it out at the most inappropriate moments - in church or at school assembly – and rubbing the bogies between his fingers, like a connoisseur rolling an expensive cigar. Hard and grown shiny with age, the bogies reminded me of a fisherman's lead shot. Barry said they tasted sweet, like aniseed balls. I took his word for it.

Another odd Eastry character was Peter Darling. About the same age as Barry, Peter too was "subnormal" and attended an Occupational Centre in Dover. His large forehead suggested Frankenstein, though he lacked the scar.

Peter was an "ambulance chaser", the possessor of a clairvoyant ability to be the first on the scene of any accident, be it major or minor. His specialty was scabs.

Once, after I'd grazed my leg falling off a slide, Peter followed me for days, refusing to go away. He was checking on my recovery, waiting for a crust to form. Judging the skin to be ready, he nagged and nagged until I let him have a go at it. In return, I received two second-hand comics, and half a bag of fluffy pear drops.

Peter used to boast, quite rightly in my experience, that he could peel a scab from another boy's elbow or knee without drawing blood or causing pain; it was all a matter of timing. If he'd owned the words, Peter would have called this "delayed gratification."

Next door to Almond, in the yard of Willow Cottage, you'd find Colin, another older boy, sitting among the dustbins, rocking himself back and forth, volunteering the animated information that his mother was coming to take him home. 'Mum's coming...Mum's coming on Saturday... Mum's coming...' he'd chant, repeating the news over and over, like a needle stuck in a groove, whether anyone was listening or not.

Years later, I discovered that Colin's mother was dead, and that Colin had seen her murdered, stabbed by his father. The authorities recommended that staff be patient, Colin would need time to get over the experience. We boys used to call him "spastic".

In Almond, for a time at least, we had Gordon, a pale, thin boy, with high cheekbones and hollow features - an El Greco ascetic with a shock of reddish hair.

I remember Gordon well. And with good reason. I remember him because, uniquely for Almond, he was a secondary school boy, aged twelve - and as such permitted to wear long trousers – and I remember, too, that he attended the same Occupational Centre as Peter Darling, along with five or six of the other older boys. Mostly, though, I remember Gordon for his odd behaviour – today Gordon would almost certainly be diagnosed with ASD, Autistic Spectrum Disorder – much of which centred around his relationship with an imaginary friend, named Paul. Between them they got me into trouble. Big trouble.

Gordon's stay with us in Almond, the records show, was meant to be temporary. His mother couldn't cope, and he needed somewhere to live until a permanent placement could be found, somewhere more suited to his needs, and his unpredictable behaviour. No consideration was given to the mayhem Gordon might have caused in the interim.

Alone among a group of strangers, Gordon, consciously or otherwise, quickly developed a range of survival strategies, all designed, it seems to me now, to get him through the day. He had his own coping mechanisms, none of which involved any thought for others. Autistic, seeing everything in black and white, he had a rigid routine and reacted badly, if not violently, to any sort of change.

School days were especially challenging. Leaving for the Occupational Centre, Gordon insisted on being first to the Dormobile. He also expected Uncle Bob to reserve a seat for him, at the back, on the right, with a space next door for his friend Paul. From here he could watch the other boys and snitch on them if he saw them misbehaving or breaking the rules.

In response, his fellow passengers began taking Gordon's seat for themselves. When this happened, Gordon simply refused to get on the bus and instead returned to Almond. 'I've forgotten to clean my teeth and brush my hair,' he'd say. Either that, or Paul needed the toilet. Sometimes Gordon just went walkabout, wandering off towards the main gate. Then Bob, mindful of the time, had to negotiate with the other boys, moving them around to Gordon's satisfaction.

The reaction, as you might expect, was far from positive. With Bob at the wheel, concentrating on the road, Gordon found himself vulnerable; he was both verbally and physically abused; sworn at, spat at; on one occasion he had to have chewing gum cut out of his hair.

After this latter outrage, Uncle Bob had Gordon sit in the front, where there was also room for Paul. An expedient solution, perhaps, but the other boys saw this as a further example of favouritism, a reward for bad behaviour. Which just made things worse.

Within Almond, mealtimes were particularly difficult. Among other afflictions, which included nail biting and thumb sucking, Gordon suffered from a drooping lower lip and was an arm waver, characteristics, and mannerisms which, through no fault of his own, were destined, from the start, to get him into trouble, especially when it came to cutting up and eating his food. Gordon, unable to restrain his limbs, fidgeted in his chair, threw his arms about and, when food did get as far as his mouth, dribbled uncontrollably.

Even the simplest request from staff would be referred to Paul. A moment's hesitation, accompanied by closed eyes and a screwed-up face, was invariably followed by the verdict: 'Paul says no.'

Auntie was furious. She was left "firefighting", reacting to one situation after another, whilst, at the same time, trying her best to follow Gordon's care plan, assuming he had one. It was the only time I saw Auntie struggling to cope, to impose her will.

Mealtime mayhem Auntie addressed by issuing Gordon with a plastic plate and cup; personal care she left to day staff. But nobody had an answer to the presence and influence of Paul. Eventually, Auntie resorted to locking Gordon and his friend in the bathroom where, she said, they were quite welcome to prattle on to their hearts' content.

But Gordon didn't give up, even at bedtime. Most boys found it hard to settle down at night, not least because, as I have said, our sleep times were staggered, from youngest to oldest. Eventually, however, with all twelve of us in our beds, whispered conversations would waver, then fizzle out; books, comics and smuggled torches would be stashed away, and, one by one, we'd drop off to sleep.

But not Gordon. Gordon just went on and on. Around midnight was when he was most awake. Just two beds removed, I'd lay there listening to him tossing and turning, muttering away, conducting a running dialogue with his invisible friend.

Worse still, Gordon seemed incapable of staying put. Most nights he'd get up and rearrange his bedding, or root around in his bedside cabinet, looking for a missing, imaginary item, before wandering off to the toilet. Then, returning, he'd stand and stare down at his mattress, complaining that Paul was hogging the bed and must move over. Half a dozen nights of this and the rest of the dorm had had enough. It was time to call upon the services of our resident ghost: the White Lady.

We'd all met the White Lady, in fancy if not in fact. Her story, as old as the home no doubt, ran through five or six versions. Some boys claimed she'd been a highwayman's accomplice, others a witch burnt at the stake. Others still opted for the one about a lost Anglo-Saxon palace, the scene of a heap of bloody murders, while a more fixed account centred on the Eastry caves, old lime workings long since abandoned and which ran under the village.

But the tale which came around most often, and the one we used on Gordon, had the White Lady as the spirit of a medieval princess who, refusing the hand of an evil suitor, found herself bricked up and left to rot in a tall tower, her shade doomed to wander until the end of time. For some reason, never addressed, her travels occasionally brought her to Eastry and, more specifically, to Almond, and the dorm.

Ghost! A single, half-strangled exclamation brought many a late-night squabble or disagreement to a halt; it was a face-saving equivalent to truce words like *fainites* or *quits* – quickly bringing about a cessation of hostilities. All it took was a bit of thinking, and the White Lady, summoned from beyond the grave, would be among us. Did you see her? Come on, you must have seen her. She was wearing long, flowing robes. Her face? No, I didn't see her face; she was hidden, under a veil. But I swear – cross my heart and hope to die – that the thing I saw was the White Lady. She came through the door and moved right down the middle of the room; drifted, floated, faded into the mantlepiece, went right through to Willow.

A description like this sharpened all our senses; indeed, it seemed that the White Lady, when stirred, was more than capable of turning nature itself on its head. The room went cold, the gloom deepened, and there was a distinctive smell, the pungent whiff of gone-off eggs or rotting meat, the perfume of death.

On most occasions, the haunting was collective, with no doubting that the White Lady was indeed present. We bore witness, though the evidence was aural rather than visual. The White Lady was heard, and the boys announced her arrival in unison. It didn't take much to set us off; a creaking floorboard, a closing door and up would go the alarm, like a cackling of geese on the Roman Capitol. Then we'd all dive under our respective counterpanes and sheets, praying that it wasn't Auntie coming upstairs.

The White Lady had impeccable timing and seldom let us down. She rattled at the windows on stormy nights, clanked her metal chains on our bedsteads and, on summer evenings, when the stuffy dorm was a haven for cheesy feet and flying insects, turned poltergeist, flinging comics and pillows across the room.

Gordon got the full treatment. Sitting at the end of his bed, I told him that the White Lady was coming for him. She always came for the new boy. Then Mark joined in. 'Stay in bed and keep quiet,' he whispered. 'Get under the blankets and stay there.'

For Gordon, the White Lady was prepared to put on a special show. No longer veiled, the apparition had turned shape shifter, carrying her head under her arm.

'She's got mad staring eyes,' I said. 'She's stalking you: I can see her. Look, here she comes, dripping blood, trailing gore; it's hanging like ropes of spaghetti.'

'Listen,' added Mark. 'Did you hear that groan? She's here, she's *here*.'

It worked. A minute or so of this menacing persuasion and, comply or die, Gordon, cowed into submission, disappeared beneath his bed clothes, and stayed there.

Job done? Well, yes and no. There was, perhaps inevitably, a price to pay for this intimidating behaviour. I'd played sorcerer, taken the White Lady in vain, disrespected her. Revenge was swift and played on my deepest fears. The very next morning, I woke up dripping wet, soaked to my skin. And not alone.

I'd never been a bedwetter, though the idea that I might start was a constant worry. I'd seen what happened to Keith, and the thought of Auntie punishing me like that filled me with horror.

Apart from the fear of punishment, I also had a young boy's curiosity, an interest in the science of it, if you like. How did you become a bedwetter? Was it an illness or disease, like measles or mumps? Some boys said you "got it" by using the same toilet seat or sitting next to a bedwetter in class.

But who were they, these bedwetters? In Almond it was Keith, and on occasion Geoffrey. My own brother Malcolm had started wetting the bed too, and there were other boys from Willow and Lime – I'd seen them hanging their bedding out in the mornings, before school. But as to the others, and how to spot them, I hadn't a clue.

Thus far I'd been spared this affliction. But why? Perhaps, I thought, I'd got away with it by attending church every Sunday, sometimes twice. But then Keith and Malcolm went to church, as did all the other boys, bedwetters or not. Ah, but were they saying the right prayers? Maybe they were singing out of tune, or pocketing the pennies given to them for the collection plate. But by following that line of reasoning, and I did, I was just as guilty. After all, Auntie sent us Almond boys off to church to offer thanks and pray for forgiveness. I just begged God to let me go home.

I hated riddles and still do; puzzles are there to be solved. But this was one mystery which declined to yield an answer; it nagged and nagged at me, refusing to go away.

Had the bedwetters of Eastry really been singled out for divine punishment? Surely God had better things to do with our time? Auntie called the culprits filthy, disgusting pigs. But then she said similar things when we "bolted" our food or forgot to clean our teeth or shoes. So basically, I came back to thinking that bedwetting was an arbitrary thing, and that unless I was lucky (and I wasn't) my turn was almost certainly going to come. One day I'd wake up to find that I'd joined the ranks of the outcasts and untouchables.

The more I thought about it, the more I became convinced that it was only a matter of time. Not that this stopped me from taking precautions. At school I trained myself to go without fluids and took care not to have anything to drink after lunch; being promoted to milk monitor helped; it meant I could avoid the spare bottles I was tasked to share out at afternoon break. And at supper time I left my glass of water untouched, later pouring away my evening cocoa. If anyone had come near me with a dandelion, I'm sure I'd have run a mile!

And the tactics worked. I stayed dry. Weeks passed and I was still dry. The days turned to months, into my first winter and the Christmas holidays. Eventually my preoccupation with bedwetting receded, though the sight of Auntie dealing with the guilty ones was a regular, and frightening, reminder.

And now, just as I'd let down my guard, it had happened. Despite the care I'd taken, I'd woken up soaking wet, and, as I have said, not alone. Laying across my midriff, blocking any attempt at escape, was Gordon.

Whenever there was trouble, something I couldn't avoid, manage, or control, I looked for a distraction. Desperate to escape, I would zone out, gazing into the distance, cutting myself off. I did something like this in the superintendent's office on my very first night and adopted a similar strategy with the heavy floor-length window curtains in Auntie's study, counting and re-counting the folds and flower patterns while she lectured me or punished me for some crime or misdemeanour, real or imagined.

In the dorm, a regular destination was the wall opposite my bed. Here, strangely incompatible with its plain, utilitarian surroundings, a large landscape painting was nailed. A rural scene, its central focus was an arched bridge, under which a flock of sheep struggled for survival amidst the winter snow. Half the animals were sheltered nearby, under a copse of trees, beech, I think. Others had pushed their way through a snow-bowed fence on to a foreground pathway or track.

The artist had captured a moment in time. But what came next? I found that by focusing on this scene, allowing my imagination free rein, I could move the story back or forward, shutting out what was happening around me, escaping the immediate environment. A psychologist would call it disassociation.

What came next was for me to decide. I could make the sheep scatter, or the bridge shudder and collapse, if I chose. The possibilities were endless.

Inspired by a school trip to Deal, and a tour round its Martello tower, I was for a long time wrapped up with thoughts of a Napoleonic invasion. Staring into the picture, I could call up a troop of French dragoons with the blink of an eye. Over the bridge, with the cracking of whips and rumble of wheels, they came; an endless line of baggage-wagons, open carts, artillery, mud-splattered soldiers and, sometimes, the Emperor Napoleon himself. Where were they going? From whence had they come?

Far from sure of my history, I was free to make of the picture what I would. But, whatever my choice, I couldn't make it last. For a second or two I was at Waterloo, my senses assailed by nearby cannon fire, smoke, grapeshot, piles of enemy dead, low groans from the wounded; the next moment a sharp word or shake brought me back.

This was Auntie in close-up. The looming glasses, the hot breath - an evil brew of sweet tea and stale tobacco - and the clicking of dentures. Looking back, I'm sure this invasion of personal body space was every bit as bad as any form of physical punishment. All I could do was close my eyes, purse my lips, and wait for Auntie to stop screaming, and step away.

And step away she did. And most times, and for most crimes, that would be the end of it. There'd be warnings and threats, of course – dark promises of the "just you wait and see" kind. Later, usually about the time I'd begun to think she'd forgotten, Auntie would summon me to the staff room; she'd stopped my pocket money or imposed a curfew, and a week of early nights.

But not this time. This time things were different. Wetting the bed was one thing, but this went far, far beyond. Another boy had shared my mattress, and he was stark naked.

What had I got to say in my defence? 'Don't bother,' Auntie said as I opened my mouth to speak. Then she hit me. 'Look at you, the pair of you. I've never seen anything like it. No, not in all my years. Put it down,' she said, and I dropped the evidence.

In one hand, I'd been holding Gordon's sodden pyjama bottoms, in the other the bedraggled remains of Keith's Davy Crockett hat. How did Gordon get hold of that? Had he visited Keith's bed as well? The thought of it still makes me cringe, even after all these years.

'Eyes front,' was the order, but a quick sideways glance revealed Gordon's body, plastered with spots. The image was absurd, and despite my predicament, I had the urge to laugh; ironically, I needed to use the toilet.

A thought flashed across my mind. Suppose this was the Dreaded Lurgy? The whole dorm had been expecting the lurgy. Rumours had gone round for weeks, and we were on high alert. How the lurgy might manifest itself, though, was a mystery. I'd always imagined it as a version of the plague, or Black Death. Perhaps, finally, this was what you got for bedwetting.

It wasn't the Dreaded Lurgy, of course. It wasn't even the measles, or the plague or the Black Death. No, the spots were something much more mundane, and for me far, far, worse. Gordon's bottom and, indeed, his lower body, was covered with a rash all right, but, as a second glance revealed, it was a rash of postage stamps. My postage stamps. Stamps from the album collection I'd taken to bed for safekeeping. Stamps made more precious because they came from Mum and Dad: and now they were ruined.

I cried. I cried because I was a young boy who'd been dragged from his bed, yelled at, and slapped round the head. Then I cried some more because I'd let Auntie see me cry.

But mostly I cried because of the stamps. The stamps were a breaking point, and Auntie knew it. She called me a cry-baby and a fool for wasting my time, and my mother's money. What did I want a pile of second-hand postage stamps for, anyway? The stamps were used, you couldn't stick them on a letter or parcel. Or could you?

Auntie insisted that the whole dorm stay where they were, shivering with cold, while she investigated Gordon's backside.

So, the two of us planned to leave, eh? And just where exactly did we think we were going? Gordon's right buttock suggested Tanganyika; the left said Hong Kong, via the Cape of Good Hope. Auntie hesitated for a moment, pondering the possibilities. Then she exploded. Far East or not, she said, *Hong Kong was not bloody far enough.*

Bedwetting was one thing. But two boys caught sleeping together...

It was time for a trip to the downstairs bathroom, and for Gordon to join the Red Hand gang. Afterwards, standing knee-deep in freezing water, we were made to flannel each other down, while Auntie sat perched at the end of the bath smoking a Park Drive, casually flicking cigarette ash and soggy postage stamps into the toilet bowl.

I tried to explain that I wasn't responsible, while Gordon excused himself by blaming a ghostly haunting, and Paul. 'It wasn't me,' he whimpered. 'Paul said...'

'Paul! I'll give you Paul.' Auntie raised her hand, then thought better of it. 'Have you any idea?' she said, then, lowering her voice, changed tack, becoming threateningly confidential. 'Let me tell you something...Let me tell you... And you'd better listen... For your own sakes...'

Then Auntie got started: a boy's body was a gift from God; abuse his gift and, well, anything might happen. Some boys had even been known to go blind. But not *her* boys. Oh no. Her boys were clean and wholesome. "A healthy mind and a healthy body," was her motto. And as if to prove her point she made us wash each other down again, insisting that this time we concentrate on our private parts, getting firmly into all those 'little nooks and crannies'.

For Gordon there was more; after being made to rinse through the sodden bedding, he was sent, wearing only his dressing gown and slippers, across the yard to the washing line. It took the weight of both of us to push open the frozen back door; outside swords of icicles dangled like stalactites from the windows.

I was forced to watch and can still remember, as Auntie intended I should remember, even the smallest details; the sharp tang of winter air in my throat and nostrils; the raw commentary of the Eastry crows; the white sheets with their wretched, red-stitched boast: *Property of Kent County Council*; and a single, cheerfully incongruent counterpane, a limp sail in orange, stark against the watery light of the winter morning. Mostly, though, I remember Gordon, struggling with a heavy laundry basket, crying with cold, slip-sliding his way back to Almond, the bedding on the line as stiff as board before he reached the back door.

The following day Gordon was moved to the opposite end of the dorm. A week later he'd gone, leaving me feeling ashamed, and very guilty.

I'd let Auntie down. She'd obviously been too soft with me. Pull another stunt like this, she threatened, and I'd be visiting the superintendent's office, where Mr. Baker would be more than happy to bend me over his desk and administer 'a damned good leathering'.

Gordon aside, perhaps the strangest boy I met during my time in Eastry was Raymond Fitzgerald. Raymond lived up at Lime with his mother, who ran the place. Former housemates, Andrew and Malcolm have vivid memories of Raymond, which largely correspond with my own.

Raymond, like Colin and Barry, was of secondary school age, physically strong, but "mentally handicapped". Puberty had set in early, hitting Raymond hard. Bodily changes were taking place, changes that Raymond could barely understand. Little wonder he seemed worried. Raymond had a nervous, anxious look about him, as though his body was in a state of constant civil war; it was a struggle with no end in sight, and no predictable outcome. Amidst this erupting chaos other things, important things, found themselves neglected. Hair, teeth (often a greenish colour, as I recall) and personal hygiene were overlooked, clothing hardly considered.

Raymond owned a dark blue, Shetland-style jumper, which he insisted on wearing, day in day out, for weeks on end. Over time it attracted all sorts of detritus; smears of earwax, bogies, scabs, off-cuts of fingernails – a random fall of bodily droppings which, mingled with debris from the meal table – breadcrumbs, lumps of porridge, you name it - left the upper part of his body resembling the unwanted remains of a ghoulish picnic.

Meanwhile, Raymond's face had taken on the aspect of an unattended wasteland, fertile ground for clumps of dark hairs, irruptions which sprang up, like the sown men in *Jason and the Argonauts*, to do battle with the armies of Acne, both sides intent on total supremacy. In short, Raymond had become a teenager.

Raymond was badly in need of a first shave, but nobody in their right mind would have trusted him with a razor. For a boy who, in common with a sizeable minority of the home's other residents, had been labelled on admission as "retarded" this would have been both inappropriate and, since he was also considered "maladjusted", tempting fate.

In fact, Raymond had, over time, developed a range of idiosyncratic behaviour patterns and coping strategies, which were little understood, if at all. Some of his more extreme tendencies, which included cutting himself, were undoubtedly a cause for concern. Mr. Baker was keeping a close eye, while the home's inspectors reported that "it is a very worrying thought, having him about the place".

Among other things, Raymond, the records show, was an arsonist, having twice tried to set fire to homes his mother was working in. I knew nothing of this at the time, of course. Even so, an intuition warned me to keep my distance.

Poor Raymond seems to have made just about everyone feel uncomfortable. In the past, attempts had been made to have him removed, but they met with only limited, temporary success. At one point he'd been sent to boarding school, at the authority's expense, but he'd absconded so often that it was eventually decided to return him to his mother. Shortly afterwards the couple were encouraged to transfer to another home, in Deal, but the move broke down. Once again, Raymond came back to Eastry.

Raymond was never far from trouble. There were dozens of incidents, one or two of which I saw first-hand. Take Grand National day, for example. Raymond, ever the attention seeker, had been keen to invite other boys to Lime, where they'd join his fellow residents, watching the big race on TV.

Auntie Fitzgerald was, understandably, reluctant; there was Raymond's earlier history to consider, not to mention the rules restricting the movement and whereabouts of his fellow Eastry inmates. But Raymond, appealing to her maternal instincts, perhaps, worked on his mother, answering her objections, slowly wearing her down. He promised to behave, he promised to change his jumper, he even allowed Uncle Bob to give him a shave. And with Auntie Fitzgerald on hand to serve refreshments and help keep order, what could possibly go wrong?

The seeds of disaster were sown by Raymond, who chose to make things more interesting, organizing a Grand National sweepstake. And at sixpence a horse, "winner takes it all", he had no trouble persuading other boys to get involved, inviting them to Lime. Mark went and I went with him. John Norley came too, along with Colin, and one or two others from Willow.

Mark wanted money for our Australia fund, or for a new pair of football boots, he couldn't decide. For my part, I didn't dare think about winning. That might be tempting fate. Still, win or lose, I'd be spending the afternoon with Andy and Malcolm. Lime was their home. Perhaps I'd get a chance to look around.

The omens were good. Met at the back door by a tidy-looking Raymond, I passed over my sixpence. In return, I was offered an old, battered tea caddy and, dipping in, fished out a piece of folded paper; I'd picked Flying

Wild, a joint favourite. Mark had Time and John had Spring Box.

It was only after twenty boys had piled into the Day Room that Auntie Fitzgerald, who'd been in the kitchen making sandwiches, twigged. But by then it was too late. Even Uncle Bob, meeting us at the door, had a ticket. He'd chosen Laffy, an Irish horse, and another one of the favourites.

'Come in, come in,' said an animated Bob, in welcome. 'Find a seat if you can.'

Ours was a timely arrival. The horses were paraded; some of the owners, Americans and Irish among them, were giving interviews; from time to time the betting odds flashed up on the screen. Soon the starter was repeating Bob's words, getting the runners and riders to line up. 'Come in, come in,' he called. Then, at last, they were off.

Peace Town, at 40-1, took an early lead, crossing the Melling Road looking every inch a winner. Purple Silk also made a good start, while my horse lived up to its name, falling at the first. Other runners, following Flying Wild's example, fell at Beeches, Valentines, or the Canal Turn. The noise level rose in response, and increased with each passing furlong, as, back in the room, our group of anxious onlookers began to lose track of their mounts. Where's Border Flight? Who's got Ayalla? George? Well, it just fell, ha-ha. 'Be quiet,' said Uncle Bob.

Order restored, Peace Town led the running; he was jumping well and into the second circuit, there seemed no reason to suppose he'd be overtaken.

Raymond for one had made up his mind. 'There's mine,' he shouted, approaching the screen. 'Peace Town's going to win.'

But no, at the second last Peace Town began to tire, the remaining runners moved up, bunching together. Purple Silk – Andy's horse - and Team Spirit, now led the running. But it was close. Excitement mounted, as it always does, coming to the final fence. Again, voices were raised, though none was as animated as commentator Peter O'Sullivan's. 'It's Purple Silk from Team Spirit with Peace Town fighting back. Fifteen yards to go and its Team Spirit... Team Spirit gets up at the very last to beat Purple Silk... Team Spirit wins the 1964 Grand National.'

A pause, a split second of silence, followed by a collective exhalation of breath, then all hell broke loose.

'I won! I won!' said Raymond, pogoing up and down.

'No, you didn't,' came a second voice.

'Show us your paper,' said another boy.

Caught out – his claim wouldn't stand the briefest scrutiny - Raymond made a rush for the table, where stood the tea caddy and its contents - a list of runners and riders and our sixpenny pieces.

Now all of us joined in; somebody had won, but we knew it wasn't Raymond. 'Grab him,' came the cry. 'Get his arms. Sit on him.' Uncle Bob sat on him.

It took three boys to open Raymond's fist, and the intervention of staff to prevent him eating the evidence. 'Get off, get off,' he said, as Uncle Bob's hand tightened round his wrist.

Pinned to the floor, the weight of a full-grown man across his chest, Raymond had no choice but to concede. 'Just get off, okay? Just get off.'

It was a strange and incongruous sight, the two combatants, one a member of staff, lying there, spread-eagled, gasping for air on the parquet floor. 'Like watching Mick

McManus,' said George Norley. 'Versus Jacky Pallo,' said his brother, rounding off the moment.

'Read it,' said Bob, offering up a half-chewed slip of paper. Raymond had picked Kilmore.

But it wasn't over. George Norley wanted his money back, and so did Barry. Other boys, frightened or upset by the violence they'd seen, had already left the scene. Others edged their way towards the dining table, jockeying for position.

Suddenly one of the lads grabbed the tablecloth, pulling the tea caddy, along with half a jug of squash and mugs, to the floor. A cascade of sixpences followed. 'Finders, keepers,' said George Norley as he got down on his hands and knees to scoop up the takings. Raymond, freeing himself from Uncle Bob's grip, joined in too, down on all fours, claiming what he could. 'Oh, no you don't,' said Auntie. 'Give it here,' she said, thrusting forward the tea caddy. 'Now, which one of you has Team Spirit? I repeat, who's got Team Spirit?'

Amid all the noise and confusion, Colin, who'd sat quietly in the corner throughout, got up and, handing over a slip of paper, squeezed his way towards the door.

'Colin, turn round. It's you. You're the winner. Come here and get your money,' said a flustered Auntie Fitzgerald. But Colin, preoccupied, was not for turning. He was off home, back to the safety, and relative quiet of Willow. 'Mum's coming on Saturday…Mum's coming…' sounded the repeat from the yard.

It was the first, and last time I went into another cottage.

Raymond Fitzgerald. What to do? Raymond was an enigma, a contradiction. Here was a boy who didn't fit into the system; a child of staff who was as needy, challenging, and unpredictable as the most difficult of his fellow residents and so resented by everyone.

The truth was that, in providing a home for Raymond and his mother the authorities had stretched the boundaries to their limit; a dangerous precedent had been set, one that threatened to tear down the iron curtain between "them" and "us", staff and inmate, which had for so long informed the Eastry ethos.

Hadn't the home been conceived and built to receive the children of the inadequate? That was the mission statement; or at least it was what we were told, and on an almost daily basis. Eastry children, almost by definition, were the offspring of careless, feckless and, in some cases, downright criminal parents. They were society's failures; yet we children were lucky; we'd been saved, taken in by Auntie and Uncle, rescued like so many stray dogs, saved from going the same way. That was the mindset, and it could hardly have been otherwise. For staff to have considered an alternative vision – to have thought about it at all – would have been to confront a bleaker truth; namely, that they needed us as much as we needed them. Little wonder then that Auntie Fitzgerald and Raymond were unpopular. Perhaps things weren't as black and white as they were given out to be.

CHAPTER EIGHT

I'd like to say that I remember all the boys I met in Eastry. Certainly, it would be fascinating to know what became of the more colourful characters. But with the cottages being run as autonomous units, and the regularity and confusion of individual comings and goings, it's only natural, perhaps, that those who have stayed with me are the boys who stood out as being "different" in some way – boys like Raymond or Peter, Colin, and Barry. Either that or they were in the same cottage, or class at school. The council's attempt to accommodate whole families has, over time, created a further barrier to memory, so much so that it is often difficult, now, to separate one boy from his brother.

I made friends, of course. But it was difficult. One night a boy would be sleeping in the same room. We'd be quietly laughing and joking together, making apple pie beds, or reading comics under the blankets by torchlight. Then, in the morning, a summons would come from the study.

And that would be that. When you got back from school it would be to find an open, empty bedside cabinet, and a bed stripped ready for the next resident. All trace of your friend would be gone, with nothing to show that he'd ever existed. When this happened to Mark, I lay on his bed and wept. We'd been friends for more than a year; we'd sat together at school, started a chess league, played football and cricket, and went everywhere together. We'd become incredibly close and, almost from the beginning, made plans for a new future "down under". And now Mark had vanished. Did he make it to Australia in the end? I'd like to think so.

What *did* become of the "disappeared"? Did they have homes and families to return to? Some children, we knew, would come back; they always came back. They were called "in and outers"; children whose mum and, less often, dad, took them away, only to return their offspring when the money ran out, leaving the family once again destitute or otherwise unable to cope. Children in these circumstances were not popular with management; they meant extra paperwork and added to the endless disruption associated with comings and goings. It was all very upsetting. Worse still, the returnees had a habit of appearing with little or no warning, coming back dirty, ragged and, according to staff, in need of discipline and retraining.

But what of the others, the inmates who disappeared, never to be heard of again? Those of us left behind were both fearful and envious. Perhaps, finally, someone had given our fellows a second chance, a place on the outside, beyond the gates. Maybe they'd returned to the heaven of a relative normality? Wherever they'd gone, no message ever came back, no shade was seen flitting about the cottage corridors or haunting the "Rec" and the changing rooms. Not one of the boys ever visited or wrote giving news – not even Mark. Perhaps he did write, and Auntie destroyed his letters.

A boy's discharge left the rest of the group unsettled, vulnerable and insecure, and was almost always followed by a period of challenging behaviour. We'd lost one of our own and his absence was keenly felt. The physical void was soon filled, of course – usually a new boy was admitted within the week; yet a gap, a black hole in our knowledge remained, a hole which, expanding, demanded to be filled. Speculating, we had to make do with scraps of rumour and conjecture, a stodgy starch of remand homes and borstal, the main course from a menu of threats and ultimate destinations put in front of us by staff on an almost daily basis. Meanwhile, Auntie herself remained tight-lipped. Another boy's affairs were nobody's business but her own.

It didn't help that the boys themselves kept quiet about their personal histories. We knew little or nothing about each other's backgrounds and, strange as it may seem, didn't ask questions about why we were in care. Half the boys had been in the system so long they probably didn't know how they came to be in a home and couldn't remember a time when things were different. Others simply chose not to say. Certainly, very few boys had visitors. No, the world outside – the past and the pain – was for the night, or moments of solitude. When we were together, we put on a brave face and focused on surviving the present, dodging staff, taking things one day at a time.

*

Of course, it was never intended, and, indeed, would not have been possible, for the cottages to be run single-handedly; Auntie and Uncle needed help. One or two staff managed by getting together, combining forces. Aunties Ireland and Cornish did this by merging Rose and May, sharing one of the dining rooms while turning the spare room into a play area for their younger boys and girls. Up at Thorn, Auntie Harris had Uncle Bob as an assistant. Mind you he only slept in, when needed – Auntie Harris didn't want him under her feet all day. Instead, he spent most of his shift on other, "general duties" and errands.

Bob, a Yorkshireman, was, like some of his charges, a polio victim and had a club foot, though this didn't stop him from driving the home's Dormobile.

Uncle Tom, on the other hand, was lucky; he had a wife to help him share the responsibilities of managing a home, Cherry being the only cottage run by a married couple. But after Auntie June started a family, she retreated more into the background, leaving the household chores to day staff, known as domestic assistants.

A domestic assistant's job description covered just about everything – cooking, cleaning, fetching, and carrying, taking the younger, infant children to school, mealtime, and overnight supervision, and so on.

Other staff had more clearly defined roles. There were deputy house parents, laundry workers, a whole host of other auxiliaries, mostly part-timers, employed to get us out of bed and on parade, marching to the same, regular, beat.

Some staff I took an instant dislike to – usually those called "Auntie" or "Uncle". Others I avoided all together. Chief among these was Uncle "Skip" Harvey, the Scout Master. Several boys had come back with broken limbs from Uncle Skip's camping trips, and there were stories of shared tents and sleeping bags, and something the older boys referred to as "night-time manoeuvres". Not for me, I decided.

Three or four staff members I remember well. Cherry cottage had Mrs. Luckhurst, with her hooked nose and bulging, thyroid eyes, features which made her look like an angry owl, I thought. Then there was Mrs. Flowers, tall and thin, who walked at a hundred miles an hour, afraid that the slightest breeze would blow her away.

A particular friend, or so I came to think of him, was Bill Cheeseman, the home's regular gardener. A tall, stooping figure, with the lines of a lifetime working outdoors etched upon his face, Bill was every young boy's idea of a favourite grandfather. He had bushy eyebrows, twinkling eyes, and when he removed his battered hat, which was seldom, it was to reveal a head of thinning grey hair, the missing strands having long since disappeared, migrating in the direction of his ears and nostrils.

Bill was on the hunt. He was looking for an acolyte, a youngster willing to listen and learn, a boy who would, in his turn, pass on a skilled gardener's secrets - the joys of propagation, the mysteries of stem cuttings, the rewards of pricking out, potting, and potting on. He wanted a young lad with vision and patience, willing to watch and wonder at the results of his own efforts, fresh growth, renewed colours and textures, new life from old. Or so it seems to me now.

The truth is that Bill was getting older: time was tight, and he was fighting any number of ailments, including arthritis and memory loss. What he most required was a willing hand to fetch and carry, someone to push a wheelbarrow and, at the end of the working day, to help track down his glasses, often found sitting on top of his head, or hunt down a missing trowel, abandoned earlier – sometimes weeks earlier - in a flower bed somewhere. In short, he wanted a boy who didn't mind getting his hands dirty. A boy like me.

I wasn't alone. Other boys, older inmates from Thorn and Willow, volunteered to help, an hour here, an hour there. And with the promise that working with Bill wouldn't interfere with my chores or general running of Almond, Auntie granted her approval. It meant one less boy to look out for, and she knew where to find me when she wanted me back. 'Go on then, clear off,' she'd say, whenever Uncle Bill hove into view.

Bill came to the home a couple of times a week, working out of an old greenhouse and small shed. There were no set days or times; it all depended on the weather. In the past his hours had been more regular; he was younger then, and he'd been employed as a general groundsman. Now the council came to cut the grass and hedges, leaving Bill to keep the borders tidy, and to potter about in his greenhouse, planting up bulbs and summer annuals, flowers for display.

And Bill's work was appreciated by both home and village; his efforts gave the home a positive presence in the wider community, particularly on special occasions - Easter, the village Flower Festival in July, Harvest Festival in October.

When he wasn't working at the home, Bill's gardening job took him to Eastry hospital, up on Mill Lane.

Bill knew all about the hospital, and its grim past. A mass of dark, forbidding buildings, the place was difficult to miss. Look up from just about anywhere in the village and there it was, a sleeping giant, a monster destined, I came to imagine, to one day wake and assert itself. "You created me," it seemed to say, "and I'm going nowhere." It was a permanent reminder of the building's original function, as the Union Workhouse.

As for what went on inside, Bill was reticent, claiming that much of what he'd discovered or seen wasn't suitable for young ears. 'I could tell you tales that would make the hairs on your neck bristle,' he said, with a shake of the head. 'But, well...'

Of course, the more Bill held back, the more I pressed. What I learned, almost by a process of osmosis, was truly frightening, carrying with it as it did echoes of my own experiences of King Hill and Newington Lodge.

A family entering the workhouse was at once split up and sent to separate areas. Women and children went to one place, the men had beds in separate wards. After that, mother and father only saw each other on Sundays, when they attended church. Even then they were not able to mix, family contact restricted to a wave, or a smile for the children.

Weekdays were workdays, twelve hours at a time, the idea being that inmates should earn their keep by hard labour - breaking stones, or unpicking rope. Not surprisingly, the local populace proved to be resistant; even the poorest of the poor had to be desperate to enter such a place; the stigma was such that often they preferred to starve.

Eventually, at the beginning of the twentieth century, a more enlightened outlook took hold, the government of the day concluding that workhouse children were better off away from such a harsh regime. Soon Cottage Homes, built to house them, began to spring up nationwide, the youngsters taken out of the workhouse and handed over to Auntie and Uncle.

Bill may have been absent-minded, but there was nothing wrong with his long-term memory. Born in the village, he recalled the development of the home well. At first there were only two cottages; evacuated during the Great War, they were given up to the relevant authorities to be used as a hospital – for Belgian soldiers or refugees, Bill thought. It wasn't until later that the other buildings were erected, and the cottage homes really came into their own. It was then that Mr. Adams arrived, and Bill was taken on to look after the garden and grounds.

Bill aside, the other staff members I remember most clearly are, naturally enough, those with whom I came into most frequent contact; those regularly assigned to Almond. One I recall with especial fondness is Mrs. Bean.

Mrs. Bean was a big-bosomed, high shouldered woman, who looked every inch the farmer's wife - which, indeed, is what she was. My first, and lasting, impression was one of overwhelming bulk; chubby arms, a wandering waistline, thick ankles and thighs, a wobble when she walked or laughed. Thus, I encountered her from day to day; a mass of quivering flesh in a floral, tent-like dress, struggling to push herself up out of a staff room chair, or, most often, in the kitchen, rolling pastry, shaking flour, rippling like a jelly.

I could go on, and the description would not be unjust, though thinking about her now, a smiling, open face, a mass of greying, once dark, tumbling hair and blue sparkling eyes are the elements of the picture that come into sharpest focus. These are the features – to which you might add a pair of big shiny earrings – which really bring Mrs. Bean back to life for me. What mattered most at the time was that she was someone to go to if you had a problem or needed a cuddle.

You would have liked Mrs. Bean. We boys certainly did. We felt safe with her; safe, warm, and wanted. Mrs. Bean's temper was predictable; indeed, she only had two moods - upbeat and manic. She was, in short, quite incapable of enforcing any sort of discipline, yet alone adhering to Auntie's harsh, regimented regime. The truth is she didn't even try; such things were simply not part of her make-up. When Mrs. Bean was on duty, rules, routines, and rotas went out of the window. Having her in the house was like a holiday, sunshine after the rain, time away from the wariness we all felt when Auntie was in residence.

Mrs. Bean had her own way of doing things and, sometimes, of not making us, her charges, do them. Often it amounted to the same thing. In the mornings she'd help us make our beds. She'd wash a boy's face, comb his hair, and fix his school tie, if she saw him struggling. You didn't have to ask, she just got on with it. At night she'd tuck you in, and sit with you while you said your prayers, if you wanted. We loved her for the care she took, and though we were hardly able to express it, for treating us as individuals - children yes, but children with needs, fears, and feelings. We loved her for her story telling, for her wartime tales and bits of village gossip. We even loved the way she mangled the English language; I for one would often be in stitches, scratching my head, struggling to grasp her meaning. Mostly, though, we loved her for her refusal to be known as "Auntie". It was an instant attraction. 'This place 'as got *Harnties* and *Hunkles* enough to sink a bus,' is what she told me. The very idea of it! Mrs. Bean said we should address her as Mrs. B. So, we did (but not in front of Auntie).

Mrs. B was a generous woman. She was generous with her time and with her love and affection. She understood children because, at heart, she was a child herself. If she didn't believe in discipline, it was, in part at least, because she didn't think discipline was needed. We used to run rings round her.

'Bring out your dead…bring out your dead…any old iron…bring out your dead…'

That was the sound; a welcome Saturday morning sound, an improvised cry assailing the dormitory windows, ushering in the weekend. Alf Bean, Mrs. B's "other half", in his usual good humour, had come for his pigswill.

It was a convenient arrangement. Once a week Alf would bring his tractor and trailer and pick up sixteen pig bins, two from each cottage, then take them back to his farm. In their place he'd deposit the same number of empties. And for the next seven days those bins stood in their respective yards, like so many disabled Daleks, used as cricket stumps, bases for tag and other games, and, of course, gradually filling up with food waste. When Alf called back to collect them, he'd drop into Almond for his morning cuppa, and a chat with "his" boys.

Alf Bean was a small, wiry man, as strong as Popeye. He'd once won a "Mr. Atlas" competition and was proud of it. He certainly liked to show off his muscles. And he had tattoos as well; on his arms and back, and one on his chest.

We had a barrage of questions. Did it hurt? How long did that one take? How much did it cost? Who's the heart for, Alf?

More often or not the response was a funny face; Alf was a celebrated gurner, a star-turn at the annual village fete. Take it too far and Alf would "go ugly", puffing out his cheeks, lifting his top lip half-way up his nose, and chasing his inquisitors round the kitchen table.

Then Mrs. B would join in. 'One of these days you'll stay like that, Alf Bean,' she'd say. And for a minute or two we boys were taken out of ourselves, and away from the world of care.

If you wanted to escape from the home, there was no better destination, it seemed to me, than the Bean's farm. The best time to visit, I imagined, was during the still heat of an August day – in my mind it was always high-summer at Glebe Farm – when I'd be free to gaze upon the Bean's farmhouse, a ragstone building topped with orange-brown Kentish tiles, before wandering about the yard undisturbed.

Midday, I thought, would be a good time. Midday ushered in a lazy, shimmering time, an hour when every living creature looks for cover. At midday all of nature would be intent on keeping cool, leaving an observer free to find his own place in the shadows, and to look at it all unnoticed.

Certainly, the farm's cat shows no interest. A fat, indifferent mouser, he lies under an old, abandoned harvester, stretching and yawning, digesting a late breakfast.

Nearby, a scatter of Orpingtons, hazy feathered triangles, seek the shade of a trailer, while a pair of chocolate-speckled Sussex hens melt into yesterday's foxholes, scrapings made in the dirt and dust for coolness and comfort.

On the far side of the yard, in an area mottled with marigolds and wallflowers, lies a pile of old rubber tractor tyres, thrown across the grass like quoits by competing giants. Under this heap is where the slow worms, adders and lizards hide. I can't see them, they're too well camouflaged, but I know that's where they'll be. I know too about the rotting rain barrel, its depth of stagnant water a magnet for hovering insects, a welcome feast for scything swallows and martins - lunch on the wing.

For me, though, this is a safe time to visit. Alf's small herd of Friesians has long since gone out of the yard, leaving only the farm dogs – two sad-eyed stragglers lurking about with a couldn't-care-less attitude on their faces - redundant until the afternoon of the day, when the cows come home for milking, and Alf Bean has his tea.

I stand still and a breeze starts up, blowing bits of baling twine and straw like tumbleweed across the tops of my sandals. Then, plop! A duck entering the farm pond takes my attention; that and the satisfied grunt of a feeding sow, back in the yard. I'm reminded of Alf's home visits, his bins, and the piglets he's named "Pinky" and "Perky".

From across the yard comes a new sound, the grating of a barn door, rocking on hot, rusty hinges. I turn and follow, slipping inside, hit by a cool cocktail of aromas; the sweet summer smell of hay, mixed with old leather, creosote and fermenting fertilizer.

My eyes, adjusted to the gloom, are drawn upwards towards the apex of the hayloft where, high up and half-hidden, a chatter of sparrows sits cracking salvaged corn seed on ancient beams of oak. Higher still, a small colony of bats hang roosting, waiting for the night, their droppings dotting a sawhorse and a pile of logs on the floor below.

Glebe Farm. I didn't see it. I was never there. Yet the picture I carried – and still carry – in my head was not altogether a fiction. Instead, it was a composite, a lingering echo of Doddington days; of hours spent playing at Cuthbert's farm, climbing five-barred gates, hiding in nettle and campion-filled ditches, helping myself to wine-dark fruit and berries - cherries, blackcurrants, elder - each according to the time of the year; it was built on memories of old tractors and trailers, barns, and bale fights, scrapes and scrumpings; being free to run and roam, finding and asking questions of anyone who'd stand still long enough to hear, and sometimes to listen as well.

That was the world Glebe Farm came to symbolize; the world I'd left behind. It was a way to hold on to what had been snatched away, perhaps never to be returned.

Physically, a tractor ride was the nearest I got to Glebe Farm. Up and about early one Saturday morning, Alf let me jump aboard and took me round the other cottages, helping to load the bins onto his trailer. He'd long since issued an open invitation for us Almond boys to visit the farm and did so again. 'Just drop in,' he said airily. 'Any time you like. You'll always be sure of a warm welcome.'

For me a "warm welcome" meant high tea - piles of Mrs. B's scones and jam, served with lashings of cream, the whole lot helped down with bottles of cream soda or dandelion and burdock. First, though, I would have the privilege of giving the other boys a tour. At least half of the Almond residents were "townies" and had never seen a farm. A visit to the Bean's would give me a chance to show off. But we never went. That sort of thing just wasn't done.

But in one vital regard at least, the farm came to us. Glebe Farm had a kitchen garden, where Mrs. B grew fruit and vegetables, so Almond had a regular supply of fresh produce. There were peas, lettuce, and tomatoes, along with rhubarb, apples, pears and plums, and runner beans according to the season. And there were eggs too, taken, still warm, from the hen house, individually wrapped and carried up to Almond in a traditional wicker basket.

Cooking back then was a labour-intensive affair, but with Mrs. B on duty there was no shortage of volunteers, boys willing to help with food preparation, or simply to fetch and carry. The job description, which is far from exhaustive, included:

Weighing ingredients (using ancient scales and individual weights), mixing and stirring, running errands, holding recalcitrant glass jars under a hot tap (a metal screw-top lid expands, quickly coming away), setting mouse traps, stocktaking the first aid box, helping prepare birthday teas (jelly and ice-cream a must), stirring a sixpence into the Christmas pudding mix, food tasting, fetching cockles in a pint mug from the fish van, writing lists for the stores from dictation ('keep the cleaning materials separate, please'), changing fly papers, tossing pancakes, cutting biscuit shapes, topping and tailing gooseberries, plugging strawberries, altering the clocks (but only twice a year), roasting chestnuts, more food tasting, taking scraps to the pig bins, mopping floors, clearing work surfaces and spillages, pouring tea, pouring boiling water over invading ants, filling salt cellars, shelling peas, removing straw and muck from eggs (using a small brush and placing in a large mixing bowl), setting the kitchen timer, setting the dining room table, swatting wasps with a rolled up paper or comic (a seasonal job, popular with everyone), raiding cereal boxes for free gifts or coupons, arguing over the former, serving cocoa from the kitchen hatch, ringing the hand bell to announce mealtimes, watching and waiting.

And for those boys too impatient to wait there were spoons to lick or cut-off crusts smeared with beef dripping to nibble, spirals of apple peel to munch on.

Mrs. B was a law unto herself, especially when it came to mealtimes. If she fancied varying the menu, cooking something different, she did, often fetching ingredients from home. My personal favourites were toad in the hole and, perversely perhaps, liver and bacon, while rabbit or pigeon pie, courtesy of the trap or shotgun, went down well with everyone.

Mrs. B did amazing things with meat. There were stews with fat dumplings bobbing up and down on the surface, struggling to stay afloat; cuts of beef topped with a suet crust made in a giant basin and served drowning in gravy; chicken pies bursting with mushrooms and peas; the list went on.

Afterwards came pudding, and more pastry - fruit pies with cherries or apples and blackcurrants from Glebe Farm, sprinkled with castor sugar and left, unguarded, to cool on a wire stand, or bread and butter pudding or roly-poly stuffed full of dried currants, fruit, or jam, for later in the week.

And always, it seemed, there was custard, a tin jug full, served with a big ladle, to be licked clean by the first boy to get to it before it disappeared into the washing up. Little wonder there was no shortage of volunteer kitchen helpers.

If mealtimes with Auntie were formal affairs, Mrs. B was much more relaxed. Yes, we boys kept to our given seats, and said Grace as a matter of course. But during the meal we chatted, told jokes, and sometimes went as far as to trade food; in short, we indulged in the sort of casual behaviour Auntie Joyce would have found unacceptable.

Worse still, from Auntie's standpoint, mealtimes with Mrs. B gave the attention seekers amongst us a platform, a stage on which to perform.

John Norley was a regular offender. Sitting at the dining room table, surrounded by a captive audience, John took the opportunity to hone his acting skills, revelling in our attention and applause.

John was a consummate performer. I knew it, we boys all knew it, but once John got going, all were under his spell. I for one was never quite able to decide between truth and theatre.

A typical, and well-remembered, routine went as follows. Half-way through dinner, during a brief pause in conversation, a strange gurgling sound started up.

Keith quickly alerted Mrs. B. 'John's choking,' he cried, in a panic.

Was John unwell? Perhaps it was a case of him crying wolf; hadn't we seen and heard it before? A purple-faced, grunting John, hand clutching his throat, soon had the dubious amongst us convinced, or at least willing to give him the benefit of the doubt. Perhaps this time it was for real. It was no act; John really was ill.

Mrs. B, however, didn't want to know; John was always playing the fool. Last week, she reminded us, it was suspected *gasket-enter-eye-tus*; John staged a miraculous recovery, seconds before Mrs. B summoned a *hambulance*. The week before John treated us to a Norman Wisdom impression (or it may have been Mr. Pastry), John stumbling over the sofa and chairs before falling to the floor, grabbing his stomach.

This time though, the agony was prolonged. John really was ill; I was sure, we were all sure.

'John's choking,' repeated Keith.

'*Heat up* and stop *hacting* the goat,' Mrs. B said from her end of the table.

'But he's choking,' Keith said.

Something must be done.

For a moment, a decision hung in the air.

Suddenly, Keith, unable to take the gurgling noise any longer, made a move. Getting up, he went over to where John was sitting, taking up position. Then he hit him. Hard. In the back.

A snort, a sneeze, and a cannonade of peas shot out of John's nostrils and went hurtling down the length of the table, bouncing off the far wall with the sort of rapid rattle that might have inspired a Wilfred Owen or Siegfried Sassoon.

'Urgh,' the group groaned in unison.

'Got you,' said John.

We laughed, of course; even Mrs. B managed a titter. Then we laughed some more. Somebody threw a ball of rolled bread. And we laughed at that too.

'You boys will be the death of me,' said Mrs. B. In danger of losing control, she made a customary appeal to our better selves. 'Boys, boys, don't do this to me, boys. Come along, Keith, sit down. And John, behave yourself. If you don't, there'll be no pudding, and I'll have to make a *raport*... Think of the paperwork; you know how I hate the paperwork.'

It was a regular thing; us *"hacting up"*, and Mrs. B calling for order, and fair play. When this appeal failed, she'd wheel out the big guns, the ultimate deterrent: Auntie Joyce. What would Auntie have to say? We knew all too well what Auntie would have to say. As for Mrs. B, I suspect that she was more than half afraid of Auntie herself.

*

Everyone, it used to be said, could recall where they were when President Kennedy was assassinated. I know because I was confined to bed with a fever, being watched over by Mrs. B. I learned what had happened from her newspaper. Mrs. B had agreed to do an extra shift; she left her Daily Mirror on my bedside chair when she popped down to help staff prepare lunch.

"Kennedy slain… Jackie splattered in blood," screamed the headlines.

I stared and stared at those words, and the accompanying picture of the presidential limousine and police outriders, for what seemed like hours. I wanted to investigate, to see and know more, and was cross with myself for not having the strength to get out of bed.

Every few minutes I'd try to make a move, inching my way down the mattress. If I was careful, I thought, I ought to be able to reach over and grab hold. "Go now," said the voice in my head. "It's easy, like hooking ducks at a fair." But try as I may, I simply didn't have the energy. Exhausted and half delirious, I was worried about the First Lady's clothes, which were undoubtedly ruined.

Later I must have slept, waking to find myself surrounded by flickering lights. I was frightened, not knowing where I was, or what was happening to me.

With the lights came shadows; huge grotesque shapes crawling over the walls and ceiling, now expanding, now contracting, threatening to swallow me alive. But I needn't have worried; it was only Auntie, who'd come up to the dorm with three or four household candles. There'd been a power cut, and she'd decided to check on me, and give Mrs. B a break. Downstairs, I heard her say, the other boys were asking when the electricity supply would be back; they were missing Doctor Who.

Auntie put a hand on my forehead, then piled an extra blanket on the bed, leaving me to "sweat it out". It was a traditional, and dangerous, remedy.

*

Under a large, round railway station clock a man in a Chinese hat and pigtails sells exotic fruits from a hand barrow. He's shouting his wares, offering bargains, treats I don't see from one Christmas to the next. There are pineapples and pomegranates, tangerines, melons, and mandarins too. Hot and thirsty, I'm desperate to get my hands on these luxuries. In my delirium, for that is what it is, I imagine myself lying spread-eagled on the floor, while the man drips frozen orange juice into my mouth from above.

But, no, it seems I am just an extra here; I'm stuck on a train, glued to my seat, with not even a walk-on part.

Yet, I can look. And I do. Then half wish I hadn't. Outside, through the carriage window, I spot my mum; yes, it's her, caught in a soup of whirling smog and steam. I'm puzzled, Mum's out of her seat. Why is she out of her seat? I didn't see her go. And that man she's with, he's a stranger. Together they move away, arm-in-arm. Are they a couple? How can that be?

I try not to look, but something compels me. No brief encounter this, the two of them, I see, are heading for the arch, walking out of the station, leaving me behind, without so much as a backward glance. A fog descends, then clears, billowing and evaporating away. It's an interlude, a gap in the clouds, forcing me to look again. At the far end of the platform Mum and her man stop at a kiosk, where he buys her flowers. A billboard repeats the story of the day.

Suddenly, I'm free. The spell breaks, the invisible force welding me to my seat dissipated. I find I can move, though doing so means treading treacle. Nevertheless, I'm not going to let Mum leave without a fight. Getting up, I struggle towards the carriage window, battling heavy feet, like a deep-sea diver lifting lead-filled boots. I try to shout, 'Wait for me,' but the window refuses to budge, the words won't come.

I'm parched; my throat feels sore, my face and neck are badly swollen, and I don't know why. I glance over at the fruit stand, then back to the kiosk; it's only a second, but in that moment of thirsty temptation Mum and her man have disappeared, fading from view. Now all I can see is a figure in black, a hunched character heaving piles of string-tied newspapers from a trolley onto the floor of an open goods wagon.

A guard appears, slamming doors. His whistle is urgent and shrill, his waving flag cinder red, the colour of the setting sun. It hurts my eyes.

A jolt, a shudder, and the wheels begin to turn. A stuttering start, a simple opening movement, is enough to trigger a frenzy of activity across the concourse.

A hidden hand pushes a pile of pineapples, and they go bouncing from the Chinaman's barrow. A troupe of bronzed pears, blood-red oranges, and florescent bananas joins them, doing somersaults, cartwheeling along the platform.

Green and white station signs that say *Waiting Room*, *Left Luggage*, and *Station Master* slide across the carriage windows, like credits at the end of a movie.

But this isn't the climax. There's more to come. In one last scene a character in a pinstripe suit and bowler hat steps forward. Recognition! I've seen this man before, and he seems to know me, too. Smiling, he raises his newspaper, and I see again the Kennedy headlines, the pictures, and the words. Meanwhile, somewhere in the far distance, a disembodied voice makes a station announcement: "Waterloo, this is Waterloo..."

Waterloo! I'm beaten back by a sudden burst of knowing, and an indescribable sense of panic and loss. In a final, desperate attempt to gain my freedom, I try to force open the carriage door. But it's too late; the platform is gone. Silver rails, the length of a groan, cross an expanding void; it's the last link, an umbilical cord stretching back to the station, and my mum.

I call out but Mum doesn't answer. There is no Mum. Not tonight, and not until I'm better, well enough to be up and about. Those are the rules. Instead, I hear the quiet, reassuring voice of Mrs. B. 'Try and sit up; there's a dear. Here, I've poured you a cup of lemon and barley.'

I open my eyes to see Mrs. B, along with Auntie and Dr. Rose, occupying the chair where earlier Mrs. B's newspaper had been. And President Kennedy is still dead. And Dr. Rose, pushing a thermometer into my mouth, says I am almost certainly going to live. I have the mumps.

The agony of separation and loss. I had that same Waterloo dream over and over during the following days. Each time I woke in a pool of sweat, pyjamas and bed sheets stuck to my body; hair plastered to my forehead. And always, it seemed, Mrs. B was there to sponge my swollen face and encourage me to drink. She was wonderful, and I loved her for it. But she wasn't my mum.

Two days later, on the Monday morning, I was moved nearer to the door, where I stayed for a week, when it was assumed that I was no longer infectious. Then staff shifted my bed back to the other end of the dorm.

*

And that was that. There was no special treatment, just as there was no vaccine. It was the same for all of us. Getting the mumps was just part of growing up. For a week or two you were excused school and Auntie's rotas, chores and inspections, and friends teased you with names like "Moon face" and "Hamster cheeks". Then it was somebody else's turn.

But I did all right. For four or five days I found myself spoiled, receiving a steady stream of visitors. Mark came up one afternoon, and brought with him his "League Ladder", a gift with a comic. We spent time working on the football results, moving cardboard team strips up and down.

Mark was a Liverpool fan, while I'd followed Manchester United since listening to the 1963 FA Cup Final. Given the success United enjoyed in the years which followed, it wasn't a bad choice (the opposition being Leicester City).

Coincidentally, Mum, like Mark, was a Liverpool supporter, though Mum's choice of a team to follow, she admitted later, had been based less on the quality of their football than the attractions of Roger Hunt's legs.

A second sickbed caller was John Norley, come bounding in, skidding across the wooden floor, throwing me his "flap banger", another gift that came free with a comic – *The Victor*, I think.

The flap banger, I should explain, was a card with a sheet of brown paper in the shape of a triangle attached to it. A violent swing of an arm and the paper flapped out, making a noise like a bursting paper bag. Four or five Almond boys owned one. John had already had his confiscated for sneaking up on Mrs. Flowers, scaring her half to death. He stole it back, then loaned it to me.

Auntie was another, more regular, visitor to the dorm. Most mornings, after the other boys had disappeared off to school, she would come and chat with the day staff, discussing President Kennedy and the events in Dallas.

Jack Ruby's gun settled nothing, Auntie said. Indeed, the whole sorry affair merely confirmed what she'd been saying for years; namely, that the country, nay, the entire world, was *going to the dogs*. She said the same thing when Harold Wilson was chosen as Prime Minister.

After three or four days, and with gathering strength, came sharper wits. Soon, familiar everyday sounds began to intrude - a radio playing, a football ricocheting off a metal bin. Then one afternoon came a new sensation; the muffled realisation that outside, snow was falling. I climbed up at the window to get a look, anxious to be part of the world again.

The wintry weather brought in Mrs. B, wind-assisted and blowing hard. '*Brrr*, it's cold out there,' she said, grasping herself in a bear hug. 'Alf reckons that storm 'as come all the way from Russia, straight from *Liberia*.'

Mrs. B eased herself down into my bedside chair. It promised to be a hard winter, she prophesied; all the farmers were saying so. Last year had been bad, but she'd known worse, not least the long, freezing winter of 1947.

From 1947 it was but a short journey back to the war, and the part Mrs. B had played in Hitler's downfall.

Almost from the start, Alf turned Glebe Farm over to growing and producing more fruit and vegetables, "digging for victory" as the slogan had it. There was more work, and extra hands were taken on.

But Mrs. B still found time to get involved in village life, and the wider community. The Women's Institute set up a National Savings Committee, money being raised for the Red Cross, with food parcels being sent out to prisoners of war. Wastepaper was collected for recycling, and tons of metal were gathered and dispatched. Then there were warship and aircraft weeks, with a plaque awarded to the village for its efforts. Mrs. B was proud to have been involved in it all, often being delegated to lay on food and refreshments.

Mrs. B had a whole trunk of wartime memories and, after a bit of a rummage, could always be relied upon to produce something dramatic – or as she would have it, *disastering*.

Many of these tales centred on the Battle of Britain which played out above her head. Every day during that high, fateful summer of 1940 had brought heavy action, Mrs. B recalled. On one occasion she saw two Spitfires from 266 Squadron shot down. Another time, after two fighter planes collided in mid-air, an enemy Me109, trailing oil and smoke, came screaming low over the trees and hedges before crashing into a field near to Glebe Farm, disintegrating as it hit the ground. Mrs. B was still cross about that one. The noise had put her hens off laying for a fortnight or more.

Mrs. B's strangest story, one which received a regular airing, concerned a Luftwaffe pilot who bailed out over the village after a dinghy inflated in his cockpit. Mrs. B had her own, typically idiosyncratic, explanation. The German pilot, she *respected*, must have been in a rush to get *hairborne*; no doubt he was *conflused* or got *sidetracted* and, as a result, misread his *destructions*. Of course, none of this would have happened if a woman had organised the pre-flight packing, Mrs. B concluded, with a smile.

Mrs. B had seen and heard it all; dog fights between Spitfires and Me109s, flights of Hurricanes sent up from nearby aerodromes – Manston was just down the road - intercepting heavy formations of Dornier bombers headed for London. Later came the "doodlebugs," V-1 rockets flying over as low as a hundred feet. It all seemed so exciting.

I had clearly been born too late; too late to meet Wing Commander Tait, who crashed near to the village, and recovered to command No.617 Squadron on the famous Dam Buster raid; too late to know Wing Commander Robert Stanford Tuck, known as "Lucky Tuck", a fighter pilot credited with shooting down twenty-nine enemy aircraft and who survived two crash landings, time in a German prisoner of war camp and escape via the Russian front to return to Eastry, where he retired after the war. Lucky Tuck was a regular visitor at Glebe Farm, calling in for fresh fruit and veg.
Of course, had I been older and wiser I might have been less gung-ho, considered the bigger picture; thought more of the pilots, on both sides, who fell to their deaths after their

parachutes didn't open, or who came down with their planes aflame, suffering hideous burns and other life changing injuries. But I had been brought up to believe, by adults armed with the benefit of hindsight, that an allied victory was a foregone conclusion, the enemy a bunch of "square heads", their air force, army, and indeed, the whole of the evil, Nazi empire inferior and deserving of destruction. Mrs. B, though, had seen both sides of the fighting; for her the experience had been close-up and personal. Perhaps that's why she dealt with it, publicly at least, by focusing on the comic, the weird and the wonderful. And who can blame her?

Mrs. B, knowing I was anxious to recover in time for Mum and Dad's Sunday visit, encouraged my recuperation, urging me to get out of bed. 'Up you come,' she said.

But that first time not even Mrs. B was strong enough to hold me. I collapsed, struggled up, staggered about like a newborn foal, then fell back heavily onto the bed.

So, Mrs. B left it until the next morning, promising that, if I could make my way to the toilet and back, she'd look in the kitchen to see if there were any letters or packages for me. I knew there would be.

CHAPTER NINE

Mum was a prolific writer. When she wasn't sending letters down to Eastry, she would be dashing off a missive to the social services or county council, mailing coupons, or entering competitions. Her specialty was the "begging" letter. Over the years she must have written dozens.

A regular target during our Eastry days was the managing director of Brooke Bond, who'd made the mistake of allowing one of his employees to put the company's Canon Street address on the back of their tea cards.

It was all very formulaic. Mum would start by praising the company's products – in this case Brooke Bond Dividend tea, good for the nerves and far superior to PG Tips or Typhoo – then give a tragic sketch of her domestic situation; how five of her six children had been snatched away from her and taken in to care; the financial cost, and hence the infrequency of her visits, the ongoing battle to get us back, and so on.

Satisfied that she had done enough to grab the attention of even the least sympathetic of readers, Mum would get to the point. One of her boys, Douglas (Mum always made sure to use our names) required just one more card to complete a set of fifty; in this case British Birds, Number 32. Another son, Edward, had been saving Flags of the World – such a good, colourful series, and *very* educational – would it be possible to send Turkey and Tunisia? Freshwater fish, planes, cars, ships, sometimes the list would run to a couple of sides of paper.

Mum struck up a regular correspondence with Brooke Bond and never failed to return a letter of thanks, remembering always to describe her children's grateful response to their generosity, and the difference the company had made to our blighted lives. She also promised to recommend their products, being more than happy to continue promoting the brand. Half a dozen letters like this, with a respectable time gap, and we boys owned every set of cards Brooke Bond produced, along with the albums to stick them in.

Afterwards, Mum moved on to Kellogg's, who were putting plastic models in their cornflakes, then targeted Robertsons, who sent a group of colourful metal brooches. They were Golliwogs, playing musical instruments. I chose the drummer, then swapped him for an Airfix model.

Mum wrote two or three times a week, her letters, and parcels – usually rolled up copies of the Eagle, Victor, Dandy and Beano – addressed to me, because I lived in a cottage on my own, with instructions to pass on her love to my brothers, along with any presents or gifts included. Sometimes Mum would add a treat for Mark as well, because she knew he was my best friend, and didn't receive any mail, or visitors.

The postal service back then was excellent, with collections and deliveries to the home twice a day during the week, and again on a Sunday morning. Yet despite the frequency of the service there was nearly always a hold-up, with little correlation between posting and arrival.

The reason for the delay was Auntie, who collected the post from the office, then hid it. I knew what she was doing. I could see the letters and parcels on the top shelf in the kitchen, waiting to be claimed.

By the end of the week, half a dozen or more items were sitting there. But when I asked – and I did, every day – all I got was 'Sorry, nothing for you this time.' The post was either invisible or, on those rare occasions when Auntie acknowledged its existence, belonged to somebody else altogether.

Auntie's denials were maddening. At first, I tried pleading with her, asking her to double check, even being so bold to suggest she might have made a mistake.

'Those rolled up comics are mine.'

'I don't think so, Douglas.'

'I can see my mum's handwriting on the wrapper.'

But it made no difference.

'Are you calling me a liar?'

'No, Auntie, it's just that...'

'Just what?'

'Just nothing, Auntie.'

After one or two episodes like this I learned to bite my tongue and wait for Sunday morning, when a whole pile of letters, cards and comics would appear, unceremoniously dumped on the Day Room table, or else straight onto my lap. Some of the mail Auntie had opened and read.

*

"Counting the hours." That's how Mum ended her Eastry letters. She and Dad visited every other Sunday, in the afternoon, after church. It was a long wait.

Everyone, boys, and girls, had to attend church, and were expected to be smartly turned out – in school uniform or, on Holy Days, Scouts, Cubs or Boys Brigade attire.

Each cottage walked down in little groups, to the sound of the bells, lingering at the church gate or porch until staff arrived, ready to shepherd us inside and into our pews. I remember I used to hang back, hoping to get the outside seat, nearest the aisle. There was more leg room, and it made me feel important, my job being to pass down the hymn and prayer books as they came round.

Hundreds of years of faith and history had been poured into St Mary's, and the church had plaques and memorials aplenty to show for it.

Yet the building was far more than a dusty museum. On one level I felt this deeply; on another I was perplexed. I was ignorant, and all too aware of my ignorance.

Basically, I was lost, unable to read my surroundings, or the service for that matter, and since neither was ever explained to me (it wasn't like school, you couldn't put up a hand and ask) I stayed baffled and confused.

Fundamentally, I knew nothing. I didn't know that the original church was Anglo-Saxon, that its tower was a Norman survival, or that the present building's main architectural style was Early English, dating from the thirteenth century. Nor did I appreciate the antique oak pews I sat in formed part of the nave, or the reason for the altar being placed at the far, east end of the church, while the font was situated near to the porch. Dominating everything, the stained-glass windows were beautiful, and intriguing, yet the figures depicted remained unknown to me. Christ crucified, yes; as to the others, well they were probably disciples and saints, though I was never sure.

I did my best to follow, and understand, the service, but a growing fascination with the past, the call of my ancient surroundings, took me away; I was too easily distracted.

Above the chancel arch, enclosed within a rectangular frame, a line of circular frescoes drew the eye. There were rows of these images – "medallions" they were called, most of them displaying flowers, roses, and irises, amongst them. These motifs, plants, and animals, all had symbolic importance. The griffin represented evil, the lion its nemesis, and the resurrection. I had no idea about this at the time; I just made up my own meanings.

Feeling excluded, it became something of a habit for me to play games with the hymn numbers displayed on the board beyond the pulpit. What did you get if you added 145 and 87, or subtracted 142 from 381? Then I'd join in with the other boys, turning the words of the week's hymns back on the vicar. "Fight the good fight with all thy might, sit on a box of dy-na-mite." Well, it was funny at the time, a childish response born out of frustration, and forced containment.

At the close of the service, the vicar blessed us all in the name of the Holy Trinity. And it was now, at the very end, that I found myself really struggling. I had anxieties and concerns, perennial questions, asked by hosts of others, congregations both past and present. I didn't know it, but centuries of theological disputes, schisms, and wars had been fought around this particular difficulty; namely, that of the nature of God, and the divinity of Christ. In retrospect, I was more than entitled to be ever so slightly perplexed. After all, I was only nine or ten years old.

To be honest, the very idea of God the Father, the Son, and the Holy Ghost (especially the

Holy Ghost), had me tied up in knots - bonds from which I have never entirely been able to extricate myself. But I put my hands together anyway. Perhaps God, or his Son, would look kindly upon me, intervening, arranging for me to go home.

God, the vicar preached, was everywhere, all at once. If true, then, as far as I was concerned, he certainly had competition. In short, the Christian god wasn't the only entity I had to look out for. There were other powers at work in the world; the Fates, lesser, older gods; I had no collective name for these forces, but of their existence I had no doubt; they were fickle and demanded respect - you ignored them at your peril.

Many of these entities were downright malevolent. Personified, I imagined them looking down on the world like Greek gods, interfering to fulfil an unknown, and unknowable plan, perhaps, or maybe just acting on a whim, squabbling amongst themselves, moving people about like tin soldiers on a plywood battlefield, or pieces on a chessboard. They could put a stop to Mum and Dad's visits with a simple shake of the head, or a click of the fingers: illness, a cancelled bus service, a burst tyre; anything might happen.

These forces had formed part of the fabric of my life since early childhood. I knew them from the books I read, or had read to me; tales, some as old as Aesop, remembered from the infants' class at Doddington, or read by Gran after she'd put us to bed at night; traditional, cautionary fables and anthropomorphic stories, like *Red Riding Hood* or *Hansel and Gretal*. Then there was *Rupert Bear*, *The Far Away Tree*, *Noddy and Big Ears* and, later, *Wind in the Willows*. Add to these the old-style nursery rhymes I'd had thrust upon me, almost from the time of my birth, and it was little wonder, perhaps, that I had reached the age of reason satisfied that I was not alone, that "out there" existed a whole universe of invisible beings.

These spirits, aspects of nature, were all around me. Nymphs and sprites, pixies, fairies and goblins; all of them, I knew, instinctively, were manifestations of the same force - the force that sent the clouds moving across the sky, that gave motion to the tides, filled lakes and rivers, and coloured woods and forests to bursting with verdant, luxuriant vegetation, autumn browns and golds, that rich profusion of nature which imbued us, one and all, with the knowledge of time passing, the regular miracle, and sadness, of the changing seasons.

Woods were special places. Larger trees lived longer than humans, and they communicated, not only among themselves, but with the animals they invited to move in with them, making the trees their home. Once upon a time, or so I convinced myself, I understood the tales they told, as they creaked, and groaned in the wind. Then something changed. Somewhere along the way I'd lost the key to this woodland language. Perhaps I was growing up? Maybe, but this didn't mean I was ready to risk denying the powers, or to betray them by revealing what I knew of their existence. Other people might not understand.

Even cut down and re-fashioned, trees kept their potency. The telegraph pole totems we boys touched on the way to school, the cricket bat I treated with linseed oil, and kept under my bed (and sometimes in it); should I have acknowledged that oak or ignored it? The spirits needed mollifying; the rituals followed.

I was incredibly superstitious, and more than ready – with no small amount of help from Auntie – to blame myself for all that was negative in my life. Suppose Mum and Dad didn't get off the bus? Would it be my fault? It would be, of course. I must have been negligent. But how? What had I done, or forgotten to do, since last time?

I had Sunday morning to worry about it, with the worst of the wait coming after lunch, which I could barely swallow. By then my head would be close to overflowing; ladders, black cats, a solitary magpie, signs and omens bouncing around my brain like balls in a bagatelle.

How to block it all out? Sometimes the only way was to sit somewhere quiet and start a slow, backward count. With half an hour to go, I'd retreat to the dorm – with permission, I had to change my clothes – and lay on the bed, arms crossed over my chest like the effigy of a medieval knight atop his tomb. "One hundred, ninety-nine - inhale deeply – ninety-eight, ninety-seven…"

At exactly five-to-two, I'd go downstairs, requesting permission to leave the home. Then came another Sunday ritual, with Auntie wanting to know where I was going, and, after I'd told her, asking whether I thought I was deserving of a family visit. I did, of course. A quick inspection – with orders to return in a presentable state - and I was off and away.

But I didn't rush. Instead, a final act of propitiation saw me walking the kerbstones, arms akimbo, making my way down the drive towards the gate. My impulse, always, was to run, but somewhere, back at the beginning, I'd set up a routine, a habit I must follow. It didn't even worry me that I might be spotted and bellowed at by staff from Cherry, Rose, or May. What was the worst they could do?

Andy and Malcolm, if they hadn't passed me on the way down, would be waiting at the roadside, outside the main gate. Edward was usually the last to appear, struggling with Ian, who didn't want to hold hands.

Together again, free at last, the five of us stood at the corner, senses on the alert, waiting for the first sight or sound of Mum and Dad's bus. Would it be a single-decker, or a double? East Kent or M & D? Then at last it came, lumbering down the hill, with angry, clashing gears, enveloped in a tunnel of exhaust fumes. 'Here comes the dragon,' was Ian's imaginative, first-time response. So, dragon it became.

The distance between stops, between the village cross and the home was short, a quarter of a mile at most, so the growling beast never managed to pick up any sort of speed. With a little practice, I was soon adept at judging the spot, the last spot, in the road where, straining, the bus ran out of options. What would it do, accelerate, pull away, or brake and come to a halt, disgorging our visitors?

*The bus has reached the last lamp post; now it's approaching the red post box. Now, now, now...*It was knife-edge stuff, the fear almost unbearable. A dry mouth; a tightening of the muscles; my heart beating against a contracting chest. This was it, the moment I'd waited a fortnight's lifetime for. Please, *please*, make it stop.

I don't think it would be possible, now, for me to capture and convey fully the desperation and anxiety of those last few seconds. Always, you see, there was the unspoken question: what if they didn't come? Suppose Mum and Dad didn't get off the bus. What if they'd disappeared, simply stepped out of our lives, vanished, never to be seen again?

The fear of abandonment was ever present. In the background, yes; but there, nonetheless; bubbling away, guaranteed to rise to the surface when I was at my most vulnerable – locked in the bathroom nose to wall. Or last thing at night, sleepless in the dorm; or, most acutely, on this, a Sunday afternoon, when I was down at the gate, watching for the bus. Mark and Keith didn't have visitors. What made me so special?

Then suddenly, Edward, Andy, or Malcolm - one of us – would spot Mum's mustard-coloured coat: 'See – look, look...'

And there was Dad, standing next to the driver, holding on to the metal rail.

Almost at once the bus, Ian's bright metal dragon, would be upon us, assaulting our noses with dust and diesel, exhaling hot fumes, swishing its doors, tap-tap tapping an idling engine.

Were there any other passengers on that bus? If so, I didn't see them. All I saw was Mum, passing down Claire – we all wanted to be first to take hold of our sister – and Dad, manoeuvring Claire's folding pushchair down the steps.

'Here we are.' A moment of hair-ruffling awkwardness, an outpouring of pent-up emotions, followed by laughter born of relief, with tears and hugs all round. 'Haven't you grown! Come on, Ned, there's no need to cry.'

Suddenly the world was made whole again; we had three hours to be together as a family.

Three hours. But where to go? Certainly not back inside, into the home. A hospital, a prison even, makes provision for receiving visitors. But not Eastry. Official callers, social workers for example, were tolerated; visiting relatives were considered a nuisance. So, without a car, and with little money, choices were limited.

The first time, I remember, Dad led us across the road, into the cornfield opposite. It was late September, harvest time, and the family sat on bales of straw eating Rich Tea biscuits and drinking squash. Andy and I were busy picking blackberries from the hedgerows when a farmer came and chased us off.

Once, and only once, disaster struck; something went wrong. Two o'clock arrived. An East Kent bus, a double-decker, pulled in, and came to a halt. Its doors opened, but Mum and Dad were nowhere to be seen; instead, a straight-faced driver met us. 'Are you getting on or are you just going to stand there gawping?' he asked. 'Well, come on,' he said, lifting his cap, and wiping his brow. 'One of you decide; I haven't got all day.'

'We were waiting,' Andy said.

'For our mum and dad,' Edward added.

Suddenly, a wide smile spread across the driver's face. 'Go on kids, they're upstairs,' he said, breaking into a laugh. 'Top deck. You're off to the seaside. Stick of rock, candy floss, "Kiss me Quick" hats - all the trimmings, I shouldn't wonder,' he called after us as we boys pushed and fought our way up the steps.

And so off we went, flying down the road to Deal, the double-decker swaying from side to side, clattering through overhanging branches and, it seemed from upstairs, just avoiding demolishing three or four garden walls before depositing its passengers, three miles and barely ten minutes later, on the promenade.

'Spot on,' said the driver, as we clambered down the stairs. He wouldn't take the coins Dad tendered for our fares. 'Go on, get the kids an ice-cream on me,' he said, dismissing the gesture with a wave of his hand. I don't know how he would have explained things if an inspector had got on.

Determined to enjoy the time, our first stop was the Wimpy bar (a recent American arrival named after "Wimpy", a hamburger-eating character from the *Popeye* cartoon) where we had a drink of pop.

Next, we headed along the promenade, Claire on her reins, Ian sat atop Dad's shoulders, just another family out for a Sunday afternoon stroll.

Attracted by its red and white awning, Dad bought us ice-creams in an Italian milk bar, a Formica affair complete with bar stools, black and white checkered floor, and hissing coffee machines. Then, with eyes already on the clock, it was off to the beach, where we boys played Canute with the incoming tide, skimmed stones, and sat for a while using Dad as a windbreak.

Afterwards, away from the sea breeze, there was time to explore the narrow, twisting lanes of the old town, where at least half the buildings, it seemed, were conversions, shops dedicated to the sale of holiday paraphernalia: buckets and spades, beach balls and cricket sets, sticks of rock and candy floss.

The last stop of the day was the joke shop, a store I'd visited with the other Almond boys. In there you could get itching powder, stink bombs, plastic dog turds; I tried or traded them all at one time or another. My favourite was the magic chewing gum; I remember buying a pack for a penny or two and giving it to Mark as a birthday present – it turned his teeth black.

That afternoon in Deal was a one off, a special treat, and remembered as such. With little money, visiting time usually found the family mooching about Eastry village.

Our first stop, base camp if you like, was the church. Today, anyone wishing to gain entry to St Mary's "out of hours", must first hunt down the key holder and explain his, or her, purpose. But back then the building was open between services, and on weekdays too. Three of the bells have been restored, and a new heating system installed, otherwise little has changed - permanence and continuity being, I suppose, part of the point.

St Mary's was a sanctuary, particularly during inclement weather. Dad, who'd been a choir boy and bell ringer in his youth, liked to sit for a while in quiet contemplation. Mum, on the other hand, always seemed uncomfortable, acutely aware that the family was sharing the place with others - a flower arranger, perhaps, or a parishioner or two preparing the church for Evensong. Often these volunteers were the same tweedy-turned-out ladies who'd come round during the morning service, offering up a collection plate while the congregation sang *Jerusalem* or *All Things Bright and Beautiful*.

For me, it was important that the family occupied the right space; the Almond pew, where I sat every Sunday morning. I needed Mum and Dad to experience the moment; to drink in the atmosphere, to smell those musty smells, to register the motes of dust floating in the sunlight streaming in through stained-glass windows, to kneel on the same worn purple hassock I'd knelt on, and to have hold of the same hymn and prayer books I'd help pass round just a few hours before. In short, I wanted their senses to be primed with everything needed to access a perfect replay of the same scene on the following Sunday, when I would be here, and they would be somewhere else.

Exiting the church, we would invariably bump into patients from Eastry hospital. The hospital, as I have said, had started life as the Union Workhouse, taking in the destitute, the elderly and the infirm. Renamed in 1948, it continued to fulfil these functions, keeping its inmates away from the public gaze, except on Sundays, when there was something of an exodus.

On Sundays, the whole village, it seemed, was populated by odd characters: arm throwers, stutterers, dribblers, and misfits; people like us.

Had these patients escaped, or were they let out, after being vetted? Maybe they were the trusted ones, allowed to wander down from the hospital for an hour or two of freedom. Or was it simply a case of "out of sight, out of mind" (or vice versa).

One Sunday, walking up from the church, we were approached by a character known, after his association with two large paper sacks, as Bags. 'Hello,' Bags said, with a rising intonation of recognition. Smiling, he raised a battered Panama hat, exposing a prominent nose, open, shiny face, and high forehead. Glancing down, I saw Bag's carriers were padded out with items of clothing, suggesting he had just come from, or was donating to, a jumble sale. It was the same collection he always had about him.

Suddenly, with only a fleeting hesitation, Bags was gone. A slight bow to Mum, and away he went, crossing and re-crossing the High Street, making his own manic, haphazard way, snaking about like a party balloon with the air suddenly released. He visited Bickers the newsagents; he paused, briefly, outside the grocers and the bank; he peered through the window of The Galleon restaurant. One by one he hurried his way to every trading outlet in the village. Then he went back and did it all again.

A glance at his wrist, a few muttered words and Bags was away. What have I forgotten? Is there time to go back to the fishmongers? Maybe, if I hurry, I'll catch the last post?

That was Bags for you. A village regular, he never went in, even when the shops were open for business. Probably the hospital had hold of his money.

Everyone knew Bags. He was part of the scenery and, in common with the other characters from the hospital, at least the ones who made it down to the village, seemed entirely harmless. All he wanted, I think, was to belong, and to be seen to belong. And he might have carried it off, had he not tried so hard. His clothing too gave him away. Put simply, he was just a little *too* smart. The hat, the buttoned blazer, his well-creased trousers, cuff-linked shirts; Bags came across as an army major who'd seen better days, a slightly faded Alan Whicker.

Of course, we Eastry boys had the usual list of disparaging names for Bags; "Spastic", "Nutter", "Loony", among them. But we were only going through the motions. Bags, we knew, posed no threat; indeed, his perambulations were part of village life, his regular appearances, like those of the postman or milkman, somehow reassuring, so that in a strange, contradictory way, he really did come to belong.

Another odd character, at the other end of the spectrum, was Snowball. Snowball had developed his own way of coping, of getting through the day. Not for him the careful study, the mimicking of others' conduct. Where Bags was an observer, trying to blend in, Snowball was a loner. He'd turned his back on the village and taken on his own challenge, left alone to cook his breakfast. Over a drain.

'Fry you bastards, fry!' Snowball's regular pitch was just along from the bakery; he was there most Sundays, a tramp-like character sporting a balding head and a straggly white beard, sitting at the side of the road, licking his lips in anticipation of a meal which never came. He was loud too, and full of encouragement. 'Come on, me lovelies,' he'd say, addressing his invisible egg, bacon, or sausages. 'That's right. Sizzle for me, sizzle.'

Snowball's frying pan was real enough, as was his sense of frustration. Sometimes, tired of waiting for his full English, he'd take to banging his pan on the drain grill. His language deteriorated too, the volume level competing with the clang of metal on metal to the point where he began to attract an audience. Most people, spotting him in time, chose to cross the road. Better safe than sorry.

*

Not everyone from the hospital was as flamboyant as Snowball or Bags; some had simply suffered the misfortune of growing old, while others, disabled, were likewise unable to live independently. Sometimes, tumbling out of the church, we came across little knots of these inmates, mostly wheelchair-bound Great War veterans, wearing their medals, parked up next to Eastry Court and the village green. It was a sad sight.

Looking back, through the soft lens of time, the scene arouses powerful emotions – images of old soldiers sitting in quiet contemplation; groups of volunteers and conscripts soaking up the afternoon sun, while just yards behind them, looming above the churchyard wall, a cruciform war memorial broadcast the names of old friends and comrades, pals who didn't come home.

What did these watery-eyed warriors think of it all now, forty or more years on? How did they spend their days? Were their heads filled with the sounds of the guns, still booming out from across the Channel; had the war left them haunted by memories of mud and machine gun fire, barbed wire, and mustard gas?

We Eastry boys used the war memorial to do step ups and play tag, little thinking about the names chiselled on the stone before us; how they commemorated real people, local men who'd worked the land and farms, before marching away to die in the fields of Flanders and France.

I wish, now, that I'd been a little older; I should have liked to have known these old soldiers, to have a privileged opportunity to hear, and record, their accounts of Mons, Ypres, and the Somme. I was walking through history; the leaves were falling, and they didn't register.

*

Leaving St Mary's behind, the family's next Sunday stop was the junior school. Here, on the other side of the gate and playground, Edward, Andy, and I would scrabble for the best position, noses pushed up against finger-smeared windows, each of us scouring the walls and tables for examples of his own, individual genius.

'Look at my map of Australia, Dad. I did that. All by myself. And it's drawn, not traced. I got nine out of ten for that, I did. Can you see it, Dad? Mark only got eight.'

Then Andy would join in. 'Well, my graph was the neatest in the class. I got a gold star. And that's my certificate for running, the one I told you about in my letter, Mum. Remember?'

One Sunday, absorbed in these competitive observations, we were surprised by Mr.

Ovenden, the school caretaker, coming in for a weekend boiler inspection. 'What's wrong with you boys, five days of schooling a week not enough?' he asked, walking on. 'I was just showing off my work,' I called after him. 'And so was I,' Edward said, aware that technically at least, the family were trespassing. 'Mum and Dad can't come any other time, they live too far away.'

Nothing more was said, but within a week my classroom, and that of the fourth form were re-arranged, their display boards repositioned, nature tables moved, and a variety of pictures and diagrams stuck onto the windows, their contents, and pupil achievements, easily visible from the outside. A word in the right ear, and Mum and Dad had their Sunday open day.

After the school, there were two or three options. One route retraced the steps the hospital inmates took, up to Mill Lane, past the old workhouse to the village windmill, the last of four, still, then, in working order.

Another walk took us along the road we junior schoolboys followed every day, to the infant's school at Cook's Lea, where Malcolm was in the reception class, and where we had our dinners.

Returning along the High Street, we passed the Premier garage, Bickers the newsagent, just about everywhere closed. Then came the two pubs - The Bull and the Five Bells. "Free House", said the sign. But there wasn't one.

Our last stop, always, was the West End Café, where we boys were treated to a soft drink, with whispered instructions not to gulp, and to make it last.

The café was a popular gathering place for the local biker community. Outside, in dry weather, groups of these motorcyclists sat round a square of picnic tables, drinking 7UP or Coke, jealously guarding their machines, parked up next to them. Careful weaving and dodging got the pedestrian visitor to the café entrance. It wasn't ideal, but it was the only place open.

Once inside, more bikers waited, lounging about a cluster of blue Formica-topped tables. Our place, when vacant, was to one side of the long counter, round the corner, out of sight, though not out of earshot.

Always inquisitive, I tried to get as close to the bikers as I could, listening carefully to what was being said, especially when it came to discussions of the relative merits of their machines, mainly Triumphs and BSAs, from what I can recall.

There was talk too of motorcycle scrambling, something remembered from Gran's house on a Saturday afternoon. I knew all the bikes; the Matchless, the Greaves, and the riders too. What could be more exciting than watching Vic Eastwood, splattered in mud, coming up the slope towards the front of a TV screen, leaping the ridges and ruts before falling back to earth, foot down, taking a sharp right, disappearing out of camera shot.

And all this accompanied by the magical voice of Murray Walker: 'He's passing Horsefield and, oh my word…Yes, would you believe it, he's lapping Badger Goss!' Murray's commentary was infectious. You could almost smell the Castrol and Swarfega.

Dad wasn't keen on the bikers – "greasers" he called them, the sort who went over to Margate or Brighton at weekends, fighting on the beaches with groups of "Mods". For my part, I was envious of their freedom and just wanted to get a better look at their machines. I liked watching them mount up and disappear down the road, engines roaring, throttles open, the sun glinting off a chrome exhaust, only to return exhilarated and laughing ten minutes or so later. And I can well remember the girls, with their leathers, white helmets, and goggles, climbing out of sidecars, breathless after going for a spin.

Never judge a book by its cover. One Sunday, a biker walked over to our table and introduced himself. 'I'm Roy,' he said. 'Like Roy Orbison.'

Laughing, Roy pulled out a pair of dark glasses. 'See?' A quick snatch of *Only the Lonely* and the ice was well and truly broken.

'Watch this,' he said, 'it's magic.' From inside an upturned helmet, Roy produced a white silk scarf which, peeled back, revealed a tiny tortoise-shell kitten. 'I nearly ran over him,' Roy explained. 'He was sitting in the middle of the road. Like a rabbit in the headlights, he was.

'You can hold him if you like. But be careful.'

'He likes you,' said Jim, another of the bikers, as I clutched the shivering kitten to my chest. 'Of course, he'll need a home...would you like to keep him?'

I looked over at Dad, who coughed.

'We haven't got a home,' Edward said. 'We're in care; pets aren't allowed.'

There, our secret was out. The cat was quite literally out of the bag. I could feel my face turn red and my stomach turn over. I handed the kitten back.

'Not to worry,' Roy said, breaking an awkward silence. 'I tell you what, who wants another drink? Or an ice-lolly. How about it, ice-lollies all round?'

Dad said it was okay. and Mum nodded, so we each had a treat and, afterwards, took turns taking the kitten round the other tables.

Eventually, a biker girl named Shirley claimed the cat for her own. 'It's a boy, I'm almost sure,' she said, giving the bundle of fur the once over. 'What shall I name him? Top Cat? Felix?' She paused. 'I know, I'll call him Taxi. Then when I go to call him in at night...'

After this incident with Taxi the cat, Roy and his mates became a regular part of our Sunday lives, standing drinks and handing out coins for the juke box, encouraging us to choose our favourite songs. I remember listening to the Searchers telling us not to throw our love away, Jonathan King informing a deserted planet that everyone had gone to the moon and, closer to home, the Beatles promoting a ticket to ride (I looked it up, and decided, wrongly as it turned out, that they were referring to a town on the Isle of Wight).

Gene Pitney's *Twenty-Four Hours from Tulsa* was even more of a challenge. Where exactly was Gene when he met that woman, the one he danced with, the one who prevented him from ever going home again? How far could you drive in twenty-four hours? I wished he'd been more specific. It worried me and still does.

The last song, the final sixpence in the juke box, signalled the end of our Sunday afternoon. All too soon it was time to leave the warm café confines and make our way back to Auntie and the home.

We tried to drag things out of course, each of us sucking on empty straws, insisting we hadn't quite finished our drinks, betrayed by the sound of bubbling air. Can't we wait until the end of this song? Don't you want another cup of tea, Mum?

But it was no good. Mum and Dad had to get the last Canterbury bus, which left the village at 5.30 p.m.

*

Saying goodbye, watching Mum and Dad as they walked away was hard, and never got any easier. But it had to be done – Mum and Dad had to go, and we had to stay.

Edward and Ian were the first to be dropped off, at the top of the drive, in front of Thorn. There were hugs and tears, and most times Ian and Mum had to be physically separated, pulled apart. It was Malling and Newington all over again.

'Hush up,' Dad would say. 'You'll have Auntie Harris out here in a minute.'

And then, as if summoned, Auntie would appear, a dark shadow framed in the light of a half-opened door. 'Now, now, what's all this?' Then came the inevitable struggle. It was a pathetic sight; Mum pulling one way, and Auntie Harris the other, with Ian in the middle, like a wishbone or Christmas cracker. It was no good of course, the prize always went to Auntie. 'Gotcha' she'd say, and Ian would be carried, kicking and screaming into the house.

Then it was Edward's turn. 'Come along, Edward,' Auntie would call, as he ran back for one last kiss. 'Don't cry, Mum. I'll look after him, I promise.' And he did.

Next came Andy and Malcolm. Andy had his own delaying tactics, making Auntie Fitzgerald wait while he went inside to fetch a painting or drawing from school, or a letter he'd written earlier in the week. 'If I give it to you now, Mum, you can read it on the bus, and it won't need a stamp.'

But the separation was too much for Malcolm. Most weeks he would turn away and go indoors without so much as a murmur, or a backward glance. For Mum this was especially hard. 'Don't I get a cuddle, then?' But it was too late; Malcolm had vanished.

With me it was different. I was last to be left because Almond was nearest the main gate, and because I lived on my own.

One Sunday, after we arrived back early (it had rained all afternoon) Auntie invited Mum and Dad in for a cup of tea. Mum was hesitant, but Auntie insisted. 'I don't bite,' she said, extending her hand in welcome. Under the circumstances, Mum could hardly refuse.

This kind, considerate side of Auntie was one I'd never seen before, and I was instantly on my guard.

'Oh, dear, you *are* wet. Come along, Douglas, hang up Mum's coat. We mustn't forget our manners now.'

So, I took Mum's coat, and Dad's and Claire's, while Auntie ushered them into the staff room. I entered the study to find Auntie sitting on the sofa, with Claire on her knee, Mum and Dad being relegated to the two armchairs opposite. Auntie smiled, patted a cushion, and put me in my place, at her side.

It was all a Sunday charade, of course, but the invitation soon became a regular thing. Auntie was insistent; Mum and Dad mustn't leave without a cup of tea and a slice of cake; besides half an hour in Almond gave them a chance to catch up with my progress. Auntie was stealing my time, and she knew it.

Begin as it may - with talk of the weather, the bus journey, and so on - slowly, slyly, Auntie would turn the conversation; her purpose, barely disguised, being to highlight the positive influence she was having on my development, an effort which, almost by default, contrasted starkly with Mum and Dad's lack of input, and poor parenting skills. And she didn't hold back. It would be "my Duggie" this and "my Duggie" that; improved punctuality, good manners, personal hygiene; incredibly, it seemed I could do no wrong.

One Sunday, Auntie produced a series of school photographs. 'Doesn't Duggie look smart,' she said. Would Mum like a copy? 'Yes, please,' came the ever-so grateful reply. 'Well, I'll cut out one of the four pictures, but I need to keep the others; for my records, you understand.'

Later, at the end of term, Auntie showed off my school report. 'Duggie's done so well,' she said. 'Just look at his marks for composition and sums.'

Auntie was more than happy for Mum and Dad to study the evidence, insinuating that it was she who deserved credit for my academic achievements. 'I'll have to ask the school if you can have a copy,' she said, placing the report sheet back in my file.

Listening to Auntie sing my praises made me wince. "Duggie?" Where did that come from? No one called me Duggie; it was always Doug, or the more formal Douglas. Perhaps Auntie was talking about someone else? She wasn't, of course, but it sometimes felt that way. I found myself discussed as though I wasn't in the room, or was invisible, or mute.

The worst thing about it was sitting on the sofa being petted and stroked. That proximity afforded Auntie the freedom, which, try as I may, I was unable to deny, to behave as she liked. An arm resting on my shoulder or snaking its way round my waist; a podgy hand squeezing my bare knee, the cold warmth of stale breath on my cheek, Auntie's very body threatening to melt into mine.

My impulse, always, was to move; to get up and cross the divide to where Mum and Dad had sat, to pick up and take Claire with me, to be where I belonged, with my family. Instead, I sat there frozen and helpless, immobilized by Auntie's casual ownership, hating myself for the hold she had over me.

Rising to leave, I'd watch as Auntie swept Claire up into her arms, smothering her in kisses; looked on as Auntie laughed and shrugged off Mum's apology for the upturned knitting basket and thrown cushions; swallowed hard as Auntie offered Claire a toffee from the sweet tin, the same tin she proffered on change-over nights, for those who'd kept their underwear clean. It was a strange juxtaposition.

Should I have spoken out? Who would have listened if I had? Mum and Dad would have been devastated if they'd known the truth. Eastry wasn't a boarding school; unhappy parents couldn't just take their offspring away. And, in any case, staff, as I was often reminded, were my benefactors; without them I'd be homeless, out on the streets. It cost money to run the home; hard working people paid their taxes to provide me with a roof over my head. Mum and Dad had given me up; I owed Auntie a debt of gratitude. Punishment or discipline was for my own good. I had rebellion in my heart, I deserved everything I got. So better keep quiet, bottle it all up, internalize the injustice. But not to forget. Never forget.

*

It was winter, always winter, when the East Kent bus came to take Mum and Dad away. My brothers had said their goodbyes, now it was my turn. Mum, prompted, promised to write as soon as she got home; I had a last chance to kiss my sister. Meanwhile, Dad collapsed Claire's pushchair in readiness - there was only one Sunday evening connection from Canterbury to Maidstone; miss it and they would be stranded.

Things happened quickly now – a snatched hug; a final, forlorn wave; the door opening, the door closing. Gone.

Ten minutes later I was back in Almond, joining my housemates in the Day Room. Little was said, the other boys seeming to sense that I needed my own space, a time to grieve, my sorrow, I'm sure, a shared sorrow.

Taking a cushion, I'd move off to one side of the sofa and stretch out, stomach flat to the floor, head cradled in my hands, opposite the TV screen. Then, with my face all but invisible, I'd cry quiet tears of sadness and frustration. Every minute, every passing second took Mum and Dad further away, and I was unable to do anything about it. All I could do was lie there, with gritted teeth and nails pressed into my palms, waiting for bedtime.

CHAPTER TEN

Auntie Joyce wrote in one of her reports that I seemed "jealous" of my sister. And on one level she was right. Claire lived at home, why couldn't I? Why was I banished here, to Eastry? When would I get out? When would the family be re-united?

I asked at the end of every Sunday visit, and Mum and Dad, humbled, did their best to answer; they *were* trying, but the place they rented wasn't suitable, or big enough, for a large family. Many years later, well into adulthood, I learned the truth: Mum and Dad had survived our Eastry years living in a cramped bedsit, sharing a kitchen and bathroom with five or six others, battling mildewed walls and constantly on the alert for stolen food and, on more than one occasion, smashed locks, and raids on their electricity meter. Claire slept on the floor.

So, I couldn't go home. There was no home, not in any real sense. And if I couldn't leave, how best to escape the deadening control of Almond and Eastry, the intrusive presence of Auntie and Uncle?

Sunday visits aside, journeys out of the home were limited. There were shopping trips, and sports matches, but mostly the world came to us.

Regular callers were the doctor and dentist, while other individuals, more welcome, included Mr. Stroud, the mobile tuck shop man, Mr. Hugget with his travelling cinema show, and Mrs. Betts from the Post Office, charged with encouraging Eastry's children to be steady savers. HM Inspector of Homes came once a year, the police more often.

The least welcome of these visitors was the dentist. The county council had invested in three mobile dental clinics – so novel that they were featured, as a double page spread, including a cut-away, in the *Victor* comic - each one pulled by a three and a half ton Austin "mechanical horse", with a legal speed limit of just 20 mph.

The detachable part of this massive combination formed the surgery; it held everything needed – a raised waiting area, a recovery bed and all the tools and equipment needed to achieve the necessary care or repair. Fortunately, there was also an X-ray machine. The idea was to bring the service to the more rural parts of the county, including schools and, of course, care homes.

Watching the dental lorry park up outside the "Rec" was always a heart-sinking experience. From inside the guts of the machine a winch released a series of heavy-duty cables. Like tentacles emanating from an alien spaceship, they spread out, seeking a power supply, the juice needed both to power the invader, and to drill into its victims' mouths. In no time at all the surgery was ready. And waiting.

Children went up to the surgery two by two, one patient directed to the waiting area, the other to the chair. A quick word of reassurance and, as if from nowhere, a rubber mask appeared, placed over your nose and mouth. 'Can you count down from ten for me?'

It was the stuff of nightmares – the smell of rubber and gas sending you off into a world of frightening dreams. Afterwards came the drift back into consciousness, the taste, a repulsive amalgam of bleeding gums and nausea, causing uncontrollable bouts of vomiting. It wasn't unusual for a patient to tumble out of the dental cabin, woozy from the gas and the effects of three or four extractions, staggering home, the air echoing with cleaning advice from a dental assistant: "Twice a day to avoid decay", was the slogan. But no one said we should stop eating sweets. So, we didn't.

The mobile tuck shop, an old battered, converted ambulance, came to the home on Thursday evening, arriving at the sound of three long blasts on the horn. Parked up midway along the drive, Mr. Stroud, a small, grey-bearded man with podgy hands and beady eyes, welcomed us, his young customers, with open arms, and did good business.

The older girls went up first, climbing into the van one at a time – with staff on hand to keep a careful eye - then the boys would walk down the drive and form a queue.

With forty or so children waiting, it must, I think, have been quite a challenge for Mr. Stroud to get his patrons in and out of his van as quickly as possible, while doing his best to relieve each child of his or her sixpence, the home-imposed spending limit.

'Got yer money?' A nod in the affirmative, and Mr. Stroud would tear a string-tied paper bag from a nearby hook and, holding it open, follow you up and down, pressuring you to make a choice. Creatures of habit, most of us boys had made up our minds in advance. Spangles, Flying Saucers, and Sherbet Dips were popular, while a handful of Black Jacks or Fruit Salad chews helped make up the difference, filling the bag.

Six shelves, three on either side, ran down the length of the van, Mr. Stroud's stock replacing the platforms originally designed for patients on stretchers, racks where the sick and injured had once rested. Two of the higher shelves held lidded jars of boiled sweets; Aniseed Twist, Rhubarb and Custard and Sherbet Lemons among them. Boiled sweets needed weighing, which gave the customer a second or two to look round and decide what else to have, while Mr. Stroud shovelled their earlier choice into the bag. Hesitate, and Mr. Stroud, fidgeting, would begin doing his own random selections on your behalf. 'How about bubble gum, or a gobstopper or two? Or a Lucky Bag. Why not have a Lucky Bag? You've still got tuppence...'

It was tempting, the Lucky Bag. At 2d a go, its distributers claimed it was a bargain, a "prize packet" guaranteed to include a "good" novelty gift, along with a choice of sweets. In truth, neither the Lucky Bag, nor its counterpart, the Jamboree Bag, lived up to expectations. Half a dozen Love Hearts, or Dolly Mixture, and a penny chew, perhaps. As for the gift, well the novelty was always something cheap and nasty – a plastic paper clip, a ring or a jumping frog, the sort of thing you'd find in a Christmas cracker. Yet, as the manufacturers well knew, few children could resist for long. It was a gamble, but eventually something worth having must turn up, surely? It never did.

In Almond, I was always one of the first in line, waiting outside Auntie's office from shortly after supper to get my spending allowance. And as I waited my mouth began to salivate. The sweet smell and taste of all those goodies - toffees, candy sticks and the rest; all it took was a toot on the tuck shop horn. It was addictive; I could feel the aniseed on my tongue, the sherbet fizzing in my throat. Closing my eyes, I was already climbing up into the van.

It was an anxious time, queuing like that. The doling out of pocket money, you see, couldn't be taken for granted. Occasionally, Auntie did the sleep-in shift next door in Willow; other times she'd take the evening off. Some part-time staff were reluctant to manage money, claiming they lacked authority; others didn't have access to a key for the cash box. If that happened, we would go without.

When she was in residence, it was Auntie who greeted us, one at a time, on the other side of the study door. Well prepared, she'd have twelve A6 lined books set out on her desk, each one containing detail of individual income and savings.

Pocket money varied according to age. The older junior boys, aged eleven, received three shillings a week, if I remember rightly. I was given two and six (written 2/6) and had to sign each time I received money from the cash box.

Of course, it was never that simple. Pocket money might be reduced or, on occasion, withheld altogether. I once went without funds for a whole month; my allowance, Auntie said, going towards the cost of replacing a broken window in the "Rec". It was Cub night and, Akala being late, we had started an impromptu game of five-a-side football. I was found clearing up a heap of shards of glass from a broken window and, after putting the incident down to Akala's tardiness, summarily dismissed.

I didn't mind that much. I'd already been banned for a week for cheating at the wheelbarrow race and, besides, my badge collection was minimal; I struggled with all those knots and could never quite get my woggle right.

A popular Almond visitor was Mrs. Betts, the "savings lady", who did her rounds on Monday evenings, after she'd closed the Post Office.

All of us boys were encouraged to save and having a sticky stamp stuck on a card in exchange for sixpence was very satisfying, especially when, like Mark and I, you had a secret plan for a better future.

Mrs. Betts was well organised, and this was reflected both in her apparel – twin set, pearls, and comfortable court shoes – and the methodical way she went about her business. Sitting down at the Day Room table, she'd surround herself with the tools of her trade; a pad of forms in triplicate; a cash box, stamp, and ink pads, blotting paper and more, all set out in apple pie order. Not a pen or pencil was out of place. When, and only when, things were exactly right would her customers come in, one at a time, to hand over their savings.

I bought my postage stamps from Mrs. Betts. Sixpence allowed me to write home twice.

The weather here is fine. How is it with you? How is Claire? Did you find her reins? Our team played Eythorne this week and Andy scored. But I suppose he has told you about that himself.

Then came a "thank you" for my comics and requests for more writing paper and envelopes, along with pleas for the used stamps needed to complete a set or collection.

Mrs. Betts has given me a Messerschmitt and the 2/6d Air Battle over St Paul's Cathedral, but I'm still missing the Spitfire. Please, please can you find one for your next parcel? Also, I need some more hinges. Must go now. Looking forward to seeing you on Sunday. PS: I swapped the Stanley Gibbons stamps for a Post Office Tower set.

Mrs. Betts, I found, was someone a boy could confide in. Yes, she came across as very formal. But this was just her workaday pose. Post Office business was important business, but once that was out of the way, Mrs. Betts let her hair down; she was available to chat, expressing a genuine interest in what we boys had been doing during the week. When I confessed that I'd been dismissed from the Cubs, she was disappointed, praising me for the work I'd done in her garden during Bob-a-Job week. 'I had you marked down for a future Sixer or Seconder,' she said, eyebrows raised.

I was disappointed too, but only about Bob-a-Job week. Those few days of freedom during the school holidays meant time away from the home, new experiences, new environments, real people, living real lives in their own homes.

Given the choice, I worked with Mark, going from house to house, competing with our fellow Cubs to see which pair could earn the most for our troop. Shopping was a regular request, as was dog walking. But a good Cub Scout is always prepared.

One or two of our "clients" I remember well. Take Mr. Potts, for example. Long retired, he was keen to talk about the village, and the home. Mr. Potts had lived in Eastry all his life, and knew Mr. Adams, the old "Super", as a friend. Mark and I spent a good hour or so with him, listening as he flitted from topic to topic, sitting in rapt silence as he talked about South Africa, where his son, a mining engineer, had settled after the war.

Finally, concerned about the time, and following hints, Mr. Potts delegated to us the task of cleaning out his budgie's cage, Polly being given the freedom of the front room while we filled a water bottle and tore up old newspapers for the floor of her enclosure.

Mr. Potts was particularly generous; as well as slipping a shilling into the Bob-a-Job envelope, he gave me some South African stamps and both of us, Mark, and I, three pence to spend on sweets. 'Keep that to yourselves,' he winked, waving us down his garden path.

On the other side of the village lived Mrs. Rowley. Mrs. B had signposted Mrs. Rowley, a friend, as a worthy cause, asking us to go along and help with her back garden.

An elderly welcoming lady, full of regret that age prevented her from doing as much as she'd like, and bemoaning the absence of her regular gardener, Mrs. Rowley led the two of us through her house to a rear courtyard. Here, on paving stones sprouting weeds and forget-me-nots, stood pots of trailing nasturtiums and geraniums, the narrow pathway leading us to a flight of three or four steps. 'Up there,' Mrs. Rowley gestured, showing that this was the limit of her mobility.

Our task was simple: take a fork and clippers from the shed and clear as much as we could in an hour. We did our best, but it wasn't easy - the rusting wheelbarrow, with a flat front tyre and a mind of its own, refused to cooperate - and there was still much left to do when Mrs. Rowley called us in for lunch. Sitting in her kitchen, Mark and I were treated to ham and chips, followed by a sweet, familiar dessert. Gypsy Tart, made with evaporated milk, muscovado sugar and pastry, was a local Kentish delicacy. Back then it was associated with school dinners. Today you can buy a version of it in Sainsburys.

The council library van visited the home once a month; for me, its arrival was as welcome, and as eagerly awaited, as the first swallow of spring. I was an avid reader, as both my school reports and Eastry records testify. The only problem was finding a place and the privacy in which to indulge my habit. Mostly I read by torchlight, under the bed sheets or, during the summer months, sitting in the yard, propped up against a pig bin. By the age of ten I'd tackled a shelf full of children's classics: *Robinson Crusoe*, *Treasure Island* and *Gulliver's Travels* (an illustrated, abridged version) among them. Then the library man suggested *Kidnapped*, and I was away again, stepping into a world of heroes and villains, storms and shipwrecks, orphans, and inheritances. And a happy ending.

Custodianship of a book was a real joy. I loved the weight, the feel of the paper, the knowledge that here, on trust, I had a means of escape; I could sit down, open my latest acquisition and, within a page or two, be transported, travelling somewhere new, somewhere exotic, and far, far away.

Not even Auntie would scold a boy for reading, although on one occasion, I remember her taking the time to warn me about the dangers of getting above myself. 'All that book learning will get you nowhere,' she said, confiscating my copy of *Animal Farm*. Icarus flying too close to the sun.

My only regret was that I was allowed to take out just two library books at a time. I would have liked four or five.

A short, blue-bearded man, Mr. Hugget came to show films in the "Rec" every other Saturday. There was a nominal 1d (penny) entry charge, but viewing was free for volunteers prepared to help set up the projectors and screen and stack away the chairs afterwards. Mark and I made sure we were among the first to arrive. Edward and Andy came along too, joining a crowd sitting down to watch a choice of war films - *The Dambusters*, *Sink the Bismarck!* or *Dunkirk*. Many of these black and white classics returned time after time; we hummed the theme tunes, lived every scene, knew what was coming next, and could – and did – repeat the scripts verbatim – usually banging our feet on the wooden floor at the same time, in rhythmic appreciation.

Every so often Mr. Hugget would bring along an offering of his own, footage taken while holidaying in Brighton or Eastbourne, popular watering places. Either that or it was a clip of a severe-looking Mrs. Hugget pruning roses in the back garden. Such was the price we had to pay for the privilege of watching the main feature.

Then one week, and quite unexpectedly, Mr. Hugget introduced an offering from Spain which, running commentary aside, quickly became an audience favourite. The setting was Malaga, where the Huggets had gone for their first overseas holiday.

The film began tamely enough, if a little shakily - shots of Mrs. Hugget enjoying a continental breakfast, followed by panoramic views of Malaga with its port and harbour and a day out with a picnic to a pile of ruins. Then came the bullfight.

And what a contrast! Suddenly, with barely a blink of the eye, the audience was transported. Now, in a scene of Kodak-captured blood and gore, we watched in open mouthed silence as a gaudily dressed matador dispatched a bull with a swirl of a cape, his short sword plunged into a forfeited body.

Next into the ring came a mounted picador; it was a picador's job, Mr. Hugget interrupted, to attack the bull with a spear, before making way for a bullfighter, who, once again, taunted the animal before delivering the fatal blow.

'But just watch this,' said Mr. Hugget. To our collective, spellbound delight another bull held its ground, pawing the sand, refusing to play along. Then the picador began to show off – 'playing silly buggers' was how Mr. Hugget put it – and the scene ended with the rider being thrown from his horse, which had been badly gored.

With the horse and bull in a stand-off, and the picador receiving medical attention, a small army of colourfully dressed attendants entered the ring, raking blood into the sand and stuffing the horse's insides back into its body, using wads of straw. Nobody would ever know how the horse felt since, according to Mr. Hugget, the Spaniards cut their horses' vocal cords.

Meanwhile, the matador stood to one side and the crowd, mainly tourists, entertained itself by throwing flowers and engaging in something resembling a Mexican wave. It was 1964, and the package holiday had arrived.

*

The times were changing, and society was changing with them. But for us in Eastry change came slowly, if at all. The care system's lack of ambition for its charges can be illustrated by the leisure time activities we were offered, almost all of which involved physical exercise, considered "character building". There was cross-country running, football, and rugby, and, for the older boys, boxing, and Judo, with a cold shower to follow.

A warm weather game, as shown by Uncle Ken's photographs, was the "water challenge". Four oil drums were set up, two in front of the trees which bordered the road into the village and two in the yard separating Almond and Willow. The containers nearest the cottages were filled with water and two teams of boys competed to transfer the water from here to the receptacles furthest away, using pots, pans, buckets; basically, any container they could get hold of. Improvisation was the name of the game, and this included pushing and shoving; all efforts to prevent your opponents from emptying their water containers being considered legitimate. Most, if not all, of the competitors ended up soaking wet and stripped to their underpants. Some boys, Edward included, ended the day naked. It was all part of the fun.

One way of escaping all this, to get out of the home and experience a change of scene, was to volunteer to help Uncle Bob, who held the keys to the Dormobile. Dover, Deal or Sandwich, where staff went to pick up supplies, were regular destinations.

One trip, which I remember well, was a December run out to Deal. It was 1964 and Bob took boys from Thorn and Almond Christmas shopping.

A wet and windy day, with darkness already descending, a ten-minute drive was followed by nearly half-an-hour trapped in the Dormobile, parked up on the seafront, waiting for the weather to relent. We sat scrawling on misty windows, watching the rain slanting down, pestering Bob for permission to get out and go.

Waiting was frustrating beyond measure. We, all of us, wanted to be out in the town, spending our savings; instead, there was nothing for it but to sit and count seagulls or gaze in the direction of the beach, studying a spread of upturned boats strewn across the shelving shoreline – *Sunny Jim, Hazy Jane, Summer Breeze* - August names oddly incongruous in December.

Having exhausted all other possibilities, we captives kept ourselves amused by singing the latest pop songs, including, with deliberate irony, *Summer Holiday.*

After what seemed like an eternity, and giving up on a change in the weather, Bob finally relented. 'Wait for it, wait for it,' he said, sliding open the side-panel door. 'Off you go, then.'

Climbing out of the van, one or two of the boys, by habit perhaps, made for the beach, the idea being to reach the shelter of the breakwaters. But those diehards who set out in that direction were at once beaten back by the wind. So, regrouping, we put our collective heads down and, raincoat collars turned up, made a hunched-back sprint towards the town centre, and Woolworths. There, while Uncle Bob looked for Christmas gifts, we boys steamed our way up and down the aisles, admiring the tinsel decorations, gazing longingly at the Airfix models, and surreptitiously helping ourselves to sweets from the Pick and Mix stand.

A final, favourite destination was the record department. Here, drawn by the sound of music, you could flick your way through the complete Hit Parade; pick up and handle, with awe and reverence, any tune from the Top Forty, 45s arranged in chart order, seven-inch vinyl copies of the songs which formed the soundtrack of our young lives.

And, on top of this, Woolworths provided a booth where you could listen to your favourites, with no obligation. I picked up the Supremes' "Baby Love", considered getting the Beatles' "I feel Fine" (it had sold out) then settled on the record I'd gone in for; Petula Clark's "Downtown". Its label was pink, the colour of Pye records, and I bought it for Mum. For Dad I chose a set of monogrammed handkerchiefs. And that was my Christmas pocket money gone.

More organized trips out, summertime activities in the main, always came with a military flavour, priority given to boys coming up to school leaving age, the majority of whom had already spent years being prepared, in one way or another, for a life in the forces. Sea Cadets, Boys Brigade members and Scouts were all expected to attend, with spare seats being offered to us junior boys.

One of the highlights was the Royal Tournament at Earl's Court in July, remembered now for its gun crew races, an arena piled high with sawdust, and the pungent smell of metal polish, cordite, and horse dung.

Not long afterwards, in September, came Chatham Navy Day and a chance to explore a fleet of Her Majesty's minesweepers, frigates and destroyers. This was firsthand stuff, and we were encouraged to go fully equipped. One or two of the older boys had cameras, and Uncle Ken came armed with his Brownie 127; others chose to record the ships – F231, D47 – in notebooks brought along for that very purpose. I can't, now, imagine why.

The dockyards covered a huge area. Looking back, I remember the impressive, gilded gates, the sprawl of Georgian and Victorian brick-built admiralty buildings, open for public viewing. Wandering about in our separate groups, I found myself standing in front of an anchor which, it seemed to me, a giant would struggle to tackle. Uncle Ken, appearing from behind, told me to stand still, then took a picture.

Close by, dating from the age of sail, a bare-breasted, gaudily coloured wooden figurehead exuded an eloquent, Sphinx-like air of mystery, her enigmatic smile providing a powerful magnet for a young boy's imagination.

The sights this weathered mermaid had seen crossing the world's oceans! And the stories she could tell. Tales of pirates and pirate treasure; Atlantic icebergs; whales and whaling ships, shipwrecks, and storms in the southern oceans. Perhaps she'd sailed to Africa, taking slaves to be traded for West Indian rum and sugar. Or maybe she had been with Nelson at Trafalgar, ploughing the waves at the bow of a man of war. I stood in front of her transfixed, my reverie broken only when Uncle Ken, having moved on, came back to get me. 'Away with the bloody fairies again,' was his comment.

And there was more, much more, a whole day's worth, in fact. There were dry docks, massive cranes, capstans as big as giant toadstools, cables thicker than Mrs. B's waist (a ship-of-the-line, I learned, carried more than thirty miles of rope, twelve for the rigging alone).

And the smell! I have only to close my eyes and say the word Chatham and I'm back there again, nostrils filled with the whiff of hemp and tar, paint, engine oil and gun metal, air borne evidence of centuries of British naval supremacy.

And I remember, too, the oily smells of a yellow naval helicopter, parked up, with its rotor blades folded back. It had settled, wasp-like, outside a temporary recruiting office, attracting would-be sailors like jam to a pot.

This is where our day ended, waiting about while the older boys, lured in by posters, leaflets, and the Siren-sound of a bosun's whistle, went in to ask about "signing on".

Before that, and last port of call, came the submarine *Ocelot*. There was quite a queue. Welcomed aboard by a squad of young ratings, our group was invited down to the mess, where a life at sea was extolled over biscuits and a mug of squash.

The *Ocelot*, we were told, was an *Oberon* class diesel-electric submarine (the smell of diesel was all pervasive) and virtually brand new, having been launched in 1962.

What was life onboard like for her crew? Basically, it was good; crowded, yes, but all sixty-nine sailors were volunteers and, we were told, there was a tremendous camaraderie. Away from port, boasted one young submariner, the men could wear casual clothes, a tot of rum was served in the evenings, and everything was done to make the crew feel comfortable. 'We've been everywhere, all around the world,' the rating confided. What he didn't tell us – to have done so would have probably breached the Official Secrets Act - was that the *Ocelot*, a surveillance vessel, spent much of its time submerged, its mission to undertake weapons testing in the deep waters of the world's oceans.

Once at sea, the ratings had no idea where they were, only that they had a duty to outwit the west's cold war bogeymen, the

Russians. For the *Ocelot* to surface was to risk giving her position away, so communication with home was impossible - no post, no telephone calls, no telegrams. Noise levels and lighting were kept to a minimum, food was eaten out of tins, and cramped hammocks had to be shared; one man climbing out quite literally rubbing shoulders with a shipmate crawling in.

Ironically, none of these inconveniences would have dented the older Eastry boys' enthusiasm, even if they had been mentioned. Indeed, confessions of deprivation and risk would, I'm sure, simply have added a touch of glamour to their imagined adventures. I too enjoyed the tour, especially the chance to inspect the vessel's torpedo tubes, the radar and the rest of its electronic tracking equipment, and to take my turn hunting imaginary battleships through the ship's periscope. But the Senior Service, I decided, was not for me. The navy meant learning to swim. And I hadn't forgotten Uncle Ken and the Dover swimming pool.

*

Everyone who was in Eastry in 1964 will remember Auntie Carol. With her brightly coloured clothes and blonde hair, cut in the latest geometric style, Carol, a small, feisty, outspoken girl of about eighteen or nineteen, was a natural for the androgynous look, the shape of things to come. None of us had ever seen anything like it.

Auntie Joyce hadn't seen anything like it, either. She took Carol in hand from day one, instructing her to cover herself up, and dress appropriately.

Arriving at work – dropped off by her mother, who drove an old Austin Seven, or on the back of her boyfriend's scooter – Carol would go straight to the staff room, where she deposited her vanity bag and made the required changes to her clothing and make-up. Basically, she went in as a Mod, and came out as a support worker, removing her jewellery, putting on a pair of sensible shoes, and donning a housecoat - though the latter did little to disguise the fact that her skirt was above the knee, with the promise that it would go even higher. When she appeared in Almond, in the spring of 1964, Carol had already worked shifts in Willow and Laburnum, supporting children of near school leaving age. Almond, I suspect, was her last chance.

Born at the end of the war, Carol, a baby boomer, started with a clean slate. Ask her about hostilities and you drew a blank; she neither remembered nor cared. All Carol knew about the war was the later rationing, and the clear up operations; bomb sites, no-go areas, and tank traps on beaches, fenced off with barbed wire, and, in our time, still mined. No soldier herself, Carol marched, if she marched at all, to the sounds of the sixties. I for one wanted to go with her.

A rebel in an age of nascent social change, Carol came to us wanting to make changes. And why not? Change was in the air, and in Eastry she found a cause. Carol took to holding house meetings, asking her Almond charges what *we* wanted to do with our leisure time. She thought we should get out more, encouraged us to have a voice, and stand up for our rights.

A suggestion that the home should be renamed, throwing off its old image, was taken up with enthusiasm. Carol arranged for everyone to have a say, staff, and residents alike. Ballot boxes appeared in each cottage, and, with Mr. Baker's blessing, we all joined in. Thinking about it now, the eventual winner "Field View" was more than a little lame, but at least we were given a vote.

Carol enjoyed a life beyond Eastry; why shouldn't we? Mr. Hugget and his war films were all very well, but there were cinemas in Dover and Deal and, closer still, the Empire in Sandwich, which showed the latest releases. And so, with Uncle Bob driving the Dormobile, that's where we went. One time it was *The Great Escape*, another *A Hard Day's Night*. Then came Sean Connery, and *Goldfinger*. We Almond boys went in as downbeat, "looked after kids" and came out walking on air, our chocolate cigarettes turned to tobacco, heads filled with girls dripping in gold paint, and Pussy Galore.

Next, Carol took us to a Dr. Who exhibition, where we got to have a go in a wheeled Dalek and met William Hartnell, the first Doctor, and in my view the best (but then I'm biased; he owned a house in Marden, where Mum was born).

But for Carol this was just the start of things. 'How would you boys like to be on television?' she asked. If there were any other items on that week's house meeting agenda, they were quickly forgotten, as a forest of arms went up in approval.

'Well,' Carol said, with an air of personal satisfaction, 'guess what: I've managed to get tickets for the *Five O'clock Club*!'

The reaction to this news was, sad to say, predictable, a "wow moment" being followed by a cacophony of questions, mainly relating to the chance of Auntie allowing us to attend.

Carol's smiling, triumphant response to the doubters (care home kids learn from the start to be mistrustful) was to produce a wad of pre-printed tickets, passing them round for inspection. Mr. Baker, she explained, had handed these very invitations over in person, just an hour before, and was even now investigating travel arrangements, and making a note in his diary.

The *Five O'clock Club* was a magazine show, aimed at the under twelves; it was commercial TV's response to the BBC's *Crackerjack* and *Blue Peter*. Produced by ATV, it aired on Tuesdays and Fridays at, yes, you've guessed it, five o'clock.

The programme's main presenter was Muriel Young, aided by Jimmy Hanley, who, as well as presenting, taught the audience how to make wooden models. The show had something for everyone: star attractions included Ollie Beak (a loud-mouthed Liverpudlian owl in a school cap) and his side-kick Fred Barker, while Fanny and Johnny Craddock taught their young viewers "Happy Cooking". Oh, and there was also a guitar slot from regular Bert Weedon. "Top of the pops" for Almond, though, was the weekly music spot.

Zoom in on a Tuesday or Friday tea time and you'd see a crowd of boys gathered round the

Day Room TV set, singing along, cheering our favourite bands, judging newcomers as "swinging" or "dodgy", thumbs up or thumbs down: Lulu, Billy J Kramer, Donovan, the Dave Clark Five; the list went on, and included several groups which, going forward, were destined to hold sway over us for years, if not decades, to come – The Rolling Stones, The Hollies, The Moody Blues, amongst others.

The band we most wanted to see was, of course, the Beatles. But this was 1964; "Beatlemania" was at its height – the Fab Four had starred at the London Palladium and gone on to conquer America. They were big - much too big for children's television and, according to John Lennon, more popular than Jesus.

But none of this put us off. A trip to London meant a day off school, two dozen or more of the home's junior aged children travelling on a specially chartered bus, amid all sorts of speculation about what to expect at the end of the journey.

First call on arrival was the ATV canteen, where we joined dozens of other youngsters for a lunch of sausage and chips, and fizzy pop.

Afterwards, we were taken, via a series of corridors, to the studio, and rehearsals. Here an important looking man, who told us he was the "Floor Manager" and who wore a kipper tie and carried a clipboard, pointed out the areas where each scheduled act or item would be presented, along with a turntabled plinth where the band of the week would perform.

Attendees were warned to look out for another man; his job was to hold up boards telling us when to clap or cheer. We had to be ready to move quickly from stage to stage, since the show was live (though the songs themselves were mimed) and it was important to create a positive, enthusiastic atmosphere. Things must go smoothly and on cue; there was no chance of a re-run.

The show itself went by in a whirl. Mostly, I remember the low studio ceilings, the spotlights, the heat, and the huge, wheeled cameras with their trailing octopus-like cables. On more than one occasion I was pushed out of the way – this was "rent-a-crowd" with a vengeance – finding myself separated from my peers.

Then, all too soon, it was over. But I didn't mind; I'd seen one of my favourite bands, the Hollies, and went home clutching a bag of sweets, along with autographs of Johnny and Fanny Craddock, scrawled on official ATV headed paper, together with memories that would last a lifetime. Two weeks later I received a badge and certificate of attendance through the post.

*

Auntie Carol lived for her music, even bringing it with her to work; a transistor radio for the kitchen and a record player, deposited, for the length of her shift at least, on the staff room coffee table.

We boys all spent time in the study when Carol was lone working. Often, if you wanted her, you had little choice; that was where the music was playing. And for me, watching through the half-open door became something of a habit.

Looking on as Carol, her housecoat thrown off and shoes kicked aside, gyrated slowly about the room was mesmerising. And wrong. A deep instinct, as old as music itself, told me this was a private moment, between Carol and herself. I knew it, just as I knew I was an intruder, yet I couldn't look away. The same voyeuristic tendency that drew me to the room in the first place kept me there, spellbound by the steady rise and fall of the record on the deck and Carol, eyes closed, arms akimbo, moving in ever increasing circles until, finally, limited space or the ending of the song brought her back to earth, and sent me scurrying away, forgetting the ready-made excuse I'd invented for being there in the first place.

For me, the experience was an awakening, the beginning of a realisation that girls were different; unknown, yet in a disturbing way, desirable. It was probably about this time that Auntie Joyce reported 'Douglas is becoming more of a boy.'

Music may be the food of love, but it didn't fill our stomachs. Friday evenings, a regular shift for Auntie Carol, meant the *Five O'clock Club*, but there was still supper to prepare. And Friday meant fish, usually locally caught Dover sole or plaice, both freely available, and inexpensive. Marine supplies were delivered to us by the frozen box load.

Afterwards, almost by way of compensation, Carol brought her record player into the Day Room. Stacked high with a collection of singles, waiting to drop from the top of a central spindle, we'd be left to listen to a selection of songs, while Auntie Carol went to clear up and tune into her transistor radio. Then the house was filled with music - Radio Caroline or Luxembourg for Carol in the kitchen, and in the Day Room the Kinks,

Stones, or Beatles for the residents. The place was more like the Cavern Club than a children's home. It couldn't, and didn't, last.

Before she disappeared (of which more below) Carol arranged for us Almond residents (she never referred to us as "inmates") to spend a week at the Warner holiday camp in Minster, forty miles away, on the Isle of Sheppey.

I don't know – and haven't been able to discover – how this holiday was funded; I do know that, in my time at Eastry at least, none of the other cottages enjoyed a summer break away, so for Carol to pull this one off was, I imagine, something of a coup. Sadly, by the time the holiday came around – the last week of July – Carol had vanished, leaving a grateful, if disappointed, Almond group to be led by Uncles Bob and Ken.

Warner's, along with Butlins and Pontins, had been a central part of the holiday camp scene for years. Its entertainment package, in common with its rivals, was formulaic, and dated; yet the campers seemed to love it. There were bumper cars, bingo, crazy golf, and a boating lake: "Come in number five, your time is up."

Most afternoons, the camp host found himself thrown into the "Olympic-sized" swimming pool; often the Punch and Judy man went the same way. Evenings in the ballroom included quizzes and "beautiful baby" and "glamorous Granny" competitions. Track down one or two episodes of the much-loved BBC comedy series *Hi di Hi*, and you'll get the idea.

The day began at 7.30 a.m., with cheesy music piped through a ubiquitous Tannoy; "Wakey, wakey, rise and shine". Half asleep, holidaymakers lay and listened as a husky-voiced female steered them through the itinerary for the day. Later, and at frequent intervals thereafter, she came on again, telling her listeners where to be, and when. Breakfast was served from 8.15 a.m., to be followed by a series of activities - boating, tennis, a three-legged race, all of it designed to take place before lunch, at twelve. "And then we have cross country at 2.00 p.m. and tug-of war. That's at three. Make sure not to miss it." With Uncles Bob and Ken at the helm, there was little chance of that.

Everyone was expected to take part; the days were carefully planned and any child, or adult, seen to be idle was quickly steered in the direction of some activity or another: archery, a Mr. Universe contest, knobbly-knees competition; it didn't matter; the message was "get out there and get involved" - and keep smiling.

But first you had to orientate yourself, to find your way about, following the footpaths and signs. And it wasn't easy, especially during the first day or two. The camp, you see, had been built like an army barracks, on a grid pattern. At its heart stood the main reception complex, which included the dining area and ballroom. There was also a camp shop, a "den" for teenagers, a day nursery for "tiny tots" and, for the under-fives, the Wagtail Club, which had its own programme of events, a separate playground, and specially trained "hostesses".

Wooden chalets, row upon row of them, dominated. With their brightly coloured doors and curtained windows they were cheerful enough, each boasting a sink, running hot water and electric lighting. And there was a chambermaid, who slipped into our rooms and tidied up while we ate breakfast, which was brought to the table courtesy of a team of waitresses. What would Auntie have to say about that!

But there was no toilet or bathroom. Wash houses were provided, one for each block, and you soon got used to passing other campers, strangers in the night, coming or going, dressed ready for "lights out", in dressing gowns and pyjamas, carrying towels and wash bags. The challenge, after dark, was how to find your way back.

Given the size of the place, dodging staff was a doddle. When it rained, and it did, a regular place of refuge was the games room, where campers could play darts, table tennis and pool, all under one roof.

Most popular were the gaming machines, rows of them, lining the walls.

The "penny falls" was my own personal favourite. Determined to win, and with limited funds, I took to stalking other, adult players, watching, and waiting, moving in when they'd given up, looking for a machine where piles of pennies overlapped and, like ripened fruit, looked ready to drop. I had some success and might have gone on to do even better (by which I mean losing my money less quickly) had I not fallen foul of the alarm system. 'Pull that bar again and you'll be banned,' threatened a young attendant.

Moving on, I tried "the crane", a machine where, by accident or design (almost certainly by design) a control arm went one way and a bucket the other. After a dozen tries, and having exhausted my supply of pennies, the engine's dinosaur-like jaws finally, and reluctantly, delivered a prize - a small cuddly blue elephant. It had taken half an hour to get hold of this unwanted gift. Nevertheless, though I can't, now, say why,

I found myself, joined by John Norley, celebrating loudly and enthusiastically, the pair of us jumping about the room with all the energy of a couple of Mexican beans. I'd defeated the machine.

One attraction I particularly remember was the fortune telling booth, featuring the trunk and head of an Ali Baba figure, captured, and imprisoned inside a glass and plywood cabinet. Place two coins in a slot and the whole apparatus would shudder and come to life; music played, lights flashed on and off, smoke bubbled up.

Then the swarthy Arab, spirit summoned from somewhere deep within, would do his stuff. A shake, a whirr, a flash from a pair of red satanic eyes and, with a clunk, a piece of cheap grey card shot out of the side of the machine, landing on the floor. My reading – along with most of the others, I suspect - suggested a bright future, one filled with health, wealth, and good fortune. "You will be lucky in love," was the conclusion. Another two pennies wasted, then.

Away from the games room, the camp shop was another popular destination, especially during damp weather. I went in every day, sometimes more than once. Other boys, too, were regular seekers among the shelves, looking for a bargain, or a gift to take home.

The store was a regular emporium, best imagined as a forerunner of today's discount shop. Miles of aisles offered everything from gob stoppers to shoe polish and tennis balls, a misleadingly casual selection of must-haves which also included a promotion on wet weather gear - umbrellas, pack-a-macs and Wellington boots; items stocked, no doubt, for the benefit of those holidaymakers who'd left home under the misguided impression that the Isle of Sheppey had, since they'd booked, been towed away and deposited somewhere further south, in the Mediterranean perhaps.

At the front, near to the tills, stood a postcard rack. On one side the cards (I bought one to send to Mum) featured local scenes; the beach at Leysdown, Sheerness Clock Tower and Minster, its promenade captured at the height of summer, flower beds and strings of coloured lights illustrating the town to its best advantage.

But a sneaky turn of the stand brought forth an alternative seaside, one populated by characters from another world altogether: curvaceous blondes with huge bosoms straining out of tiny bikinis; globular ladies in massive swimming costumes lording it over short hapless men with bald heads and moustaches. 'Saucy,' was John Norley's sniggering verdict on these comic illustrations. Uncle Bob, catching us in the act, was less inclined to laugh them off. 'Adults only,' he said, turning the rack towards the wall, and pulling us away.

Friday night was Campers' Night; there was bingo, a fancy-dress competition and, to round things off, a sing-along which, this being the last evening, ended with Vera Lynn singing "We'll Meet Again," followed by a drunken, table-tipping conga, a groping "Auld Lang Syne", and a staggering trip back to the chalets.

Earlier, at lunch, Uncle Ken, cradling a second pint of pale ale, summed up the holiday. He was not happy. 'Don't you boys know how to enjoy yourselves?' he asked, skipping through the events programme. The Eastry contribution to a fun week had, he said, been negligible. Yes, Geoffrey had come second in an egg and spoon race, and three or four boys – though not me - had excelled in the swimming pool. But that was three days ago, on Tuesday. Could any boy, hand-on-heart, claim to have contributed to camp activities with enthusiasm? It wouldn't do.

Ken, you see, was obliged to keep a daily diary, his written report to be handed in upon return to the home. What would Mr.

Baker, not to mention Auntie Joyce, have to say?

The coming evening, Ken insisted, offered a last chance for us to redeem ourselves (and, no doubt, justify staff overtime and expenses), to make an impression, go out with a bang. Tonight, one of us, Ken determined, would take part in the Junior Fancy Dress competition. 'Cheers,' he said, raising a half-empty glass in my direction.

'Let me see,' Ken said, stroking an imaginary beard, and ignoring my pleas to be excused. 'You could go as the Lone Ranger. No? Then how about Long John Silver? Actually, I think you'd make a good Long John Silver, Terry; though, come to think of it, getting hold of a parrot might be a bit of a challenge…'

At this late stage, I thought, finding any sort of costume would be difficult. Then Uncle Ken had an eureka moment. 'I've got it,' he said, with a self-satisfying rub of his hands. 'Get me some old newspapers.'

Junior Fancy Dress. There were, I think, six or seven competition entrants: a Tarzan with a brown-gravy tan; Little Bo Peep (elaborate crook, but no sheep), a French onion seller, prone to falling over his bicycle (adult size, borrowed for the occasion) and a heavily made-up Count Dracula, all crepe cape and red plastic fangs, among them. Each of us, it seemed, was competing for the first prize, "a free all-inclusive weekend at a Warner's Camp of your choice".

Drawing the short straw, I was slated to go on last; the wait a stomach-churning eternity of fear, accompanied by an overwhelming urge to hide, or run away. Finally, my turn came and, shaking, I stepped out from the wings onto the stage. Fifteen minutes of fame? Not for me, and certainly not this way.

'Don't be shy,' said the camp host, beckoning me forward. There were one or two titters, and a wolf whistle, followed by a shout of encouragement from Uncle Bob. 'Come on, folks,' said the man with the microphone. 'Give the lad a chance. Ten out of ten for originality, if nothing else.'

Blinded by the light, I could barely see beyond the first few tables. But all eyes, I knew, were on me. Meanwhile, mine were locked on a distant glitter ball. The whole thing was worse than one of Auntie's inspections.

Picture the scene. Imagine an audience of perhaps two hundred families; young children, frazzled mothers, and well-oiled fathers, invited to show their appreciation for a pale, lanky kid who stood before them barefoot and dressed in nothing but a tabard of poorly taped sheets of newspaper and a paper hat; the headgear being too small, badly folded, and in imminent danger of coming apart. Oh, and let me not forget the final addition, the *piece de resistance*, the dangling placard with its string-tied legend: IN THE NEWS.

'Inspired,' Uncle Ken called it. I just wanted the ground to open.

*

Given such episodes of ridicule and ill-treatment, staff punishments, times when I'd been given no choice or say in my life, you won't be surprised to learn that I often dreamed of escape, of running away.

And I was not alone. One evening, sitting on the swings, Mark produced a penknife. 'I've got a secret,' he whispered, grabbing hold of my hand. 'We're friends, aren't we?'

'Yes, of course,' I replied, though, I admit, with no little trepidation. 'Well, stay still and do as I say,' Mark said. It seemed that, if Mark were to share his secret, the two of us must be more than friends; we had to go to the next level: to become blood brothers. 'Keep still,' Mark said and, tightening his grip, cut a line across my thumb. 'Now you,' he said, passing the knife to me, and I did the same. Then, we pressed our thumbs together; there, the deed was done.

Afterwards, while I sucked on my wound, Mark revealed his secret.

'Some of the boys have got stuff hidden,' he said.

This "stuff", it turned out, was concealed under a floorboard in the staff toilet, right under Auntie's nose, and was, Mark revealed, being added to on an almost daily basis, the cache currently consisting of a torch (minus batteries), half a dozen sticking plasters, a map of Thanet, and pieces of cutlery stolen from the kitchen. Survival rations included acid drops and a packet of Spangles.

Ironically, none of these items, useful or not, was needed to affect a breakout, Auntie being quite relaxed about our Almond comings and goings. Indeed, she was so sure that her charges wouldn't abscond, or, if we did, that we wouldn't go far, that, when the mood took her, she was quite happy to send a boy, unaccompanied, on an errand from the home to the village.

A regular destination was the hardware store. 'Ask Mr. Butler if that tin of elbow-grease I ordered has come in, will you? And while you're at it bring me a left-handed screwdriver,' she'd add with a sly smile.

Tantrums, and threats to run away, Auntie met with the same self-assured composure. Going somewhere? Well, Auntie wasn't about to stop you. 'Here,' she'd say, opening the back door, gesturing the would-be escapee out, 'be my guest.'

Alternatively, the culprit would be told to wait. 'Not in that much of a hurry, are we? Give me a minute and I'll make you up a packet of sandwiches and find a penny for the toilet.' Having made her point, Auntie would walk away. But she didn't forget.

Of my brothers, the only one to try to escape was Edward. Egged on by one Kevin Philips, an older boy and regular runaway, the pair simply walked out of school, jumped on a Deal-bound bus, and didn't come back.

The way Edward told it, years later, the whole episode was far from an adventure. 'I don't remember any sort of plan,' he said.

What he did remember, or chose to remember, was recounted reluctantly, and with no little embarrassment.

'There were chips, then a walk along the promenade and, later, half an hour or so watching three or four anglers fishing from the end of the pier.

'Soon I began to worry. It was nearly eight o'clock, the sky was darkening, it was bedtime. We were certain to have been reported missing; the police would be looking for us. I wanted to go back, but Kevin had none of it.

'He said there was no money left for the bus. Turned out he'd used the last of our money in the arcade. The plan was to spend the night on the beach.

'So,' says Edward, 'we jumped down onto the shingles and, hugging the sea wall, began walking, heading towards Walmer, getting rid of our school ties and caps as we went. After a while, we came upon a row of fishing boats, sitting above the tide line, hauled out of the water for the night. Finding the smallest, we pulled back the tarpaulin cover and dropped down on to an assortment of ropes and buoys. And that's where we spent the night.

'And that one night was enough,' Edward said. 'Hours of cold and discomfort, the noise of the tide and the seagulls settled things. As soon as there was some light in the sky, we climbed out of the boat and retraced our steps into town. Thinking about it now, it was almost as if we were being mocked by the last vestiges of summer: flowers on the traffic islands circled with flowers; hanging baskets on lamp posts, rows of boarding houses, their foyer lights still burning. The day was waking up - a milk float, a road sweeper, a dustcart, the world turning regardless.

'Kevin spotted a policeman standing in the doorway of Boots; crossing the road, we went and handed ourselves in.

'My next memory is sitting shivering in the back of a police car. I remember worrying that we'd have to pay for new school ties and caps. Then I fell asleep.'

Edward's tale was told in a minor key; he was anxious that events weren't exaggerated, distorted, or embroidered. 'I was no hero,' he insisted. 'It was a stupid thing to do, and not something I'm proud of.'

And the punishment? 'I was given the "nose to wall" treatment, an hour each day, every evening for a week, marched out into the yard and pushed, face forward, up against the brickwork. And there I was made to stand, arms at my sides, while the other boys played around me. The order went out;

I was to be ignored, and Auntie Harris made sure to position me where I could be seen from the kitchen window.

'And there was another, unforeseen, side to my punishment, which involved Ian. Bewildered, he'd take my hand, tugging at my shorts, crying heavy tears of frustration when I wouldn't turn around. "Why are you looking at that wall, Teddy. Aren't you allowed to play with me?"

'I had little choice but to shoo Ian away, calling for one of my housemates to take him indoors, or over to the swings. That was my real punishment; Ian's upset and the realisation that I'd broken my promise to Mum to be there for him.'

But at least Edward avoided the cane. It was Kevin who took a beating, but then he'd gone off before. And he had a habit of persuading other boys, often younger and more vulnerable, to accompany him, usually with promises of sweets and treats, but sometimes with threats of violence if they hesitated or refused.

The police came to the home when Kevin and Edward absconded (they were always quick to visit the home then); the police came when George Norley "mooned" the occupants of a Ford Anglia on the way back to Eastry from a trip out (unluckily for George the car contained two officers from the station in Dover; they followed the Dormobile back to Thorn, where, afterwards, George was severely punished); the police came when Pamela Smith, a fourteen-year old from Laburnum set fire to another girl's hair; they came when Mary Hicks, also from Laburnum, and her friend Cheryl (transferred to Eastry from a remand home, where she'd been incarcerated after trying to drown her baby sister in the bath), ran away, being caught shoplifting in Ramsgate; and the police came again when Auntie Carol's record player went missing.

It was Mrs. B, dropped off by Alf for her Saturday morning shift, who insisted Carol report the theft. And it was Mrs. B who provided Sergeant Stone, sent out from the Dover station, with a description.

'It's lovely, Sergeant; so *compacted*, so modern. I said as much to Alf, only last week,' said an animated Mrs. B.

'Alf, I said - Alf, that's Mr. Bean, my 'usband - that gramophone of Carol's is *bleautiful*. I said so, and I don't mind *hadmitting* it. It's *high fidelio*, I said. *State of the Ark*. Why, the sound comes out of the lid, thank you very much. And what's more it's *electrocuted*, and *fully portabled.* It has a case and a handle; you can pick it up and take it anywhere.'

Mrs. B, realizing she had just confessed to motive, if not opportunity, suppressed a girlish giggle. 'I hope I haven't dropped myself in it,' she said, glancing over at Auntie Joyce.

'It's an Alba,' a dejected Carol said.

Anything else?

'Yeah, it's red and has a sixpence taped to its arm; it stops the needle jumping,' John Norley added.

'Very *sentimental*,' said Mrs. B.

John began to whistle the *Z Cars* TV theme. Auntie Joyce gave him a death stare. Sergeant Stone took notes.

Auntie Joyce was steaming. She'd been away for a couple of days - in hospital undergoing "a procedure," rumour had it – and remained "under the doctor". Returning home to find a squad car sitting outside was not part of her agenda.

'I haven't even had time to take my coat off,' Auntie said, taking her coat off.

Then came the interrogation. Which of us, apart from Carol and Mrs. B, knew anything about a record player? When was it last seen, and where? John? Geoffrey? Auntie wanted answers. I raised my hand, quietly admitting to listening to music emanating from the staff room. John, and Keith followed. Sergeant Stone, deferring to Auntie, took more notes.

We boys were all under suspicion. And not without reason. A sizeable minority of Eastry's inmates had form. They stole from one another; lifted things from shops; anything not nailed down would disappear. Yet despite this penchant for theft, our favourite guardians, and especially Auntie Carol, were off-limits. We'd never steal from Auntie Carol. She was young; she'd been good to us; she was on our side. And, besides, "portabled" or not, where would a boy hide something the size of a record player?

As it happened, the thief, an opportunist who'd climbed in through the staff room window, found himself apprehended the following weekend, trying to offload the stolen Alba in Dover market. And no doubt the law and the local magistrates dealt with him accordingly.

But it was Carol, the victim in the affair, who suffered most. It was Carol who'd left the staff room window open, not locking up before bed, and Carol who'd allowed her charges into the study, with potential access to confidential files.

And who'd given Carol permission to bring a record player to work in the first place? No one.

Add to this the neglect of her chores and Carol was finished. Within days she'd joined the ranks of the "disappeared".

Was Carol sacked? Maybe, I thought at the time, she'd been given a second chance, transferred to another home. Somehow, I doubt it.

*

None of this, nor any other negative aspects of Eastry life are to be found in the reports of Her Majesty's Inspector of Homes, certainly not those I've managed to gain access to, dating from 1964 and 1965, and which concern Almond and Thorn.

The inspector's report for 1965 makes especially interesting reading, as much for what it leaves out as anything else. It records that the boys billeted in Almond "seem happy and well cared for", and praises Auntie Joyce for her work and dedication.

Overall, the account is a positive one, the only criticism concerning Almond's bathroom. No, not the abuse, nor the cold, or the long, lonely hours inmates spent locked in; just a note highlighting the towels; the boys' towels, individually labelled, were kept on the same rack, which was unhygienic.

"One of the old school," the inspector writes of Auntie Harris, reporting on Thorn. She is judged "dependable" and "steadfast" and praised for keeping her cottage "spotless".

Ironically, Edward recalls, the result of all this industry and diligence was that Thorn under Auntie Harris came to resemble a hospital rather than a home – a place to be endured, rather than embraced. It was certainly no place for a sensitive boy in need of love and affection.

'I wish now that I'd spoken out,' Edward says, discussing inspection day. 'But somehow the abuse and neglect we boys suffered had become normalised; it was part of everyday life, no more than we deserved. And, anyway, who would have believed me?'

What angers Edward most is the acclaim Auntie Harris received for the care she took with Ian. 'If only the inspector had known,' Edward sighs, with a sorry shake of the head.

Ian suffered especially. Once or twice a week, her older boys having gone off to school, Auntie Harris would lock up and go out for the day, visiting a grown-up daughter, who lived in the village. Before turning the key, she'd take Ian, four years old and too young for the infants' school and put him out to "play" – with instructions not to disturb the neighbours.

A pat on the head, an apple or biscuit thrust into a reluctant hand, and Auntie was off down the drive, lugging a heavy canvas shopping bag, leaving Ian at liberty to play in the drains, launch a raid on the pig bins, or find new and interesting things to do with worms and slugs. Often, he'd be left alone like this for hours, until Auntie came back or Uncle Bob and his Dormobile returned from the afternoon school run.

Years later, Ian himself relived the experience, recalling how, unattended, and increasingly cold or thirsty, with only the porch-covered boot room or outside toilet for shelter, he learned to use the lid of a shoe polish tin as an improvised drinking vessel, dipping it into the toilet bowl to fill with water.

Time had made Ian philosophical, and he joked about having shown some initiative. He'd even turned his hand to snail racing, though being outside in the cold and wind damaged his hearing, and he suffered from earache well into adulthood.

CHAPTER ELEVEN

How many days make an academic year; how many hours add up to a school term or, for that matter, a school week? I haven't made the calculation, but school, for me, was special; indeed, it was central, vital; it offered freedom, escape from the world of care, a chance to learn, to develop and be recognised for what I was; an individual, a person in my own right. Indeed, school embodied such a welcoming, and non-judgmental environment, that today even the journey, and especially the orchard, evoke powerful memories.

I could make my way to the orchard in my sleep, and have done so many times, though in my dreams I'm always alone.

Out of Almond I go, fitted out with my new uniform, walking up past the sports field and the football pitch, its goal posts looking forlorn and strangely incongruous on this, a school day morning.

Through a gap in the fence – a natural place for a gate, though one was never provided - and I'm on to the pathway, which leads down to the world beyond. It's hallowed soil this, a rough track of rutted ground, a pilgrim's way of compacted flint and chalk formed by legions of scholars, generations of juniors who have traversed this route swinging satchels, laughing, and fighting their way to the village school for a chance, which not even Auntie or Uncle could deny them, of receiving some basic education, to breathe in the same rarefied air as their peers from beyond the institution, and to experience a few hours of relative normality.

As I walk, the home is on my left; on my right, and topped by barbed wire, a fence runs down the slope, separating me from a herd of cows. Beyond that fence are water troughs, starlings, exposed tree roots. A heifer looks up, a second, equally nosy, swishes its tail. Tongues roll, then, as I pass, heads go back down.

Further along, a row of copper beech trees runs up the ridge. My eye is drawn towards the middle distance where, not half a mile away, the tower of St Mary's floats above the rising fields. Up down, up down; the very act of walking causes the church to move, rising and falling, like a boat at anchor in a distant harbour. The tower, the clock, the flagpole, the top of the clock, the pinnacle of the pole, the pinnacle of the pinnacle. Then the building is gone, and, on the other side of the path, the playing field, and the home with it.

Now the track narrows and a rough hedge of thorn, Old Man's Beard and blackberry, a whole summer's growth, reaches out from either side, threatening to snare me in its wild embrace. Straying brambles scratch my arms and legs and, as I negotiate them, spring back, propelling me forward.

Then, all at once, I'm through and out into a widening, open space. In front of me, beyond the first of two stiles, stands the orchard, its gnarled old trees, branches heavy with fruit, coming at me through the haze of a September morning.

It's a hushed, secluded spot, this place I have come upon - all gauzy spider webs, silver snail trails, and secretive, flitting birds. A scatter of rabbit droppings, impossible to avoid, pellet the path. My nostrils fill with the cider-smell of fallen apples which lie, wasp and worm eaten, fermented in little heaps, or mashed to brown on the floor. A million motes of water droplets hang in the air, while swollen flies squat on silky blackberries, waiting for a lemon sun to burn away the mist, bringing warmth to a world of autumn hues - yellow, red, and russet.

Dreams aside, a shake of the kaleidoscope brings us to another day, another time and season, and more particular memories.

Early winter and the orchard stiles are slippery. All around the muddy footprints of November sit, frozen in white. Blown leaves from the nearby beech trees cling to the fence, while the trees themselves, stripped bare, stand defiant, like soldiers holding out during a long winter siege.

And I remember especially a Monday morning in December when some of us boys, faced with the alternative, persuaded Auntie to overlook the weather conditions, sanctioning an expedition from the home to school.

The team started out bravely enough, four or five of us, kitted out with scarves and mittens, kicking our way through the snow, throwing snowballs, laughing, and joking at the novelty of it all. But by the time we reached the top of the field the wind had gotten up and the snow and hail, sharp like needles, began slanting into us with a real sting. So, we put our heads down and, finding what remained of the fence and path, battled on, seeking the shelter of the orchard below.

And what a world it was, down there in the hollow. Here everything had changed; the place strangely familiar, yet brutal, brittle, and locked in, the very air too silent to be real.

And the snow. It was softer now, floating down in heavy feathers, like the aftermath of a pillow fight between the misbehaving offspring of those winter gods - Odin or Thor, rulers from the north. As for the wooden stile, that was gone, buried. We didn't climb it; we threw ourselves over the top.

White remembered days. Reaching school, it was to be congratulated by the headmaster for making the effort. Then our little group of adventurers waited, shivering against the weak heat of a radiator, until staff came to take us home.

On days like these, spring seemed an impossibility. Yet gradually, imperceptibly, the days began to lengthen. Christmas came and went, then New Year. Soon my prayers were answered, as the days became longer.

Here my pocket diary, handed out at the end of a December carol service, reinforced what I could see all around me, its pre-printed pages replete with sunrise and sunset times, daylight increasing by two minutes a day as the winter retreated, giving ground, ever so slowly – and not without a fight.

In the orchard, an invisible hand prepared the way, leaving behind the hazy blue burnt twigs of a bonfire, rising smoke filling the air with the smell of apple wood.

Soon the grass beneath the trees began turning chlorophyll green; snowdrops and tiny star-headed anemones patterning the ground; catkins dangling in the hedges. Then, following my February birthday, the March wind arrived, blowing away a year's evidence of schoolboy transit; empty crisp packets and chewing gum wrappers all gone.

Imperceptibly, but inevitably, the false start of April gave way to the annual miracle of May, when patches of bluebells appeared beneath blossoming orchard trees. For me, this was a time both of hope and melancholy - summer was coming, 1964, and I was a year away from Doddington.

An enchanted place like the orchard, must, I thought, have an entrance code or key, an "Open Sesame" of some kind. And so, it proved. Lodged end-on in one of the stile posts was a single farthing piece, a quarter moon of silver jammed into a gap formed by a natural split in the wood. Set at face level as you climbed, the coin could hardly be missed, the surrounding surface being shiny, worn and grooved, like a flagstone at a martyr's tomb. Clearly the farthing had been there for a time; other boys, I discovered, had long since followed the superstitious habit of touching it, both going out of the home, and coming back.

In truth the orchard – all the boys called it the orchard – was nothing to write home about (though I'm sure I did): a few stunted plums and pears and some apples – Coxes and Bramley's, eaters, and cookers; a dozen or so trees, enclosed in a small paddock, a box of land no bigger than the penalty area of a football pitch. And beyond the orchard, over a second stile, came the back gardens of a row of terraced houses which, in their turn, abutted onto the road.

It wasn't far. At busy times you could hear the traffic through the overhanging tunnel of a high hedge, the onward route taking a pedestrian out onto the pavement and road beyond. There, in the mornings, you might bump into the younger Eastry girls and infants, Malcolm amongst them, who walked, escorted by Auntie Cornish, to school via the main gate.

*

My class teacher was Mr. Desborough – aka "Daddy Long Legs", "Daddy Desborough" or, more tellingly perhaps, simply "Daddy".

Mr. Desborough was a tall man; six-foot two or three, I should think. At nine or ten years old, gazing up from my classroom seat, he seemed like a giant. His clothing too reinforced a sense of height, the grey-checked suit he wore being at least one size too small, suggesting that, like us, his pupils, he was still growing and would one day burst free.

Collecting together my memories of Mr. Desborough, fragmentary now, I remember especially his curly, greying hair and his way of prowling the classroom, waving his hands about like a mad professor – Mr. Desborough seemed to spend all day on his feet – his sleeves shooting up towards his elbows. When he sat down, to mark class work or take the register, his trouser legs also went on their travels, moving up towards his knees, exposing inches of white hairy leg and patterned socks.

What age was Mr. Desborough? Was he married? Did he have a family? I didn't, then, give a thought to his personal life. Indeed, I don't think it would have surprised me to learn that "Sir", along with the school's other teaching staff, was permanently trapped inside the school building, being hung up in a classroom cupboard overnight, only to be brought out by Mr. Ovenden, the caretaker, in the mornings, stood in front of the blackboard, handed a piece of chalk and generally primed ready to start all over again. I owed, and owe, Mr. Desborough a great deal, but the idea that he might have an existence outside of school never crossed my mind.

Mr. Desborough, being the upper junior class teacher, taught English, Geography, Arithmetic, Science, and other subjects, including PE and Music. He threw himself with enthusiasm into all of them, knew how to get his pupils to listen, and managed, for the most part at least, to get some learning into our heads without resorting to extreme measures.

His favourite subject was history. Saxon invasions, Viking pillaging; vivid stories and brutal battles, told Mr. Desborough's way, gripped and quieted the whole class. Indeed, it would have been difficult not to become engrossed in a history lesson when it was delivered by Mr. Desborough.

Yet it wasn't all blood and gore. Yes, there was a lengthy list of England's kings and queens, whose reigns and dates we must remember - we would, after all, be tested on them; but it was the lives of the ordinary people, which, Mr. Desborough insisted, really mattered. Alfred may have burnt the cakes, but what about the poor woman who'd left him to watch over them?

Mr. Desborough was constantly on the lookout for new strategies, for keeping his class "on task". Starting a timeline, he had the keenest among us pin a continuous strip of paper - Bayeux Tapestry style – at waist level all around the classroom, breaking either side of the door. Then, when we tackled a subject relating to the past, or, indeed, current affairs, the class was taxed with seeking out evidence and illustrative materials, often by way of homework, our mission to find maps, drawings, pictures, or photographs to be added, with dates and exposition - a sort of "show and tell" - during the next lesson.

With just about every invader arriving in England via the Kent coast, field trips to nearby Dover and Deal were obvious choices, and produced all sorts of evidence, while Richborough, said to be the landing place of the Emperor Claudius in AD 43, seemed a good starting point for our tapestry. I received a gold star for my written account.

One of my sources reports that children from the home were a challenge; they fidgeted in class and lacked concentration and application. There was, no doubt, some truth in this – it would be surprising if there weren't – yet several factors mitigated against non-engagement or disruptive behaviour. Credit for this, during my time at least, must go to Mr. Desborough, and his inclusive teaching style. There was no discrimination; indeed, this would have been difficult, since half the class – half the school - originated from the home. Also, there was always the unspoken threat, seldom enforced, of a pupil being sent to the headmaster. Mr. Fright (yes, really) only had to pick up the telephone and Auntie or Uncle would know all about it.

This was the sixties and, as I have already said, change was very much in the air, in the field of education, as much as anywhere else. Teaching methods were being reassessed, which left the very fabric of the school inadequate, classrooms dating from the 1850s, and designed for rote learning, proving unsuitable for pair and group work, the sharing of ideas, coming together as a team. The old Victorian desks, bolted together in pairs and set out in rows of eight, facing the front, belonged to the past, along with the building's separate entrances for boys and girls. It was the end of an era, time for a new beginning.

Changes came quickly. Returning after the 1964 Christmas holidays, it was to find a near total transformation. The school itself, church-built in Victorian Gothic, still stood, but that was as far as it went. Mr. Desborough's classroom, all the classrooms, had been stripped, the ghosts of generations of junior school ancestors exorcised. The squeaky old desks, with their ink wells and name-scratched surfaces, were no more. In their place came octagonal tables, modern chairs, display boards, and free-standing, colourful storage units, having individually labelled trays. Even the curtains had been taken down, replaced by adjustable blinds. The only nod to the past was a large map on the wall, almost a quarter of it painted in pink, the colour of a vanished empire. Sometimes it's hard to let go.

Despite these changes, there was still a gender divide when it came to playtime. The girls played at skipping and hopscotch, while we boys, locals and home kids together, followed, and sometimes invented, our own competitive games.

In the summer it was cricket, improvised by chalking stumps on the school wall. There was no umpire; instead, we used a tennis ball, made wet with a soaking from the playground fountain. A round damp mark on the chalk meant out. No arguments.

Half-way through the autumn term came conkers, which because of the short season and, it must be admitted, the potential for inflicting pain on an opponent's knuckles, was taken up with enthusiasm. The secret of success, passed down through generations of schoolboys, relied on preparation. First gather your conkers, then soak them overnight in vinegar, before oven-baking them for twenty minutes or so. Finally, string these potential "sixers", preferably using an old boot lace, and there you were, ready to go.

So how to gain access to vinegar and a hot oven? Fortunately, for Almond, we had Mrs. Flowers to bargain with. The deal was based on fear – her fear of all things arachnoid. Mrs. Flowers was convinced that, strategically placed in corners or windowsills, conkers, or rather the chemicals they exuded, offered a way of dealing with that terrifying autumn intruder, the common household spider. Country lore, folk tales? All we boys had to do was surrender a dozen or so wrinkled leftovers.

Winter term brought the playground fountain back into focus. A cold, clear December day, long awaited, brought ideal skating weather. Time to make a slide.

It was a school tradition, collecting water from the fountain in cupped hands, sprinkling it on the ground, creating an ice rink. A short run up and a skater could slide along - for at least fifteen feet or so - before coming, shoulder first if you got it right, up against the buffers, the shock absorber of the classroom wall. Wrapped up in coats and scarves, groups of rosy-cheeked boys, and sometimes girls, waited their turn. "Not too hard, not too hard" was the panicked cry, as gloved hands launched a squealing participant forward. Most children ended up on their bottoms, though I don't recall any real accidents, or staff interfering to break things up.

Perhaps the most competitive break time pursuit was "flick cards". This could be played all year round, though not when the weather was wet, or windy. It went like this. First, agree on the tea cards to be deployed. Then, having set them up at an angle against the base of a convenient wall, compete to knock the cards over. Watched by an audience of waiting, would-be participants, two challengers, having divided out their remaining cards, stood back and took it in turns to flick them at the targets. The rules were negotiable. Some boys preferred to play from a kneeling position, while others stood. All sorts of wrist actions were tried, and perfected.

In another version of the game, the winner kept only the cards covering, or partly covering, those that had been knocked over. Sounds simple, and it was, but the game quickly became addictive, winners amassing large numbers of cards, which were carried about in bundles tied together with elastic bands. Dirty or dogeared, it didn't matter, they all counted when it came to bragging rights. Having your cards confiscated, for whatever reason, was considered a disaster, so much so that the prospect may even have helped promote good classroom behaviour.

I could use up pages and pages describing my school days. But to be frank, my experiences, I suspect, would not be too dissimilar to your own. As tempting as it is, I'm sure I'd end up going off at a tangent, losing myself in yards and yards of nostalgia. Basically, though, the point I want to make, what I remember most, is the sense of inclusiveness; yes, we classmates were competitive, all children are, but everyone wore the same uniform, there were no ranks and no distinctions. We were a group, and got along as such, at least until the end of the day. It was then, and only then, that unison and shared interests were shattered. The bell went, satchels and coats were retrieved, there was a jostling rush to get beyond the school gates, out onto the street. There, segregated, village friends, often met with affection and exuberance by mums or dads, went one way, while us "looked after kids", waving goodbye, returned to the home, to Auntie and Uncle.

CHAPTER TWELVE

At the end of the summer term, my second, Mr. Desborough offered to loan me a book. It was HG Wells' *History of Mr. Polly*. 'Give it back after the summer break,' he said, taking my return in September for granted. 'And let me know how you get on. I think you'll enjoy it. Wells mentions Maidstone and the Medway; places a Man of Kent like yourself will appreciate, I'm sure.'

As far as I remember, Mr. Desborough never got his book back. Nor did I return to school for the autumn term. Instead, I joined the ranks of the "disappeared". I went home.

*

Auntie had it all carefully planned. One morning, a week or so into the school holidays, Uncle Bob turned up, parking his Dormobile out front. His task, following Auntie's instructions, was to get her charges out of the cottage. "Take them to the beach, I don't care where; Ramsgate, Margate, you choose." It was left to Bob, who decided on Camber Sands, to get us boys organised.

Everyone was excited. Two or three of the lads, keen on crab fishing, asked if they might buy lines and nets. Others, including myself, searched the boot room, angling for buckets and spades, lobbing them into the hallway, emptying last year's sand onto the floor.

Then Auntie stuck her head round the study door. 'Send Douglas to me. I want a word.' Then she disappeared, back into her lair.

What had I done this time? Standing at the window, her back towards me, I looked on as Auntie ran her fingers down the curtains, engrossed in the activity outside. Behind her, beyond the open window, I could hear Uncle Bob, taking a head count, heard the boys respond as their names were called. Next came the sliding of the van door, the turn of the key in the ignition. Any moment now they'd be gone. Why didn't Bob notice my absence?

Looking on as the vehicle moved away, Auntie turned and, taking a couple of steps, paused, straightening the study hearth rug with her foot. 'Don't worry about that lot,' she said, finally making eye contact. 'You're not going with them. *You're* going home.'

'What?' I gasped. For a moment, I could hardly take it in. All I could think of was what was happening beyond the window, and Camber Sands.

'Not "what" *pardon*,' Auntie said. Have you learned nothing during your time here? I said, *"You're going home.'*

I stood there incredulously, scarcely able to process the information. Going home? Getting out? After all this time the very idea of freedom seemed too good to be true. When was I going? Where, for that matter, *was* home? Why had Mum and Dad hidden this news from me, from my brothers? I saw them only last Sunday; they said nothing.

'There was a delay,' said Auntie. 'There was furniture in storage, a grant for bedding, and other costs. Nothing was certain, the council couldn't agree an exact date, *I've* only known about it for four or five days.'

So, it was true, I was leaving, going home. I had a sudden and light-headed urge to rush outside and shout my freedom to the skies; to stop the departing Dormobile, jump in front of it, wave my arms, insist on saying goodbye.

I wanted a big final scene, a last farewell. 'I didn't know, I promise I didn't know. I'll write, of course I'll write, I'll send you all my news.' But it was no good. Not for nothing had Auntie waited until the last possible moment to call me into the study. That, after all, was how things were done; this way none of the other Almond boys would see my departure. By the time they got to Camber Sands, they'd have forgotten all about me, I thought. It was the last time I'd see any of my housemates and friends.

'Well don't just stand there, take this,' Auntie said, and thrusting a cardboard box in my direction, ordered me upstairs to remove all evidence of my existence.

'Oh,' she added, as I turned for the door, 'don't forget your locker. Your books, toys, and stamp albums, all of them. I want it all gone. You're to report to the office without delay.'

'And my brothers?'

'Just go.'

And that was it. My world, the known world, was turned upside down in an instant, in the blinking of an eye.

Even the dorm, nominally out of bounds during the day, wore a different face. For me, the dorm meant bedtime, night hours when housemates held belching or farting competitions, told dirty jokes, made apple pie beds, or invoked the ghost of the White Lady and other creatures of the night. Walking in now it was to find a room full of light, the windows thrown open, rows of curtains waving in the breeze. All twelve beds, mine included, had been stripped; sheets and counterpanes lay in a series of piles, awaiting removal. A floor polisher stood, abandoned, next to the mantlepiece. Two or three neglected dusters sat, alongside a tin of Johnsons Wax, on the nearest bedside cabinet. Further along, a deserted cup of tea, long cold, rested on a windowsill. 'Mary Celested,' I said, addressing an empty room. It was pure Mrs. B.

Mrs. B. I was going to miss her terribly. Disappearing without saying goodbye just didn't seem right.

There were other staff too; Bill, Mrs. Flowers, not to mention my Almond friends. As strange as it may seem, I had mixed feelings about leaving, or at least about the manner of my leaving. It had all been so sudden. Getting out wasn't supposed to be like this. I'd always imagined myself playing to an audience of inmates, being cheered on as I stuck my tongue out and raised two fingers to Auntie. Yet when it came to it, going, never to return, was something different altogether. The home, you see, meant security. It had taken two years, but I'd begun to toe the line, fell into a routine, knew what it took to fit in, to avoid punishment. Almond had become the place where I belonged. Did I deserve better?

Half an hour later I found myself trekking down to the main gate and office, counting the kerbstones, keeping to the established, self-imposed, rules.

Suddenly, halfway towards the exit, came a moment of panic. I was leaving, going home, but what about my brothers? Auntie had said nothing about my brothers.

I needn't have worried. Edward and Ian, shouting and waving, soon caught up. Andy and Malcolm, dispatched minutes before, were waiting outside the storeroom. There, someone had been sorting through the possessions taken away two years previously, and we were each handed a string-tied brown paper package of washed but, by now, well undersized clothing.

Afterwards, standing on the verge, the five of us stood peering down the road towards the village, just as we'd done on all those Sunday afternoons. This time, however, there was no bus bringing Mum and Dad; no, this time it was Mr. Waller and his Austin we looked for.

For me, the wait was agonising; every oncoming car brought anticipation, then disappointment. Ian, though, had decided that it was party time. 'We're going home,' he yelled, jumping up and down. Then he jumped up and down some more. 'We're going home, we're going home.'

Ever wary, I put a finger to my lips. Even now, at the very end, to celebrate the family's freedom seemed premature. Staff might overhear; our joy at leaving might be seen as ingratitude. Who was to say that the decision to release us couldn't be overturned?

Mr. Waller's arrival brought great relief, and a collective, quiet, cheer. Escape began, now, to seem real. 'Wait here, boys,' our rescuer instructed. Then, plonking his trilby down on Ian's head, he disappeared into the office. Five minutes later a member of staff came out and beckoned us in.

Line up, strip off, and get ready to be examined. It was time for a final inspection, this time conducted, in a very casual fashion, by Dr. Rose.

A sense of déjà vu hung heavy in the air; the older of us boys, I'm sure, each reliving his own sharp and painful memories of having been here before. True, there was no cane wielding Mr. Adams or tea guzzling Dr.

Brocklehurst this time round. And no Auntie Harris, Auntie Fitzgerald, or Mr. Baker either - none of them feeling under any obligation to wish us farewell. Yet the room was just as it had been two years since: the aquarium, the trophy table, the cane on the wall. And Ian clutching Archie, his teddy bear.

My thoughts went back to that first night – the first of hundreds, as it turned out. I lived again the humiliation of those inspections, shuddered at the memory of all the later occasions I'd stood in front of staff, half-dressed or naked.

I recalled, too, my first evening in Almond, and my first meal - a runny egg and soldiers, washed down with a lukewarm mug of powdery cocoa, followed by another inspection. The image of myself kneeling over the bath, while Auntie examined me for nits is, like so much else from Eastry, something I've never forgotten. If I close my eyes, as I did at the time, I can still feel those hands, a stranger's hands, on my head; smell the stinking liquid she massaged into my hair; hear the impatience in her voice as she ordered me to keep still. The delousing was conducted using an ultra-fine comb, with a newspaper placed on the floor to catch the lice as they landed. 'Ouch, that hurts,' I said as the comb scraped across my scalp. 'It's supposed to,' came the clipped response.

But today, the last day of July 1965, was not a time for agonising over the past – that would come later – no, this was a time to get away, to go home.

Edward went back into the office to collect a raft of school reports and post office savings books, and I followed. Dr Rose produced papers; files were handed over. There was small talk and banter; Mr. Waller, uncharacteristically, turning down a cup of tea. 'Which one of you was sick last time?' he asked, as we made our way to his car. 'Me,' I confessed, raising my arm. 'Well, sit in the front, and wind down the window.'

With a final wave, Mr. Waller turned his vehicle westwards, to the village and then beyond. A minute or so later we were gone, homeward bound.

*

Granville Road. What can I say? The property Maidstone Borough council gave us was an old, three-storey Victorian town house, one of five. Originally there were six, and our house, at the end of the row, was number five. Then came the Blitz, and the bombs. The end house, number one, the Germans destroyed in 1941. All that remained was a large crater – great for sliding down on a sheet of cardboard – the house shored up with scaffolding. The whole row, condemned, was due for demolition; three of the remaining houses were already empty, yet we were moving in.

Mum's persistence had paid off. She'd pestered and pleaded and when that didn't produce results, she decided to force the council's hand by getting pregnant again. Finally, someone took notice, social workers and health officers began to visit the bedsit in Boxley Road; reporting back that, with a baby due, Mum's housing situation was unsustainable, and was affecting her mental health. The Terrys began to come up in Housing Committee meetings. But it was a close-run thing. For weeks, if not months, a decision hung in the balance. Some council officials argued for, others against; rent arrears and nuisance behaviour were on the agenda. Eventually, Granville Road was suggested as a possible solution.

Had someone worked out that providing housing, especially a property not on the official waiting list, was more cost effective than keeping the Terry children in care, I wonder. Who knows? In any event, the emotional and psychological effect of indefinite separation, if considered, went unrecorded. Instead, the official paperwork focuses on the dilapidated state of the building under consideration, with one housing officer, a Mrs. Gurney, recording that the place was "terribly damp" and hardly fit for human habitation, and certainly not a suitable place for a newborn child. It is difficult not to conclude that we were being fobbed off, set up to fail.

Eventually, the council produced an offer. The deal was quite simple. Dad had to show that he could run a tenancy; keep himself in employment, pay the rent when due, and ensure that his children were fed and clothed properly. The potential reward? A four bedroomed house on a post-war council estate. Two years' probation was the offer; in the event those two years became four.

Mrs. Gurney's assessment of what awaited us, recorded and waiting for me to find, years later, was spot on. When Mum and Dad went to view the property, a carpenter was sent for; the front door was warped, and the back door was hanging off its hinges. The week after we moved in, a man came to replace broken window glass, yet the third floor of the house remained untouched and unvisited; there was no electricity up there, and when the wallpaper was pulled away, the plaster came with it. The window frames had lost their putty and let in daylight, and the weather. When Mum gave birth to sister Janet she was removed, returning to the family six months into her young life, when conditions were considered safe.

Those conditions included cockroaches, rats and fleas; when it rained, a Niagara Falls of water flowed down the hill that was Peel Street and poured in, flooding the basement kitchen and the sitting room, pushing rafts of excrement up and out of the downstairs toilet (there was no bathroom) a slowly moving log jam broomed on its way out of the back door. The positive side? Well, it wasn't Eastry.

*

A new home meant a new school. And school meant learning to prevaricate, to muddy the waters. Take television. Sometimes we had TV, and sometimes we didn't. If the rental went unpaid a Rediffusion man would take the set away. When that happened my contribution to class or playground chat was limited; I learned to go with the flow, or, if cornered, to adopt diversionary tactics.

Every lesson, it seemed, was designed to trip me up. An attempt by the teacher to teach us averages was an immediate cause for alarm. How much pocket money do you get? Put your hand up if you receive more than two shillings. I tuned in to the others; five boys had two shillings, three pupils three. So, I said two and six. I'd just begun to concoct a story about my disposal of this sum of money when we moved on. In English we were asked to produce an essay about the summer holidays. I handed in my exercise book filled with pages detailing a family trip to Cornwall, a vacation which owed more to Enid Blyton's *Famous Five* than anything approaching the truth. In short, it was a complete fantasy.

Even the most mundane situation threw up a challenge, a potential mountain to climb. Take school dinners, for example. Why, Michael Higgs inquired, was I the only boy who didn't hand in his dinner money when the register was called on a Monday morning? Well, I said (I'd rehearsed this one) my dad's rich. He pays in advance, sends in a cheque to cover the whole term. Little lies, common to all school children perhaps, didn't amount to much, but they added up. In no time at all they became bigger ones. Soon I had invented a whole new history for myself. Under scrutiny, and recalling Uncle John, I informed Andrew Saward, another inquisitive classmate, that I'd arrived in Maidstone from Cyprus, where my dad had been working undercover for the government, on Her Majesty's Secret Service. Afterwards, in a panic, and expecting further questions, I reached for my atlas, then went to the school library to research all things Cypriot. No easy task.

*

One day, June, from King Hill, turned up. Finally, after months, if not years, of legal wrangling, her compensation had come through and, celebrating her good fortune, she'd travelled down from London to visit Mum, with a new man, and a new car. June also brought news of Pat, speaking proudly of how the Malling rebel and friends had helped set up a commune in the East End, and, ever on the side of the oppressed and vulnerable, became involved with a newly formed homelessness charity.

There were gifts too, including a record player, and a collection of LPs - Elvis, Gene Pitney, Roy Orbison; American music the Hut Thirteen women had sung along to in King Hill. Mum accepted them with thanks, but, three years on they already belonged to a different time, the music which filled our home now – via the pirate ships Caroline and London – was much more progressive and experimental.

I missed June's visit. But I didn't miss her car. It was a Red Mini-Cooper, parked right outside our front door. Andy spotted it first, as we came round the corner, on our way home from school.

'Who's...that?' I asked. 'Any ideas? Recognise it?'

'Dunno,' came the reply.

'Leg it' I said, and the pair of us scurried off in the direction of the town centre. 'We'll leave it half an hour, then come back and see if the coast is clear.'

It was a plan of action agreed on right back at the beginning.

Yes, we made a game of it; we were spies, or fugitives, escaped prisoners, out to right a wrong, or, coming right up to date, Napoleon Solo and Illya Kuryakin, agents of U.N.C.L.E, dedicated to battle the forces of an evil empire, which in 1965 went by the name of THRUSH. But game or not, we were always on alert.

And that was how we dealt with things. Any vehicle stopping near the house, you see, was suspect, and signified potential trouble. Perhaps it was Mr. Iggulden, the School Board man, in a new car? More likely it was a housing officer or rent collector; then again, we hadn't seen Mr. Tremain from the NSPCC for a while.

Maybe a debt collector or bailiff had gained access or, worst of all, and seldom mentioned aloud, a social worker had turned up. Basically, we'd learned to equate any parked vehicle with officialdom, with people having power: bureaucrats or professionals licensed to pry, to report and chastise or, if the mood took them, have us removed.

The spectre of the home was ever-present. And for me, of course, Eastry meant Auntie Joyce. Try as I may, I couldn't forget her parting words, her vision of my life away from Almond, an experience she warned would be nasty, impoverished, and short. 'You'll be back,' she'd said. 'Your sort always come back.'

Auntie was wrong, I didn't go back. However, this didn't mean the abuse, the guilt, and trauma I'd suffered at Eastry were erased. On the contrary, they lived on, buried deep within my psyche. In adult life this led to mental health issues, to depression and anxiety, the causes of which took years for me to recognise, and, with help, come to terms with.

I was constantly on my guard, suspicious of everyone, determined to hide the stigma associated with my past. I became suspicious, disbelieving, and mistrustful, questioning the motives of everyone, particularly those in positions of authority. Never try to con a care leaver; isn't that what they say?

Over time, even physical contact, a fundamental human need, became a challenge. Basically, I couldn't bear any kind of intimacy and became hyper-vigilant, flinching at the lightest touch. A proffered hand, the threat of a hug or a congratulatory pat on the back – which I was sure I didn't deserve - and I would switch to fight or flight mode, suffer an adrenaline rush, begin to panic, and experience an overwhelming urge to escape, to run away.

Today, I've stopped running, at least long enough to put my story down on paper. If, in doing so, I have done those former Eastry residents, and my friends and housemates in Almond any sort of justice, then I am content.

Acknowledgements

I would like to thank the following for their help in bringing this work to fruition.

Firstly, my editor Alison Williams for her for patience and diligence in pulling things together.

Next, Mary Matthews of Three Shires Publishing for her experience and guidance, without which I'd have struggled to get over the line.

Finally, I would like to pay a special tribute to my friend, author Judith Barrow for her kindness, enthusiasm and support, freely given.

All royalties earned by the author from this publication will go to BBC Children in Need.

About the Author

A graduate of the University of Wales (Aberystwyth) Doug has spent much of his adult life working in Further Education and Youth Work, focusing especially on young people who are disadvantaged or at risk of homelessness. He has been associated with a range of organisations, including the London based Foyer Federation, the charity Shelter, and the Welsh Senedd. He has travelled extensively in Eastern Europe and accompanied groups of young people on educational visits to Romania, Hungary and Poland.

Doug now lives in Pembrokeshire, where he enjoys spending time with his children and four young grandsons, Gwilym, Arthur, Gwion and Oliver. He continues to advocate for the vulnerable and those in need of care and support.

Printed in Great Britain
by Amazon